OVERLOAD

OVERLOAD

HOW GOOD JOBS WENT BAD
AND WHAT WE CAN DO ABOUT IT

Erin L. Kelly and Phyllis Moen

Princeton University Press

Princeton and Oxford

Published by Princeton University Press
41 William Street, Princeton, New Jersey 08540
6 Oxford Street, Woodstock, Oxfordshire OX20 1TR

press.princeton.edu

Library of Congress Cataloging-in-Publication Data

Names: Kelly, Erin L. (Erin Lee), 1970– author. | Moen, Phyllis, author.
Title: Overload : how good jobs went bad and what we can do about it / Erin L.
    Kelly and Phyllis Moen.
Description: 1st. | Princeton : Princeton University Press, [2020] |
    Includes bibliographical references and index.
Identifiers: LCCN 2019027049 | ISBN 9780691179179 (hardback) |
    ISBN 9780691200033 (ebook)
Subjects: LCSH: Quality of work life—United States—Case studies. | Employees—
    Workload—United States—Case studies. | Work-life balance—United States—
    Case studies. | Organizational change—United States—Case studies.
Classification: LCC HD6957.U5 K34 2020 | DDC 331.20973—dc23
LC record available at https://lccn.loc.gov/2019027049

British Library Cataloging-in-Publication Data is available

Editorial: Meagan Levinson and Jacqueline Delaney
Production Editorial: Kathleen Cioffi
Text Design: Leslie Flis
Jacket Design: Karl Spurzem
Production: Erin Suydam
Publicity: James Schneider and Kathryn Stevens

This book has been composed in Arno Pro and Gotham

Printed on acid-free paper. ∞

Printed in the United States of America

10 9 8 7 6 5 4 3 2 1

For Graham, Noah, James, and William

CONTENTS

⌘

PART I. THE PROBLEM

PART II. A POTENTIAL SOLUTION

PART III. LOOKING AHEAD

OVERLOAD

Part I

THE PROBLEM

Chapter 1

⌘

OLD RULES, NEW REALITIES

The way we work is not sustainable. Sherwin knows this well. He has twenty years of experience as a skilled information technology (IT) professional and is one of the many professionals and managers we interviewed in a Fortune 500 company we call TOMO. Sherwin has a hybrid role where he designs new software solutions to address business problems but also participates directly in developing that new software; he's both a big picture thinker and attuned to the details of writing solid computer code. On the personal side, Sherwin is a divorced dad with two daughters who live mainly with him. He is also the point person for his elderly mother, who is deciding whether it is time to move into a nursing home.

Sherwin's family caregiving feels manageable; it is his workload on the job that is overwhelming. Sherwin estimates he works about 70 hours per week. He starts work with calls at 5 a.m., pauses to get his kids ready and off to school, works a full day, prepares dinner and supervises their homework, and then routinely works, at home, until midnight. The long hours and intense pace are perhaps not surprising given the managers he reports to. Sherwin's manager, Tanay, describes himself as a "super workaholic" and says his own boss (who sits two levels above Sherwin on the organizational chart) pushes teams so hard that he is "trying to get blood from a rock."

Sherwin is dedicated to his job and often excited about it. He enjoys the technical challenges of his work and appreciates the "tremendously talented people in this group . . . Wow, these guys are smart!" The feeling is mutual: Tanay conveys his respect for Sherwin's intelligence and skills when we interview him separately. But despite appreciating much about his job, Sherwin knows the way he works is toxic. He recognizes that "never being able to get [all] the work done—[takes] a tremendous toll on me health-wise." His work patterns make it harder for him to take good care of himself. "You're staying up late, you're eating," and "the last thing in my mind was to get up and work out. Too tired." In fact, Sherwin recently had a heart attack, luckily a fairly minor one. He tells us:

> I didn't even realize it, just went into the doctor because I was not feeling well and they ran an EKG and they did some tests and said "You had a heart attack yesterday."

Sherwin was out of work for about four weeks to recover from this health crisis, but it has had a lasting impact. As he says, "I'm looking at things a lot differently in my life," and he hopes to work differently to take better care of himself.

The way Sherwin works and lives exemplifies the *overload*—the feeling of having too much to do in too little time—that so many professionals and managers confront today. These employees are privileged in terms of their pay, benefits, and the ability to work in clean and comfortable offices. They are generally treated with respect, with their contributions and ideas recognized.[1] These would seem to be "good jobs" in many ways. University of North Carolina sociologist Arne Kalleberg suggests we assess job quality by considering earnings, benefits, job security, and opportunities for advancement as well as how much autonomy or control employees have, how meaningful and interesting the tasks are, and how hours and schedules fit with the rest of life.

But these professionals and managers find that what had been good jobs have morphed into something more intense and less secure. New communication technologies foster an always-on, always-working culture. Managers and coworkers know they can contact employees anytime, anywhere, and they often do reach out before and after official workdays. Moreover, globalization, automation, and artificial intelligence make it clear to even the most educated, experienced, and skilled workers in a variety of occupations and industries that their jobs are changing radically, and may even disappear. Earnings and benefits are still relatively generous, but there is an increasing price to pay. Good jobs, previously characterized by relative autonomy and security, have become bad, with rising workloads, a sped-up pace, and escalating expectations that seem impossible to meet.

Is this the future of work, shaped by warp-speed connectivity, ratcheting demands, and eroding security? These ways of working will either break organizations or break people. Outdated policies and expectations collide with the intense realities of the digital revolution and the global production of "knowledge work" (as well as manufacturing goods) to exacerbate burnout, stress, and poor health. Most businesses continue to demand 9 to 5 (or 8 to 6) desk time *in addition to* early morning calls to offshore colleagues, last-minute but all-too-common work requests at 10 p.m., and ubiquitous emails, texts, and instant messaging.

Alongside changes tied to new technologies and global competition, US companies are routinely merging, reorganizing, downsizing, even disappearing. This leaves all employees—even skilled professionals and middle managers—unsure whether they will have their jobs next year or even next week. Those who survive layoffs experience even more overload as they attempt to cover the work of their downsized coworkers. The firm resolves to "do more with less," and employees try frantically to make that happen.

Our interviews and surveys in TOMO's IT division demonstrate that overload harms workers. That is probably not a surprise to readers, and it is very clear to the professionals and managers we interviewed. Kunwar, a manager who supervises almost thirty employees and is also a wife and mother, explains that her 10 p.m. meetings mean her "entire evening is actually ruined" because she is "on edge" and busy preparing for the call. Similarly, taking a "status call" meeting at 5:30 or 6:30 in the morning on Saturday or Sunday, as she does regularly, affects the whole weekend day.

> You're not able to relax a lot, so it's definitely taking its toll on people's health and stress levels and maybe blood pressure without us knowing it. Sleep—not being able sleep—or not taking the time even to go and exercise. I'm definitely constantly thinking about work.

But we also see that overload creates problems for the organization that employs these professionals and managers. Working at breakneck speed means the work product is not as high quality as it could be. The problem is not a lack of talent but a lack of time. Firms that rely on knowledge workers seek to recruit and retain creative people who can innovate. But creativity and innovativeness are simply incompatible with burnout and exhaustion.

A manager explains that the software developers who report to him are frustrated because "different people are pinging them for information" all day. They are interrupted from writing their code because questions come at them via the chat software the company uses. These IT professionals feel "they go through the whole day, the whole week without doing what they were expected to do" during regular work hours, so they work late nights and weekends (like Sherwin) to try to catch up. The manager sees how this fast pace affects teamwork too, reporting "simmering tensions" because the team members are working under too much pressure to address any concerns.

> The pedal is pushed continuously . . . It's like full throttle. Keep moving [laughs]. You get hurt? Tough. Let's just get it [done] . . . I'm not saying I'm ignoring you, but sorry—we gotta get it done.

We ask if this pressure is due to a big deadline we know the team is facing in a few weeks (in September) and he explains that the intensity is routine:

> We had it like that for June. We have it like that for September. I see that already December is coming [along] that way.

Overload and the clash of old rules with new realities are not private troubles that employees and frontline managers can fix for themselves by getting up earlier, deciding on their own to not read email in the evening, or scaling back on family obligations. Solving these problems requires inventing new ways of working to promote sane and sustainable jobs, fostering effectiveness on the job, *and* insisting on a higher quality of life for workers of all genders, ages, educational levels, occupations, and life stages.[2]

We believe federal safety nets and labor regulations should be updated to address the new intensity and precarity of work, as well as the growing inequality in the United States and elsewhere. But corporations and other employers can also do something about overload. Drawing on our research with an interdisciplinary group of scholars called the Work, Family, and Health Network, we identify creative and practical ways to reshape how work works, which we call a dual-agenda work redesign. Dual-agenda work redesigns prompt employees and managers to look at how work can be changed in ways that benefit employees (and their families) and also benefit the organization. We demonstrate that those changes work well for employees, their families, and also the organizations that employ them.[3]

This study establishes that things can change for the better. Innovative initiatives like the one we describe can create a new normal. In that new normal, employees have greater authority to make their own decisions, managers and coworkers recognize and support the realities of life outside of work, and everyone focuses less on when and where the work happens and more on working effectively and efficiently together. Working "smarter" includes dropping some tasks and meetings and turning off technologies from time to time. We show that the rules, everyday practices, and expectations can be changed, even though, as our research in TOMO reveals, redesign is hard to sustain in the face of other organizational changes like new leaders in the executive ranks.

The status quo can seem intransigent. But there are ways forward to more sustainable, enjoyable, and effective work lives if we have the will, power, and imagination to push for that. This is, ultimately, a promising perspective on the future of work.

Who We Studied and How

We investigate overload and its consequences with data collected in a variety of ways—surveys, company records, ethnographic observations, and in-depth interviews—and we also summarize related research conducted by others. We then utilize evidence from a pathbreaking randomized field experiment to understand what can change and how.

Our study unfolds over about five years and includes data gathered from about a thousand employees and managers in the IT division of a large, Fortune 500 tech-focused company we call TOMO. The company isn't headquartered in Silicon Valley and it isn't known as a super exciting place to work, but it is generally viewed as a good employer and a decent corporate citizen. When we first started visiting TOMO offices, the fields of cubes seemed familiar to us from many white-collar workplaces we have observed as well as from pop culture. The IT professionals and managers we met are often middle-aged, wearing jeans or casual slacks and button-down cotton shirts or crisp sweaters, and largely white or people of South Asian descent. They fit with our cultural stereotypes of an engineer, though there are more women (roughly 40%) in IT at TOMO than in many tech organizations. What is less familiar, though, is the emptiness. On many floors, a third or more of the cubes are vacant, a visible reminder that the firm has repeatedly downsized workers as it expanded offshore and relied more on technology to automate or streamline the work.

This workforce includes people in a variety of IT-related occupations—software developers, quality assurance staff, project managers, and the analysts who translate the needs of clients into project plans for the other IT experts to build. Employees and managers are paid quite well, with an average salary over $90,000 in our IT sample, and their benefits were historically generous. In addition to the good salaries and benefits, employees at TOMO appreciate the generally respectful work environment, the intellectually challenging work, and being located in middle-American cities that have reasonable costs of living and attractive amenities. TOMO IT professionals have formidable technical skills, but their experiences are more akin to professionals and managers in other large US firms in the middle of the country than to those working in more famous tech companies in Silicon Valley or New York City. People in TOMO's IT division tend to stay with the company, assuming they are not downsized. On average, our respondents had worked at TOMO over fourteen years.

We have deliberately focused on technical professionals and frontline managers who are in "good jobs," but who are not among the most elite workers or at the very top of the wealth distributions. These professionals and managers mostly have college degrees, earn salaries well above the median US salary, and receive good benefits as full-time employees. Recent studies of work often investigate either end of the occupational spectrum—those struggling in hourly service jobs, like retail or fast-food jobs, or those working in elite professional services firms, including well-known management consulting companies, financial firms, or "big law" practices.[4] We choose instead to study the middle, to concentrate on workers with college educations and earnings in the upper-middle class who are neither economic elites nor employed by the leading firms. The stories of intense work, insecurity, and overload that we hear in TOMO are probably familiar to many. Certainly when we share our findings with white-collar workers, professionals, and managers from a variety of different industries, people nod in recognition and often smile ruefully, recounting their own experiences of overload. We believe the people we studied at TOMO represent a much larger population of employees and managers in the United States today; their stories tell us about the realities of today and the possibilities for the future.

Our study involved multiple components and multiple people over a long time period; we conducted this research as part of the Work, Family, and Health Network, an exciting collaboration involving scholars from multiple disciplines at universities and research centers across the nation. Throughout the book, we share findings from published papers written by this team of scholars. However, the evidence we present here draws primarily on our own analysis of the tough realities facing these workers and the promise and challenges of organizational change in this firm and others. The two of us were in and out of the company for meetings, observations, interviews, and briefings with executives and others. Our research team included several "embedded" social scientists who were based in the firm to do participant observation, organize the rollout of repeated survey waves, conduct about four hundred interviews, and coordinate the training built into the dual-agenda work redesign we call STAR (for Support. Transform. Achieve. Results).[5]

Half the teams in the IT division at TOMO participated in the STAR redesign initiative while the other half served as the control group, who continued to work under the usual company policies. This experimental design makes our evidence strong: teams were randomized to the STAR "treatment," and so the employees in the two groups reported the same strains, stresses, and attitudes at the beginning of the study. Comparing how the experiences and attitudes of those in the treatment and control conditions change over time reveals the effects of STAR. Our research team was committed to a rigorous design and to checking our own assumptions and hopes; the field experiment gave us confidence in assessing what changes and what does not with STAR.

This book describes the results of trying to change the informal norms and formal rules regarding when, where, and how work is done. STAR aims to give teams and the employees within them greater control regarding their time, how they meet project goals and deadlines, and how they use (or turn off) technology to get the job done and still take care of themselves. STAR also encourages managers to actively convey their support for their employees, recognizing their priorities and responsibilities both on and off the job. At the same time, organizational concerns are also important. STAR aims to make changes that do not interfere with getting the work done and that may even help the company perform better.

Studying organizational change as it happens in a real corporation is both challenging and gratifying. This research design allows us to exploit two very important lenses on the social world. First, when an organizational change like STAR is implemented, members of the organization are confronted with the question "How might it be otherwise?"[6] The way that work has traditionally been organized is not the only reasonable, rational, or feasible arrangement. It is simply the status quo, devised in the middle of the last century when technologies, tasks, workforces, and expectations were very different. The STAR process makes it clear to multiple stakeholders that the rules of the game can be changed. In fact, taken-for-granted policies, practices, interaction patterns, and assumptions are examined, rather than being assumed to be rational or optimal, through the collective, reflective process of this work redesign initiative. Professionals and managers in the STAR treatment group gain permission and indeed are encouraged to reimagine how they could get their jobs done in more sane and sustainable ways. We observed that questioning occur and tracked what happened as employees and managers in STAR chose what to change, experimenting their way to a new normal. We hope this book prompts a similar reflective process for the reader, encouraging you to think critically about the way work is organized and how we can foster better ways of working in all kinds of jobs and in all industries.

Second, a key precept from social science is that we learn about social systems by trying to change them. Kurt Lewin, a famous organizational scholar, said, "If you want to truly understand something, try to change it."[7] Efforts to change work organizations prompt reactions—and those reactions are very informative regardless of whether the change succeeds in the intended ways. Our research design permits us to capture changes in practices, in interpretations, and in relationships, as well as how planned changes can derail. In our case, TOMO went through a merger during the course of the study and was acquired by a more conservative firm (which we call ZZT). The eventual revocation of STAR in the aftermath of that merger tells us almost as much about the corporate world in these intense, insecure, and shifting times as we learn from the successful implementation of this initiative.

Reimagining Work in the Twenty-First Century

We use the case of organizational changes at TOMO as the centerpiece for a broader analysis. The first section of the book dives into what we have come to see as a key problem of our time, overload. What is overload and what are its consequences? How has overload become so ubiquitous? Defining the problem is important for identifying real solutions. Our own understandings of the problem evolved through this study. Although we have both investigated work and family concerns for much of our academic careers, we now believe that the core concern for many professionals and managers is not *balancing* work and family obligations, but rather how to manage all that one is asked to do *at work*.

In other words, we locate the root problem not in the ways work and family connect and conflict but in intensified work itself. This is an important shift in the framing of the problem. We have come to worry that a work–family framing is problematic because then the problem is seen as a women's issue or as primarily the concern of working mothers along with some involved fathers.[8] But overload affects men and women workers at all ages and life stages. Work isn't challenging only for mothers, for fathers, or for those caring for aging partners or parents or confronting their own health challenges. Younger workers—often millennials with no family responsibilities—still feel they "should be working all the time," while many of the baby boomers we interviewed felt overloaded and burned out too.[9] Overload is pervasive and these intensive ways of working put health, well-being, productivity, and innovation at risk.

The second section of the book introduces and evaluates a potential solution to address overload and foster new ways of working. We investigate a particular initiative we call STAR as one example of the dual-agenda work redesign strategy. The changes prompted by STAR may include shifting schedules, working at home when feasible, questioning meetings and "low-value" tasks so that people can focus on the core of their work, and more. These work practices can be viewed as workplace flexibility, but we also investigate how flexibility means different things in different contexts. We need to craft forms of flexibility that actually help workers, rather than just pressing them to be always on and always available or asking them to give up good careers in order to get the flexibility and control they need.

The third section of the book examines possibilities for redesigning the way we work. Here we go beyond the case of STAR at TOMO. Organizations can do better for their employees while also doing better for the business (as we demonstrate in the second section). We identify pockets of change, exciting innovations in corporate and public policy, but we also recognize the challenges of making meaningful institutional change happen in a variety of contexts that reach a wide variety of workers. We conclude by sharing multiple avenues for creating more sane and sustainable work.

There is a path forward, and this study points to real possibilities for crafting new ways of working that do not take today's craziness for granted. But before we get there, we need to learn more about the problem of intensive work and the feelings of overload.

Chapter 2

⌘

OVERLOAD

Overload Up and Down the Chain

Randall is a software developer, a single white man in his early forties who has a trim dark beard and a bundled sense of energy. He recently purchased a home he is hoping to renovate, and he enjoys watching and playing sports too. But he spends 50 to 70 hours per week working, leaving little time for those pursuits. He explains his recent schedule as working 8:30 to 5:30 in the office and then more:

> [On] a lot of these projects, they expect you to be to be working from 8:00 [p.m.] to midnight. And if you weren't on that 8 to midnight call, the next morning you hear about it. "Hey [knocks on the edge of the cube], where were you from 8 to midnight?"

Randall feels pressured to be on late-night calls, after putting in a full workday in the office, because someone—presumably a manager with authority over Randall—has "decreed" (in Randall's words) that he and the rest of the team should be on these calls. Randall describes the TOMO IT management style as "more of a dictatorship than anything" and says, "it's not an enjoyable work environment at all."

Randall's frustration arises in part because he believes he is not really needed on these late calls. He does not recall providing any concrete input to the technical problems discussed in recent weeks, "yet every night, I'm here 8 to midnight." But even when he is contributing to the evening calls, Randall views this schedule as exhausting and excessive. He feels "owned by" the company because the work demands set by "them" took over the rest of his life. He recalls:

There are times when I would go home from work at 7 p.m. and purposefully take a nap because I knew I was going to be working from 9 p.m. to midnight. At that point, I lived for the company, you know? I didn't take that nap for me. I took it for them . . . I had to take a nap because I knew I was going to be up all night with them. And that was every night.

Besides fostering resentment, these work patterns create practical problems. Randall reflects back on a recent period when his team was in "crisis mode":

And I was on speakerphone and I'd just go to the bathroom flush the toilet—do whatever. And it's like, "You took up my life, what am I supposed to do?" You know? And I know everyone on a call can hear me living my life.

But you give me 3 hours a day to sleep? That's just stupid. If that's how your relationship with a company is, you're really—you're not happy about it.

Randall's manager, Jonathon, is a white, middle-aged married man, with three children at home. He supervises a large software development group and reports to the director, Vanessa.[1] Jonathon is proud of the work he does as a manager and he believes his job matches his skills well. Jonathon is also devoted to his family and his community activities in a suburb about an hour's drive from the office. He tries to keep his work hours reasonable to leave time for those commitments.

But the stories he tells and the interruptions during our first interview with Jonathon reveal how difficult it is for him to get away from his work. When we ask him whether and how his work affects his personal life and health, Jonathon first claims to have strong boundaries. But he immediately describes how work intrudes into home time, with his phone buzzing during the interview to illustrate how often he is interrupted:

When I go home, I go home and I don't do anything else, except when the pager or phone rings. I refuse to log in at home. I refuse to. When I'm home I'm with my family and with my kids.

And the only time that I make exceptions for that is [phone buzzes] is when that happens. Or when [phone buzzes] my boss is calling me. Or when I have a meeting that I've accepted and scheduled. Like tonight at 9:30. But that's pretty late, you know. My kids are winding down and everything at that time and they know I gotta get on a call and do my thing.

Jonathon dislikes how his work overload affects family time, and he believes his wife's health has been harmed by the calls he gets late at night. He tried leaving his phone in another room but then he gets called on his home phone line, "which wakes everybody up 'cause it's louder."

The reality of being interrupted on his drive home, when he is home with the family (awake or asleep), or when he is at a Scout or church event, contradicts Jonathon's stated values about prioritizing family time and community involvement. Jonathon is an officer in two different community groups, and he recalls a recent cook-off he had helped organize. Vanessa, his boss, called him during the event:

But what'd I do? Not answer the phone? I mean, I answer the phone. It's Vanessa. She wants to talk about something. So I talk about it.

Yet these calls with his boss are not productive or efficient. He will drift away from family and community time to take the call. But, Jonathon says with a chuckle:

The next morning, I can't even remember what she said [phone buzzes]. I can't even remember what we even talked about [phone buzzes] on some of that stuff. Because I'm in information overload.

Jonathon also reflects on what he hopes for his children in light of his current overload. He talks with them "about career paths" and has brought them on tours of the TOMO building. They are curious about different IT roles, and he recognizes the appeal.

By comparison to other industries, it tends to pay better than average. At the same time, there's a price you pay for that. And I don't want my kids to be in this industry, quite frankly.

Vanessa, the director who manages Jonathon, Randall's team, and several other teams, has a somewhat different perspective—but admits that these jobs are intensive. She estimates that the managers under her work between 45 to 50 hours per week on average, but

> they need to be accessible 24/7, 365 days a year. And if they're going to be out of town, unavailable because of vacation or because they're going to be gone for a weekend or something, then they need to let me know.

Vanessa is clear that being unavailable for work questions is the exception, rather than the rule, even outside of the traditional workday.

Vanessa seems to place responsibility for overload on the frontline managers and their employees. She says that work hours should be determined by the projects and deadlines that a team faces, what she calls the "commitments" that they make.

> If you make a commitment, if that takes you—if you have to work 70 hours one week, well then, next time don't make that commitment.

Yet it isn't as simple as turning down work or setting longer time lines. We heard over and over that managers and employees worry that setting more reasonable commitments or moderating their work hours will make them look bad and make them more likely to lose their jobs.

Overload as the New Reality

These examples from Randall, Jonathon, and Vanessa capture what is happening in professional and managerial workforces across the United States and other advanced economies: even those workers who make good money and work for a respected organization face jobs that are becoming more intense and harder to contain. Availability via phone, email, text, and other technologies is expected over and above the requirement to be in the office during the standard business hours of, at a minimum, 9 a.m. to 5 p.m. There seems to be little time fully off of work, little mental space to recover and recuperate. And the time spent working is often pressured—a frantic attempt to try to keep up with more and more work. Companies, as well as nonprofits and public sector organizations, are staffed in a lean way with pressure on employees to be responsive and agile, despite the growing demands. We learned about these realities in one context, the IT division of the Fortune 500 company that we call TOMO, but the experiences of overload are increasingly evident across industries and occupations. You may well recognize overload and the practices that produce it from your own life.

Overload involves long hours of work, but we cannot fully understand the situation if we only consider the number of hours worked. Many people assume that Americans (and also others working in rich industrialized countries) are working longer and longer, but the trends are actually more complicated than that. When we measure the *average hours worked per week* for those who are employed, we see few changes in recent decades—despite the sense of speed-up and time famine. But averages mask variations in workers' experiences, of course, and we have seen a bifurcation in work hours in the United States since the 1970s. More people—especially professionals, managers, and those earning higher salaries—are working very long hours, often measured as 50 or more hours per week. At the other end of the hours distribution, the United States has a sizable group of workers putting in relatively few hours. Many of these hourly workers would like to work more than they do. Shifts in work hours (at both end of the hours distribution) were more dramatic in the 1980s and 1990s and have moved less since 2000.[2]

When we look at *annual hours worked*, there has been a more dramatic increase over these years. In 2013, the average annual hours worked in the United States was 1,836 hours, up over 183 hours since 1975. That is an increase equivalent to four additional 40-hour weeks per year. Much of the change in annual hours worked reflects a move among women to working more weeks per year. And because women are more likely to be in the paid labor force, are more likely to work full time, and are working more weeks each year, there are many *families whose total hours* in paid work have increased.[3]

We also need to consider how work is experienced in terms of work effort or intensity. Counting the hours worked isn't enough to fully understand the weight of the job and its impact on employees, families, and communities. Trend studies suggest there is increased work intensity in the United States and in many European countries (especially the United Kingdom, France, and Ireland). Work intensity is measured by survey questions about needing to work hard, to work fast, feeling pressured by deadlines, and not having enough time to finish one's work. Perceived work intensity also increased throughout the 1990s; then it seemed to level off until it rose again in the aftermath of the Great Recession.[4]

Our specific focus is on overload, which we define as *the sense that work demands are unrealistic, given limited resources.* This is the classic definition of stress: too many demands, coupled with too few resources (such as time or staff) to accomplish what is needed or expected.[5] The stress arises from not meeting others' expectations, but also from not meeting one's own expectations. At TOMO, 41 percent of IT professionals and 61 percent of their managers agree or strongly agree with the statement that there is "not enough time to get your job done." A related issue is feeling the need to work very hard or very fast, particularly when a change or speed-up is perceived.[6] The professionals and managers we study are vulnerable to overload, but they are not alone. A recent national survey finds that over a third of employed Americans agree or strongly agree that there is "too much work to do it well" in their current jobs.[7]

Intensive work practices and the sense of overload they engender are a source of chronic strain. Excessive work demands leave people stressed in part because they feel they have little control. There seem to be no options for changing the situation. Randall (the frontline employee introduced at the beginning of the chapter) and Jonathon (the manager) both convey that sense of limited control. Work demands are ratcheting out of control and yet "they" (presumably upper management) insist on conference calls at all hours of the night and expect subordinates to interrupt personal, family, or community commitments whenever a boss calls or texts.

These conditions are often seen as intractable, as "just the way it is" and sometimes as just the way it has to be. Is that true? It is a fair point that IT systems need to be maintained and technical problems need to be addressed quickly. Those real operational needs justify the push for nearly constant availability across TOMO's IT division. But long work hours and quick responses during nonwork time are also routinely expected outside of IT, including in professional service organizations (like consulting and law), in direct customer services (like hospitality and retail), in healthcare occupations (from surgeons at the top to nursing assistants at the bottom), and elsewhere.[8]

In the IT setting, the expectation of near constant availability is strong even when there are no urgent technical problems. Instead, the need reflects management expectations that employees will respond quickly to a question that a manager, coworker, or client brings forward, even when the issue is not actually time sensitive or tied to an urgent technical fix. That is the case in other occupations and industries too. One important implication is that the experience of overload depends on the social norms regarding when, where, and how work is accomplished and how workers are evaluated, not only how much work is assigned or how many hours are worked.

Four Dimensions of Work Intensity Contributing to Overload

Overload, again, is the *subjective sense* there is too much to do, given the resources (including time and other people) on hand. But there are concrete, *objective work practices*—specific dimensions of work intensity—that converge to create the sense that work demands are spinning out of control.[9]

The Weight of Long Hours

Overload is clearly tied to long work hours. Georgia, a manager of testers who perform quality assurance work to ensure software will operate as planned, routinely works 12-hour days and sometimes even more:

> I usually am online from about 6:00 in the morning until usually, actually about 6:00 in the evening. And depending upon what's going on, if we're involved in anything really big and meaty or big and ugly, I may be on 24 hours a day. Or at least, on and off, 24 hours a day.

Time spent working crowds out time for other things—even basic things like getting groceries or taking reasonable breaks. Like Randall, Georgia brings up the bathroom when she reflects on her thinking about her current work routines:

> This sense of "Oh my god! Something has got to give here! Surely I can find 5 minutes to, you know, run into the bathroom." . . . I have felt a sense of being really stretched over the last few months.

Employees in other fields outside of IT report similar challenges with taking basic breaks. A recent *New York Times* story that describes professionals and managers who plan to retire early—in their thirties or forties—quotes a pharmacist:

> "There were days when I had 12- or 14-hour shifts where I didn't use the restroom, where I didn't eat, because so much work was piled up on me," Mr. Long said.

In addition to nurses, doctors, and teachers who share stories about managing to find time for bathroom breaks and snacks on the run, one survey finds that around 40 percent of professionals regularly take lunch breaks away from their desks. And a quarter of those surveyed agree with the statement "I eat alone to multitask better."[10]

When long hours are sustained over a long period, they wear workers down. The IT professionals we study sometimes talk about variations in workload depending on the stage of the software development cycle and the difficulty of a particular project. In one of our first focus groups, Jarla explained that the workload had "peaks and valleys." But we soon hear that the rhetoric of peaks and valleys does not match the current reality. Jarla's coworkers in the focus group point out that valleys have not happened recently.

REBECCA: We haven't had a valley for . . .

KARI: Years.

REBECCA: Yeah, over two years. And for me that is definitely impacting sleep. I have unexplained hives. I've been to the [hospital name] clinic. They don't know. I only can sleep with tranquilizers at night, so we don't know if it's stress or not.

Our survey of almost 1,000 TOMO IT professionals and managers confirms the connection between the number of hours worked and subjective overload. We label a respondent as overloaded if they agree or strongly agree that there is not enough time to get their job done. Sixty-five percent of those working 50 or more hours per week report overload, compared to 35 percent of those few in our study who usually work less than 50 hours per week. In statistical models that adjust for other risk factors, we see that working 50 or more hours per week doubles the risk of reporting overload.[11]

Having a child in your home or being a caregiver for an adult relative does not predict a sense of overload among these IT professionals and managers.[12] This is important because talk of work stress and the strain of long hours often emphasizes employees' desire for work–family balance. We see the work domain (and not the combination of work and family responsibilities) as the primary source of strain. Even those who have few family responsibilities report considerable overload. Work is the driver of overload, sucking up time and focus regardless of one's family or personal circumstances, with widespread health and well-being consequences for people at all ages and life stages.

Always-On Availability

Professional and managerial work is unbounded today. New communication technologies mean an employee or manager can be reached for work matters anytime and anywhere. Vanessa lays this out explicitly, saying "so they need to be accessible 24/7, 365 days a year" and referencing the smartphones that make it possible for her subordinates to be accessible for work tasks or questions at any time. This can be couched as flexibility, but what is expected is *employees' flexibility to respond* as requested to work intrusions. Our perspective is that the new communications technologies, including smartphones and cloud storage, make it feasible to respond to questions at any time or any place and to coordinate work around the globe. But the technologies are not the real problem, or at least the root problem. Overload arises from management expectations that employees and managers will do whatever they are asked, no matter how many hours have already been worked or when those requests come in.[13]

Even though we do not want to put all the blame on technology, it is true that email, smartphones, and other connective technologies mean people can *try to* live up to those always-on expectations. Brice, a manager who puts in about 55 hours per week and often arrives home after his kids are in bed, notices the comments he receives on Monday morning. His coworkers or managers seem surprised he has not responded to emails sent over the weekend.

> That has become more and more of a culture expectation now. Overtime and weekend work seems to be like the norm today.

Hayden, another manager, says about his team: "We've been on 24 by 7 for the last five years." What does this mean? Obviously no individual is working 24/7 for years on end, but Hayden's five employees may be called at any moment, and that level of availability has been expected for the last five years. (It wasn't the case for the first fifteen years Hayden worked for TOMO, when there was a significantly larger workforce.) Hayden's team does not monitor the technical systems for problems or investigate day-to-day issues as they arise—that falls to a production support team that is officially on call. But Hayden's team gets pulled in for complex issues or problems with "heavy impacts to the business," as he puts it, and those could arise anytime. Hayden tells us about "SWAT calls," where his team will frantically try to figure out the technical problems, facing "unbelievable" stress as they work through the night.

Availability expectations also make it hard to actually take the relatively generous vacation time that TOMO provides or to be fully away from work when officially on vacation. One software developer decided to take some of her vacation time in short, two-hour chunks to attend her daughter's soccer games in the late afternoon. She blocks her calendar well in advance and counts this as official vacation time. But her manager will call her "pretty much every time" that she leaves early for the game, she reports. To borrow sociologists Dan Clawson and Naomi Gerstel's term, we have a situation of "normal unpredictability" in which workers are asked to deal with "the pervasiveness of routine disruptions" and continually expected to shift their own plans in response to shifting requests from work.[14]

The expectation that you will be checking emails and taking calls as they come in affects employees even beyond the time spent on those tasks. One study finds that doing email "after work" makes it harder to detach mentally and increases feelings of burnout. In fact, these negative effects are found among workers who feel they are *expected* to be responsive, regardless of whether the employees *actually open* the emails.[15] (We put the term "after work" in quotes because there are fewer boundaries between what is work time and what is personal, nonwork time, making common survey questions about work interruptions after a regular day less sensible than they once were.)

Our survey also confirms a connection between working during "nonstandard" but increasingly common times and the sense of overload. Sixty percent of those who are working 10 hours or more per week during the evenings, nights, and early mornings feel overloaded, compared to 41 percent of those who do less work outside the traditional business day. Moreover, 68 percent of those who work at least half of their weekend days feel overloaded, compared to 42 percent who do less work over the weekend.[16] Overload is high for those working longer hours overall, but higher when work is stretched out, done at all hours across the week. Looking more broadly at US workers, we see that our IT professionals are not alone in their work patterns. American workers put in longer hours than workers in European industrialized countries, and they are also more likely to work outside of what were previously considered to be standard hours. One out of three Americans does some weekend work, and one out of four works some at night.[17]

We have emphasized the high availability expectations for professionals and managers; for these workers, being available often means putting in long and stretched hours. Yet availability expectations are also high for other workers, in a somewhat different way. In service sector jobs in retail, hospitality, and healthcare, for example, workers are expected to be always available, to take whatever shifts they are assigned, and add more hours if requested. Because these workers are paid hourly and receive much lower wages than the IT professionals we are studying, that variability in the number of hours worked puts their tight family budgets under more pressure.[18]

Here too new technologies facilitate these shifts in how work time is organized, but the underlying issue is management pressure to be available. Scheduling software now allows companies to make "just-in-time" adjustments to schedules. With easier forecasting of customer demand and close tracking of revenue and labor costs, these technologies allow frontline managers to change workers' work schedules at a moment's notice. If there are fewer customers than expected at a local restaurant, wait staff are sent home one evening, and those workers earn less that week than they'd hoped. If a few more patients are admitted to a unit in a given hospital or nursing home, then nursing assistants may be asked—and pressured—to come in at the last minute or to stay for a second shift. In warehouses and transportation (including Amazon and other companies that send goods directly to customers), shifts are routinely cut or extended in response to the volume of orders that need to be shipped that day to make the promised delivery time.

Those additional hours may be appreciated because the extra money is welcome, but unpredictability in work schedules makes it very hard to maintain stable routines and to take good care of yourself or your family.[19] Despite the challenge of unpredictable schedules, these hourly workers know they need to make themselves available for work at almost any time or they risk getting scheduled for fewer hours (and bringing home less pay).

Multitasking and Split Attention at Work

What can you do when you have more work than you can handle? In addition to working longer hours and attending to the phone and email at all times, many employees and managers try to fit more work into a given hour by multitasking.

At TOMO, geographically distributed project teams mean that the vast majority of meetings are actually conference calls. Managers and employees can attend multiple meetings *in a single block of time*. This can happen when individuals log on, listen or contribute, then quietly log off a call to get on another call or when they take off a headset to talk with a coworker in person. This is the high-tech version of stepping in and out of meetings. This can also happen when someone listens to two conference calls at the very same time. One of the most vivid moments of our early shadowing of these IT professionals was when we first saw someone listening to two calls at once, with a different headset playing each call into a different ear.[20]

Even when only on one conference call, TOMO employees and managers rarely devote their full attention to the meeting. They routinely listen to a call while using the internal chat message system. (TOMO used Instant Messenger or IM at the time; Slack is a popular example of internal chat today.) Sometimes this is a shadow meeting where people "ping" each other on IM about who will raise a question or push a particular point, but these side conversations are often about a different project altogether. And meeting time often turns into time to review and respond to emails, just because there is no other time available. Georgia explains:

> I sometimes sit here on the phone for 10 to 12 hours a day and that's on the phone. That's not work I'm doing outside of all my meetings.

Multitasking during calls is so expected that those leading the meeting routinely say a person's name a couple of times before asking a question, to give that person time to start paying attention. Employees sometimes ask for something to be repeated and admit that they have not been listening, either making a joke out of it or just stating it without comment. In an interview, Hayden mimes what it is like to be distracted during a call and then to refocus:

> And I'm as skilled as anybody else [at multitasking]. I'm like okay [looking at one thing on his desk], that's okay [looking at another thing across the table], that's—"I heard my name!" [laughs and sits up straight]

Interruptions occur routinely, even aside from calls and meetings. Employees are generally expected to be "green on IM," which indicates that they are available on the internal chat system. Questions from coworkers and managers come in—nearly constantly for senior professionals in technical lead roles—via IM as well as in person and by email.[21] Pinging someone on IM is preferred by many because it feels less formal than email, which automatically creates an electronic paper trail of the discussion. But IM is also understood as a real time exchange (or synchronous, in the terminology of communications scholars). So an IM question is expected to be answered almost immediately, particularly if the person being contacted is marked as being green. Coworkers also stop by their colleagues' cubes to talk, although those old-fashioned interruptions vary depending on how the team is split across office locations and cities.[22]

Quick responses are expected in many work groups even when the technical issues are not actually urgent. For example, Monica manages a team of IT architects who do big-picture planning regarding the next technical systems. These workers would not be involved in responding to technical outages or other crises, and Monica is unusually flexible regarding where her employees work. Yet she expects a quick response—under 15 minutes—whenever she pings an employee by IM, unless she knows that person is in a specific meeting or training session.

Employees and managers realize that these work patterns are not efficient and sometimes complain that the best time to do their "real work" is in the evenings and nights. They can plan the new application, write the code, or summarize data from test cases when there are fewer interruptions and fewer scheduled meetings. But high workloads push employees to try to cram more work in whenever they can, during the day too. So employees and managers continue to multitask and interrupt others in the hopes that they will be able to make it through all they are asked to do.[23]

Conventional Expectations for Face Time

In many work groups, the expectation of being available outside of standard daytime hours comes on top of requirements to be in the office from at least 9 to 5. In other words, new technologies and globally distributed work processes mean many employees and managers are living with a new model where work stretches across time and space, and yet are also constrained by the old model that rewards "face time" and being visible to one's manager and other people higher in the hierarchy. Old rigidities of the workday are overlaid with new expectations of unbounded work, contributing to overload.[24]

Kathleen, a development manager who is working on a high-profile project, describes the way face time works:

> There's definitely an expectation that as long as the boss is here, I need to stay . . . It has this ripple effect. If my boss is still here at 6:30 [p.m.], I'm still here. And then my team feels like they still need to be here. And so that's definitely a cultural thing.

Kathleen believes there is a risk for those who leave earlier than expected, even if they are getting their work done.

> If somebody's going home consistently at 4 o'clock, they're a target. They're a target for a layoff. You know, or "They're not doing their job," or they're [pause]. Even if they put in an eight-hour day.

We cannot say whether those with less face time are actually more likely to be laid off—but those concerns drive employees' behavior and managers' expectations of what is appropriate for their subordinates.[25] Kathleen's team had just worked late nights—both in the office and then later at home—for several weeks to meet a deadline. When we asked whether her subordinates could take time off during the day to recover some of the time spent working late at night or in the early morning, Kathleen responds, with some regret:

> No. And that's the only thing. It's not that I tell them they can't, but if they did, it would make them stand out. You know, 'cause nobody else does. So we don't manage that very well. We expect them to be here all day no matter what is going on early in the morning or late at night.

Kathleen's team is not unusual. Many professional and managerial workers work at home *in addition to* full, regular workweeks in the office. Mary Noonan and Jennifer Glass analyze two nationally representative data sets and find that "telecommuting is not being predominately used as a substitute for working onsite during the first 40 hours worked per week."[26] In other words, options to work at home are often used to extend the workweek among those facing high workloads, rather than the time worked at home replacing time worked in the office.

Another manager, Austin, who reports to the same vice president as Kathleen, informally grants time off to compensate for long hours and allows his employees to work at home, even though his vice president dislikes the practice. His boss assumes those working at home are "goofing off," according to Austin, but he sees it differently:

> Yet, really, in a job like we've got—especially when you're on call and you're up all night—you can't be expected to come and sit in the office all day.

Early in our study, senior managers at TOMO convey doubt when employees choose to work at home during the official workday—but the very same employees are routinely pushed to work at home at night, in the early mornings, and over weekends. Austin sees this collision of the "old-school" organizational culture and the new expectations of being on call and "up all night" as unrealistic. His solution is to allow his employees to do things differently—what we call flexibility as accommodation—rather than to challenge the predominant expectations about the way his team should work. For employees who have a less supportive manager than Austin, rigid face-time expectations amplify the exhaustion from putting in long hours and being nearly constantly available, making the sense of overload even starker.

Implications of Overload for Health and Well-Being

Why does overload matter? The quotes in this chapter make it clear that intensive work practices and overload are burdensome and frustrating for employees and managers. These practices also have real implications for health and well-being, for personal and family life, and for organizational performance.

Management scholars Joel Goh, Jeffrey Pfeffer, and Stefanos Zenios recently synthesized what is known about work "exposures" and health.

Scholars have long known that those who earn more tend, on average, to have better health, but what else matters besides pay? Goh, Pfeffer, and Zenios identify ten specific work conditions that predict poor health, as measured by self-reported ratings of physical health and mental health, having a chronic condition or illness that has been diagnosed by a doctor, and mortality. Our professional and managerial sample at TOMO is hit by at least six of the ten detrimental work conditions. Four of those hazards have been discussed: long work hours (per week), longer work shifts or work times spilling into possible recovery time, high demands that prompt working fast and feeling under pressure, and a sense of limited control over how the work unfolds and how it fits with the rest of your life. Two more work hazards are also quite evident among these professionals and managers. Work–family conflicts are common, as we describe in the next section, and job insecurity takes center stage when we ask why these employees work so intensively.[27]

The research tying certain work conditions to poor health would not be surprising to the professionals and managers at TOMO. They are living it every day. Their stories help bring these health hazards to life, showing us how intensive work translates into real consequences for health and well-being.[28]

Overload and Poor Health Behaviors, Chronic Conditions, and Health Crises

Melissa, a testing manager, tells us that her team often talks about the health implications of their jobs:

> About not having enough time to work out anymore or enough time to get good rest, or eat right. So everybody's complaining about putting on extra weight [laughs].

She goes on to mention how her employees choose sleep over working out and rarely find the time to make and bring healthy food to work.

> They grab and go or they run across the street. And I'm guilty of it too. I mean we've commiserated about it . . . I know my blood pressure is high.

At the time of this interview, Melissa routinely works over 60 hours a week and gets between 200 and 500 emails a day. She coordinates closely with offshore workers, mainly in India. She is on conference calls early most mornings (usually 5 a.m.) and works in the office from her first call until at least 5 p.m. She also has less frequent nighttime calls and works many weekends, because new software programs or applications launch (meaning they go live on the network) then. Melissa shares that the last time she "hit the exercise machine" was before her team got the applications that left them overwhelmed for the last year. Unfortunately, about two years after our first interview with Melissa, she had a stroke she describes as "blood-pressure induced." She went on disability leave but did not recover enough to return, and so she was forced to retire early, in her mid-fifties.[29]

Work stress makes it harder to stick to healthy habits and to avoid bad habits. Casey, a white married woman in her thirties, finds it hard to stick to her exercise plan and eat healthy—even though she identifies as an avid athlete and a "recovering workaholic" who is trying to keep work hours under control these days. She also admits that "happy hour is a problem" at times of high job stress, because she will "want a drink after work." Sylvia is a white woman in her early fifties who works about 50 hours a week and supervises about fifteen employees. She smokes, though previously she had quit smoking for three years.

> Every single time I've quit, what does bring me back to smoking is job stress. Every single time. Without a doubt.

Sylvia, and others who smoke at TOMO and in other workplaces we have observed, seem to value the smoking *break* as well as enjoying smoking itself. Because meetings run into each other, workloads are high, and questions come in constantly, Sylvia and others routinely skip lunch.

> So when I am really stressed, I just get up and go outside [for a cigarette]. And that's my habit.

Monica is the manager mentioned earlier who expects her employees to respond to her pings within 15 minutes, yet this white woman in her fifties feels the burden of these work practices herself. Monica jumps in before the interviewer can even ask the question of how work affects her personally or with regard to health. She links her work practices to her health and the transformation of her body:[30]

> I can tell you the toll it's taken on me in the last two years. I'm on six pills now [listing the medications]. I'm seeing a cardiologist now [chuckles].
>
> I have seen a chiropractor. He said, "You're in IT, aren't you?" I said, "Yes. How do you know?" [And he responded:] "From the way that you hold your head, your neck, and the stress internalized physically in your body."

Our survey of almost 1,000 TOMO employees and managers confirms what these interviews suggest. Reporting overload (by agreeing or strongly agreeing that there is not enough time to do their job) and working more than 50 hours per week both predict worse mental health. Overloaded employees and those working longer hours report significantly greater burnout, stress, and psychological distress (how often someone feels sad, nervous, restless, hopeless, worthless, and that everything is an effort).[31] Unpredictable schedules and always-on availability for work also affect well-being. Specifically, employees who describe their schedule as variable but feel they have little choice in their work hours also report significantly higher burnout, stress, and psychological distress. Not surprisingly, these employees have lower job satisfaction and are more likely to be planning to leave the firm soon.[32]

Overload and Sleep

Many professionals and managers recognize the toll on their health is partly due to the way that their work affects their sleep. Recall Sherwin's reflections on his work patterns and limited sleep before his heart attack, Randall's resentment when he was only getting three hours a night to sleep (due to late-night calls), Jonathon's recognition that pages and calls interrupt his wife's sleep as well as his own, and Rebecca's story about unexplained hives and needing medication to sleep. And those are just some of the sleep concerns we heard.

Pauline, a manager with about 150 employees and contractors who report to her, describes how limited sleep and limited time away from work affect her employees. She points out that people often push through a stressful week with the idea that they will relax, recover, and catch up over the weekend.

> Well, my teams don't have that . . . You never have the sensation that you are not on the clock.

Kavi, a South Asian man in his thirties and the father of two young children, describes how stretched hours and nighttime calls affect his own health and well-being. When we interview him, he has just returned from vacation. This year he decided to not check email while on vacation, and "believe it or not, I really slept well," he says. Kavi's relief was short-lived, though, because he had already been back on a late-night call and work worries were already affecting his sleep:

> We had a really rough call with VPs [pulled in] on some issues. And then I just couldn't sleep. I'm thinking this morning: there is a correlation with [that call]. I think it's stress-related sleep.

Kavi connects his poor sleep to his distraction during the day:

> There are times when I'm talking to myself . . . It's just work-related stuff and my wife tells me, "Who are you talking to?"

Sleep issues are widespread in this professional workforce. Our Work, Family, & Health Study colleagues asked over 600 IT employees to wear actigraphy watches that measure sleep objectively and in detail, capturing both time sleeping and sleep interruptions. Nearly two-thirds (65%) show evidence of what scholars call "sleep deficiency." Forty-one percent are awake at least 45 minutes after falling asleep the first time during a night, 18 percent are averaging less than 6.5 hours of sleep a night, and 22 percent respond to a survey question by saying they never or rarely feel rested upon waking. Some workers report two or three of those conditions.[33]

Our survey data also point to a connection between overload and sleep issues. Sixty-three percent of those who say they have too much work to do usually slept less than 6.5 hours, compared to 40 percent of those who do not feel that overload. Working 50 or more hours per week also makes it more likely to sleep less than 6.5 hours per night. And both subjective overload and long hours predict poor-quality sleep and greater difficulty getting to sleep.[34]

Implications of Overload for Family Relationships

Long work hours, always-on availability, and the need to put in face time in the office mean that work often spills over to affect personal life and family time. Both our survey of TOMO employees and managers and previous studies of other workforces demonstrate that those working longer hours and those reporting work overload report significantly greater interference or conflict from work to family life or personal life. They are also more likely to say they do not have enough time with their children, their spouse, or for their family to be together.[35]

What about the fourth dimension of work intensity that we have highlighted? Multitasking is quite also evident at home, and it too seems to affect interactions with family and friends. When these professionals and managers are home, phones may be buzzing with texts, pings from instant-messaging applications, and actual calls for more urgent matters, plus there is pressure to check the emails that are piling up. These overloaded professionals and managers end up splitting their attention between work and personal interactions even when they are physically at home, often annoying family members.

Consider Kunwar, a South Asian woman managing more than twenty employees who is married to another IT manager who works long hours himself. Kunwar's preteen daughter is not satisfied with her mother's presence because her attention is split.

> And my daughter sometimes will be frustrated where she'll scream and say, "You guys have very stressful jobs. You're not talking to me." Well, you know, I try to be with her, but I'm on email. And it sort of makes her frustrated.

Stella, a fifty-something manager of software developers, also describes split attention:

> I do the very same thing, you know, sitting on the couch with the laptop, working while everyone else is in the family room doing whatever it is they're doing. The good news is you're there with them. The bad news is you're half there and half doing something else.

We call this *focus strain*, in addition to the time strain that is understood to be a critical part of work–life challenges. Focus strain occurs when professionals and managers try to cope with high work demands by bringing work into family time and spaces.[36] Tanay, the manager referenced in our opening story about Sherwin and a father and husband himself, describes how new technologies foster focus strain among his direct reports:

> I get a lot of stories about people who get that [new message] and then their kids are talking to them and they sort of zone out. Their spouses and their kids get mad because they're not paying attention, because they're looking at this email that they got from their boss on the phone.

While these IT professionals and managers and their families may dislike this "normal unpredictability" of interruptions and unexpected work, it is now routine.[37] Montgomery, a manager and a white man with grown children, explains that his employees are accustomed to long hours and long weeks:

> We've got the working seven days a week straight stuff pretty much under control.

He says the "biggest impact" on family life comes from work that is "unplanned" and occurs on the weekends or nights. Thornton echoes this annoyance with unexpected work on the weekend, noting that this gets his employees "more fired up than anything." He says they (and he) react quite differently to weekend work if they are warned it is likely on Thursday or Friday, as compared to getting a call on Saturday morning. Thornton feels that his time with his preteen daughter is fleeting, and he wants to be available to her for the "Daddy times" that are left.

Despite these frustrations, we hear a sense of resignation in our interviews. IT professionals and managers expect their work to be demanding and believe they must respond accordingly. New communication technologies mean that checking in on work after hours is routine. These professionals and managers have even trained family members (especially spouses) to accept this as part of their jobs. Joseph is a manager of a team of project managers (PMs), each of whom tracks and monitors the work of several different software development groups. He describes regular weekend work but says his employees' families accept that:

> Most of the employees kind of joke about it, about how their weekend is pretty much shot . . . Fortunately (at least this is what they tell me), their families understand that's part of the job. It's what PMs do.

Spouses just do not expect much unencumbered time, even though they may be deeply frustrated by the long hours, interrupted personal time, and chronic overload.[38] The routine nature of extended work and work done at home, during official family time, is clear in Henry's comment:

> If I go home before 6:30, my kids are surprised. If they don't see me on the computer over the weekend, they're surprised, saying "Oh, you don't have work now?"

Is There a Gender Story?

Too often, discussions of work intensity are framed primarily as a desire for better work–family balance. In recent years both the popular press stories and academic research have focused on *role conflict* (investigating how work and family responsibilities do not fit together), and that is certainly important. But we are now convinced that the more acute problem, which affects many people at all ages and life stages, is *role overload*.

Defining the problem correctly is important, because it affects who sees these issues as relevant and how broad a coalition might be mobilized to seek solutions. Work–family and work–life concerns are generally understood in many organizations, in popular culture, and sometimes also in academic research as women's issues.[39] But it is not just women (mothers, wives, or caregiving daughters specifically) or women and some involved fathers whose health, happiness, and personal lives are affected by escalating demands, long work hours, and expectations of working full days in the office while *also* being responsive nights, mornings, and weekends. The burden is felt even by single men like Randall, who resents how work intrudes into his personal time, affects his sleep, and poisons his feelings toward his company.

Both women and men are hit by today's always-on work world. Among TOMO IT professionals who are not in a supervisory role, women and men are equally likely to put in at least 50 hours of paid work each week, equally likely to work at least 10 hours a week during nights or early mornings, and equally likely to work at least 4 weekend days per month. Women who are managers average 49 hours per week, and male managers average 50 hours per week. So the women working in these IT positions at TOMO are working in ways that are very similar to the men working in the same types of jobs in this firm.

Despite the broad reach of intensive work practices for the men and women working at TOMO, women seem to be hit harder than their male counterparts. Our survey data reveals gender differences in reports of subjective overload. Among IT professionals, 36 percent of men agree or strongly agree that there is not enough time to get their job done, while 48 percent of women do. Among IT managers, 40 percent of men report overload and fully 74 percent of women managers do.

Why would this be, when our interviews reveal that many men report being overloaded and exhausted, as we have shared earlier, and when work hours, nonstandard hours, and weekend hours are similar? One possibility is that there are gender differences in the *willingness to report stress or strain in surveys*. Women consistently report more stress, distress, and depression in surveys that include well-being and mental health questions (and that is true in our TOMO sample as well).[40] A question about having not enough time to get a job done may prompt a gendered social desirability bias in which respondents, perhaps unconsciously, adjust their responses to meet social expectations. Men face strong cultural expectations to be fully committed to work and successful breadwinners, and our culture's emotional rules link masculinity to stoicism.

So men may be less likely to admit—both to the field interviewer conducting the survey and perhaps to themselves—that they are overwhelmed by any aspect of work or that they find it difficult to do their jobs.[41]

Another possibility is that women's greater overload reflects *differences in their total workload—capturing both paid and unpaid labor*. These women are working full time (and overtime) in their paid jobs. The time and energy they spend on family responsibilities and caregiving on top of that may add to their sense that there is not enough time for work—or for anything else. Even though overload is centered on the work domain, having too much to do at home may make people feel more swamped in general. The men we interviewed seemed to be heavily invested in their family lives and many described specific involvement in their children's lives. But many of these stories focused on activities—on Scouts, sports, church groups, showing up at lessons and performances—that represent a "public fatherhood" that Carla Shows and Naomi Gerstel have described as the ideal among men in the professional class.[42] Only a few of the married fathers we interviewed seemed to have the *primary* responsibility for routine household and childcare tasks, or revealed they did significant "mental labor" (such as coordinating and anticipating school or sports deadlines, doctor's appointments, and more). This family-focused mental labor is often unequally distributed and drags on women's well-being, as sociologist Shira Offer has found.[43]

Our interviews also suggest that women are more aware of and concerned about bringing home their stress and bad moods from work. Mothers and wives are expected to be emotionally available and attuned to family members and to regulate their own emotions in support of others during family interactions. McKenzie reports, generally, about her team:

> They're working very, very long hours. And they're frustrated all day long. So when they get home, they take it [i.e., that frustration] to the house.

McKenzie continues with a story about a woman on her team with children at home:

She told me she got home and everybody was looking at her . . . try-ing to measure what kind of mood Mom was going to be in. And if she got started on work, she got herself [worked up]. It's like everybody was scattering, you know.

This crossover of bad moods from work to home is familiar to McKen-zie, who laughs as she recalls ranting or roaring about work to her hus-band when he has no idea what she is talking about.

In contrast to McKenzie's laughter about spewing her emotions from work at her husband, other women feel guilty about bringing negative emotions home to family members—even when they recognize that the source of their stress is a specific work situation. Kunwar, who earlier described her daughter "screaming" about the long hours and split attention of her parents' jobs, feels unsupported by her manager. He is "not a people person," she says, putting it nicely, and she recounts being yelled at and "feeling very small" after interactions with her boss. She works hard not to take those feelings out on her subordinates at work, but Kunwar feels terrible that her mood affects her family. Her subordi-nates can "go to HR," meaning the human resources department, but she feels guilty that her family has to just deal with her emotional outbursts.

I have taken it out on my family. I have. On my little child. I've gone home and yelled. That's not nice, right? And then there have been times when I've gone to my room and cried because of the demands.

Kunwar is quite emotional in the interview too, saying that her "stress level" and short fuse mean:

I feel like I'm not a good mom at times. I try [crying], try to be a bet-ter wife.

We assume that men sometimes bring their work stress home as well and rant or vent about work to family members. But we did not hear regret about taking it out on family in our interviews with men. This is consis-tent with survey research that finds that women, who know that our culture holds them responsible for a happy home and family, often feel more guilty about work interference with family time and are more distressed by the ways that work affects home life.[44]

Finally, men's and women's experience of work overload may differ because *men are more likely than women to have a spouse who is devoting most of their time to home responsibilities.*[45] Again, overload is about work demands and resources but may be affected by who is available to take care of the home and family demands too. Women in the TOMO sample are less likely to be married or partnered (73% vs. 89% of the men) in the first place. Among the married and partnered workers, 29 percent of the men working as IT professionals or managers have a spouse or partner who is not employed—and so available to take on more at home—as compared to 15 percent of the women. And women are more likely to be married to someone working 50 or more hours per week; that was true of 37 percent of married women and 13 percent of married men.[46]

When women do have a spouse who has scaled back at work, they also find some relief. For example, Kathleen is the development manager working in an especially intense group who described face-time pressures. Her husband works in IT as well and quit his "crazy hours" job a few years ago to start his own business. Kathleen appreciates that he is available at home much more than she is:

> He can be there with the kids for baseball games, things after school, and they're not home alone in the afternoon . . .
>
> So that's been really, really helpful. And also he's pretty much taken over like the—he does everything. He does the laundry. He cleans the house. He cooks the meals. I mean he's like Mr. Mom, you know, because I come home and I've worked a 12-hour day and I'm just wiped out. So he takes on a lot of that, which has helped.

Research by Noelle Chesley and Karen Kramer confirms that it is common for men who are focusing on family responsibilities to be self-employed or working as contractors rather than being a full-time stay-at-home dad who is completely out of the labor force.[47] McKenzie, who recounted venting to her husband, also shares that his self-employment makes her life easier even though they do not have children.

So he went out on his own and now we have the luxury of him working part time and it is truly amazing. It was a total change in lifestyle . . .
I'm so glad that my husband has his own business now. Because if he
worked full time and I work full time, I don't know what we'd do.

So is there a gender story? We have made a two-pronged argument:
that intensive work is a real problem for both men and women working
in professional and managerial jobs, and yet this situation seems to translate into a heavier sense of overload for women than men. On the one
hand, current work practices are not only or primarily a problem for
women or for those who are doing the work of caregiving for children
or other family members that has traditionally fallen to women. Our interviews reveal that intensive work practices and overload have real consequences for the health, well-being, and personal life of people in all different situations. And on the other hand, there is some evidence in our
survey data that women feel more overloaded, more stressed, and more
conflicted in the face of this work intensity. Drawing on a rich literature
on gender, work, and family, we note that women may feel this overload
and strain more intensely because they are more willing to acknowledge
those feelings (and admit them in the survey), because they are doing
more at home or feel they should buffer home and family from their own
negative emotions and stress, or because women are less likely to have
a spouse who has changed their work situation to provide some relief on
the work front.

There is also a deeper way that gender is implicated in this system of
intensive work and overload. When organizations structure good jobs
(meaning jobs with high pay and good benefits, high status, rewarding
or meaningful work, and advancement opportunities) so that these positions are nearly all-consuming, there are implications for gender inequality. The underlying premise of that system is that paid work is the
primary focus of adults' lives. The people who are more likely to be able
to work in these ways are traditionally men, particularly those with wives
at home. Other people—including those with day-to-day caregiving responsibilities for children or dependent adults, women who are

pregnant or nursing, and those with compromised health—find it much harder to work so long and so intensively, and to be always available for paid work. As feminist organizational scholar Joan Acker put it over twenty years ago, the very idea of a job assumes a "disembodied worker who exists for the job." Acker continued: "The woman worker, assumed to have legitimate obligations other than those required by the job, does not fit with the abstract job."[48] In other words, work organizations are gendered in subtle ways at their foundation when they assume the paid job is the only or primary focus for a given adult. And that is usually the assumption, implicitly if not explicitly.

When we look at the broader workforce, women are still somewhat less likely to prioritize paid work over all else—which sustains gender inequality. Sociologists Youngjoo Cha and Kim Weeden examine nationally representative data and find that men were about twice as likely to work 50+ hours in 2009 (although recall that the TOMO sample does not have much of a gender gap in work hours). Given the intensive expectations regarding both work and family obligations, some professional and managerial women do leave their jobs—though we understand this more as being pushed out of inflexible and unworkable situations rather than as opting out. Wives are more likely to leave their own jobs when men are working very long hours (but men married to women who work extreme hours are no more or less likely to quit). Those difficult decisions, made by individual women and by couples, end up reinforcing gender inequality. In fact, our interest in this project was driven in part by the idea that challenging overload and these institutionalized expectations would render professional and managerial work more feasible for more women and legitimize family care for more men.[49]

The intensive work practices also assume that workers have healthy, able, even vigorous bodies. Legal scholar Catherine Albiston reminds us that work is defined, culturally and legally, in contrast to disability.[50] Despite policy changes like the Americans with Disabilities Act that aim to support workers with disabilities, there is an underlying assumption that workers are able-bodied. Although IT work is knowledge work that would not be rated as physically taxing or dangerous if evaluated on the stated occupational requirements, workers with disabilities or those facing physical challenges that affect their energy and stamina may be unable to work in ways described here. We see that some older workers struggle with the long work hours and disrupted sleep—although we see younger and middle-aged workers are also affected by intensive work demands that wear down their bodies and their psyches.

The assumptions that workers are able-bodied and have significant physical stamina intersect with the dominant cultural expectations for men in US culture. Men are or should be physically strong and able to tough it out, even in physically challenging situations. Sociologist Marianne Cooper explains that the men (primarily software engineers) she studied in Silicon Valley enacted their masculinity simultaneously through technical prowess and through a willingness to work to exhaustion "in order to display the depth of one's commitment, stamina, and virility." She claims that "presented with an overwhelming challenge, it takes masculine capabilities to complete the mission, to overcome the odds." Our study includes both men and women in IT, and the IT workforce we study is more balanced in its gender composition (with roughly 40% women in the IT division of TOMO) than is the case in many tech companies. Our interviews do not ring of masculinity claims as much as some other reports of "bro culture" in tech firms do. Still, men are likely aware that their masculinity could be questioned if they seem to lack stamina, are unwilling to put work above all else, or otherwise appear weak even when faced with extremely high work demands.[51]

We have described a situation where even in good jobs, management pushes for doing more with less and new technologies enable an always-on culture that is unhealthy and unsustainable in the long run. As Georgia (one of the managers quoted earlier) said, "Oh my god! Something has got to give here!" What has given thus far, in this organization and in so many others, is employees' ability to set boundaries around their work and find time to rest, recover, and take care of themselves and their loved ones.

Employees arrange—and constantly rearrange—their lives to do whatever is needed or asked of them on the job, at almost any time and with almost no limits beyond those imposed by their exhausted bodies.

Many professionals and managers are caught in the vise, squeezed between conventional face-time expectations (where it is important to be visible and visibly busy in the office) and new technologies permitting work to occur anywhere, anytime.

How did this happen? And why do these professionals and managers put up with it? We turn to those questions and the impact of overload on business outcomes next.

Chapter 3

⌘

HOW WE GOT HERE AND WHY IT MATTERS

Is overload, and the work intensity behind it, inevitable? Our answer is no, but it is also not easy to challenge the circumstances that produce overload and this intensity. Particular management decisions drive the intensive work practices and overload we see in professional and managerial jobs. People at the top of organizations are asking more and more of employees but offering fewer and fewer resources to help them meet those escalating demands.

Common theories for explaining long hours and high investment in work often look to employees and pay less attention to employers and to the broader context that pushes companies in this direction. Financial markets reward cutting labor costs but often ignore the longer-term costs of intensive work and overload, at the same time that new technologies create new options for moving work to other countries or turning to machines and AI to do this knowledge work.

We are interested in the space between individual workers and global markets. What specific management practices create this situation within an organization? How does it seem reasonable to ask people to do more with less? And why do professionals and managers, clearly privileged in education and status, not resist the ratcheting up of workloads and always-on expectations? How are these employees both coerced and convinced to accept this speed-up?[1]

In analyzing employees' and managers' experiences, we also learn something important about how the current practices affect the firm. The company is getting more hours of work out of their workforce—without additional pay, since these salaried workers are not paid overtime—by pushing IT professionals and managers to take on more tasks and ramp up the pace of their work. That may seem to be a smart strategy, but in fact there are real downsides for the company, as well as for workers and their families. Pushing harder and working longer means that professionals and managers are stressed, less likely to be innovative, and less likely to do high-quality work, or even to remain with the company.

The (Missing) Policy Context

This period of high work intensity is also a time where workers (of all kinds) seem to have little power to push back against these demands. Early in the last century workers also experienced long hours and harsh work conditions, and probably felt overloaded too. Corporations spawned by the Industrial Revolution adopted agricultural patterns of expecting their workforce to work from sunup to sundown six days a week. Piecework, together with minimal wages and few labor protections, meant that working intensely was necessary to earn a sufficient income. Workers could be and were fired at will if they seemed to work at too slow a pace (and sometimes lost their jobs for trying to organize their peers to fight for better conditions). The urban, industrial ideal was that the father's wages would provide financial support for the family; wives and children took care of household chores as well as often taking on additional piecework, so that the men and the young, unmarried women could put in their long days in factories.

Then came a period of change, where work intensity and overload were actively tempered. With the crisis of the Great Depression fresh and building on years of struggle by labor movements, policies like the Fair Labor Standards Act of 1938 created new standards and benefits for many workers. The United States created its first federal regulations regarding an eight-hour workday and overtime, minimum wages, safety regulations, and workers' compensation funds for those injured on the job, plus the benefits for older people and the disabled established by the Social Security Act. Unionization was recognized in law through the National Labor Relations Act. Many workers benefited, and new expectations emerged. For example, the 40-hour workweek became our cultural default, synonymous with a full-time job.

Still, many workers were not covered by these labor protections. The most egregious exclusions left out domestic workers and agricultural workers, jobs that were largely held by African Americans in the South. Historians have noted that including those occupations (and those primarily black workers) would have made it much harder or impossible to pass this law at the time when racial exclusions were explicit and predominant in the South.[2] Professionals and managers were also excluded for different reasons. They were viewed as either independent of the employer, in the case of professionals, or as agents of the employer, in the case of managers. That understanding of the workforce and the relevant divisions within it justified the exclusion of many salaried workers from the hours and overtime wages provisions of labor laws.[3] Americans now use the term "exempt" colloquially to refer to most salaried workers, referencing these exclusions from the Fair Labor Standards Act.

Even among those who were covered, these labor laws did not set maximum hours of work or provide guaranteed time off via paid sick days, paid vacations, and paid family and maternity leaves. Those breaks from work are provided by law in other rich industrialized countries, but available only in the United States through corporate benefits or legislation passed by some states and localities in the last twenty years. More generally, other countries often set working time arrangements by law or through negotiations with unions, whereas the situation in the United States is "unilateral," with employers setting the rules.[4]

Explaining Overload: Three Perspectives

Understanding this context is critical for understanding overload. Scholars should pay more attention to the limited leverage that professionals and middle managers have today. Instead, many focus on the apparent puzzle of why professionals and managers work very long hours and so intensively when they are not overtly or explicitly forced to do so. Their explanations look to the employees themselves and describe internalized, softer forms of control.

The first explanation, common in popular press accounts and inspirational biographies of business leaders, is that some people are "driven" and extremely passionate about their work. Their personalities and their love for their work lead them to invest so much of their time and energy in their jobs. A less positive portrayal is that those working long hours are workaholics who have given their all to their work, relinquishing other aspects of their identity and other engagements with the world in the process.[5] But explanations rooted in personality would not predict the widespread patterns of intensive work that we see or the persistence of these practices among those people who feel overloaded, exhausted, and even "owned" by the company.

The second explanation focuses on the rewards—from business organizations and from society—that accrue from working intensively. In the United States especially, but also in other countries, hard work is valorized. In her study of women in elite finance jobs, sociologist Mary Blair-Loy developed the idea of a "work devotion schema" that motivates and legitimates working so intensely. These work patterns are thought to signal an individual's devotion to their work. That devotion, in turn, is believed to reveal the person's moral commitments—to hard work and ideally to their work as a calling. Another sociologist, Allison Pugh, interviewed workers in a wide range of jobs and finds: "Like many Americans, most [of her respondents] laid claim to intense work commitment as a core part of being an honorable person." Working intensively has long been expected of middle-class men, though we argue that the expectations have ratcheted up considerably. Sociologist Marianne Cooper's interviews with men doing IT professional work in the late 1990s are particularly relevant to our case; she argues that these technically proficient and privileged men work intensively, putting in long hours because being the "the go-to guy"—dedicated and willing to sacrifice valued personal family time—demonstrates and affirms a specific type of nerd masculinity.[6] But long hard days are increasingly expected of women and men alike.

From this perspective, workers are self-motivated and self-disciplined to work long and hard because doing so allows them to reap psychological and economic rewards—the satisfaction of doing a job well and with pride, but also financial and career rewards because businesses offer higher salaries, bonuses, and promotion opportunities to those who work in these ways. Those beliefs that one's work devotion reflects moral worth, the social validation that comes from others noticing and praising one's intensive work, and the material rewards are all mutually reinforcing.[7]

In these explanations, workers are seen as having internalized what management would want them to do. They feel that they have willingly chosen to work so intensively. Scholars call this normative control, which is contrasted with more explicitly coercive control in which it is evident that management is pushing for certain behaviors. Of course, management is working, behind the scenes, to foster normative control. Organizations deliberately create cultures that encourage high commitment to the firm, specifically, and to one's work identity more broadly. For example, sociologist Arlie Hochschild's classic study of one large manufacturing firm recounts how management crafted an organizational culture that affirms and appreciates employees, which motivates them to work long and hard. Many of these workers even experience work as a haven from family life where relationships are more stressful and less encouraging than those with coworkers. In these cases, working long hours and buying into the organizational culture proves that one is a full member of the organization. That sense of community membership is seductive, drawing workers in and justifying their intensive work.[8]

A third explanation jumps from internalized norms and identities to macro-structural changes in the economy and in technology. The claims here are that a set of interrelated changes have put increased pressure on workers, even though those workers are less likely to be protected by union contracts or informal firm commitments to lifetime employment. One important change is the push for firms, particularly those publicly traded in stock markets, to meet certain financial targets each quarter or year. Firms are increasingly oriented to maximizing shareholder value and short-term profits, rather than being managed and evaluated in terms of long-term growth, stability, or contributions to a healthy community. (This increased pressure is called financialization, though that term is used in many different ways, or the shareholder revolution.)

These financial pressures often lead management to cut costs by cutting the workforce or shifting work to cheaper labor markets.[9] Technological advances render these changes economically and pragmatically viable; you cannot ship your professional or technical work to India or to Bulgaria without technologies that facilitate sharing information immediately, privately, and securely. In global IT, we see the intersection of greater insecurity (because US workforces have been cut as the offshore workforce expanded) and new coordination tasks (because production is integrated across global teams) that exacerbate overload. In other knowledge-work industries, global teams prompt stretched work hours and new coordination tasks—although there may be less perceived insecurity if the globalization reflects expansion into new markets. And increased insecurity now arises from automation and AI, as well as from global labor chains.[10]

These macro-structural changes mean that workers have less power in the labor market, leaving many workers feeling that their jobs are more tenuous and their economic security is at risk. This insecurity is well-known for manufacturing workers losing out to production workers in other countries. But we see that even those in highly skilled professional and managerial positions now feel insecure and find it difficult to resist management pressures to work longer, harder, and at all times of the night or day. Top management is increasingly interested in the "ends" of cutting labor costs in an effort to meet short-term financial goals; tax law and labor law both make that a smart strategy. Technologies provide new "means" to trim the expensive workforce based in the United States or other developed countries. As sociologist Arne Kalleberg recognizes, "workers have few options but to consent to managers' demands that they work hard, especially when unemployment is high and there is a sizable reserve army of unemployed workers ready to take one's job."[11]

Today, the reserve army of workers who might take your place includes not only those who are unemployed in the United States or your home country, but those who are looking for work and gaining new skills in "emerging markets" around the world and those who will do the work as a "gig" or freelance job rather than expecting a job with a stable salary and benefits. Automation and AI may mean fewer human workers—even the ones earning the cheapest wages—will be needed in the future. Malcolm Harris's analysis of "the making of Millennials" reviews the growing inequalities and economic anxieties that have "made employees both desperately productive and productively desperate."[12] Millennials may be particularly hard hit by these changes in worker power and management strategy because they have been less likely to make it into "good jobs" early in their careers (and have more student debt contributing to their economic worries). But the stress of rising insecurity and inequality compels frantic work across generations, including among the professionals and managers of all ages at TOMO.

Much of the economic research and more quantitative sociological studies have looked at trends in firms' economic strategies and examined whether there are parallel trends in employees' reports of their work hours, intensity, and stress. But they only hint at the connections between the macro-structural changes and individuals' experiences. In other words, the tie between the big picture and people's lives is proclaimed but not shown. There are rich empirical (often sociological, qualitative) studies on the dynamics of internalized control, where many of these workers have taken on the task of driving themselves. But it is time to update that research. Is normative control, with its internalized expectations, still the primary driver of long hours and overload? Or have globalization, digitalization, and downsizing stripped bare the façade of normative control, so that the external forces encouraging intensive work and overload are evident and these work practices feel coerced, rather than chosen? Our research answers those questions and empirically traces the path from macro-structural changes to the lived realities of overload.[13]

The Case of IT Professionals
and Managers at TOMO

The question of why top management would expect employees to put in long hours, be available at almost any time, and put up with escalating demands may seem obvious: most professionals and managers working in the United States are paid a salary that does not go up as their hours increase, even if they work beyond 40 hours per week.[14] So the firm pushes hard to get more work from each employee, assuming that more hours for the same salary will mean greater output per dollar paid. Labor costs are tracked and monitored carefully as part of top management's efforts to meet certain financial goals watched by the financial markets. Stock prices are often expected to go up when cost-cutting measures like downsizing and shifting to offshore labor are announced.[15] Particularly in the United States, where employee benefits make up a large part of total compensation because large employers like TOMO pay a significant portion of healthcare costs, management is tempted to cut people from the primary US workforce and replace them with offshore workers, with contractors in the United States who do not get benefits, or with new AI tools.

Management can follow this business model because workers' capacity to resist is limited. High-performing employees may flee a firm with chronic overload to look for better conditions elsewhere. Those exits have real costs to the firm when deep expertise on particular systems is lost and those groomed for leadership leave. But many workers wonder if they could find a job with the same pay and benefits but less overload, and they worry they will lose their current jobs, like so many of their peers. Job insecurity often means the survivors of downsizing and offshoring accept the additional work (including the coordination, training, and monitoring with cheaper staff) that is piled on above and beyond their previous job requirements.

We use the case of IT professionals and managers at TOMO to examine how intensive work and overload is fostered by certain management practices and staffing decisions and to consider the implications for the firm, including calling out the unrecognized costs of these management practices and staffing strategies. We expect that similar analyses in other industries would find similar dynamics, and we describe research on other industries at the close of this chapter. But first we focus on the case of IT because this industry is on the cutting edge of distributing knowledge work across time and space, using technologies to distribute and coordinate work, and embracing automation and AI in white-collar jobs.

Our respondents at TOMO offer a vivid picture of how these strategies work to create compliance with unreasonable expectations, but they also reveal the unacknowledged problems with the current practices.

Unrealistic Time Lines and Implications for Quality

To understand how intensified work and overload are produced at TOMO, we must understand how software applications and programs are produced. The ideal software development process at TOMO and many other IT organizations is both linear and interdependent (details on each job are provided in appendix 1). The general process can be extrapolated to other professional services and project-based knowledge work.[16] The software development process begins when the business clients and technical experts jointly identify a business problem that IT might address. At TOMO, most clients are internal—other parts of the company. For example, the business-to-business sales force might need their software updated to track customer interests differently. Or a particular software product might need to be revamped to track external clients' use and bill them appropriately. In that case, the IT division's client would be the TOMO business unit that sells and services that product, not the external customers or end users. During the planning stage, a program manager and system engineers learn about the clients' needs and then these technical experts develop the technical specifications and requirements that lay out what the proposed IT solution will do.

Developers, who are more formally called software development engineers, write and debug code, with their code tested at various stages by testing or quality assurance (QA) staff. Once new applications are launched, production support employees maintain and troubleshoot the many applications and programs that have been developed in-house or linked to in-house systems. A well-functioning application or program requires that employees in each role do their job well or the project will have real problems. In order of their involvement, analysts need to have a good understanding of the end users' needs, preferences, and quirks; architects and systems engineers must effectively plan how to integrate new code into larger systems; developers need to write working and preferably clean code; testers should catch problems early, before the release or launch; and production support staff must have a thorough understanding of the software (and its goals) as well as quick strategies for getting an offline system up and running again.

One core problem is that the time lines for producing the new applications or programs are no longer realistic, according to the IT professionals and managers we interviewed. Kathleen is the development manager in charge of a high-profile set of applications who told us about the cultural expectation that she should be in the office as long as her boss is there. Asked about her employees' concerns, she says:

> Probably number 1 is we're not doing realistic time lines. There's a fine line with balancing what the business and the executives *would like* and what the true window that all of the people working on the project *need* . . .
>
> There's a lot of pressure to meet the time lines. So sometimes I'm hearing [from employees] that we're not giving them realistic time frames to do their work.

Often deadlines are set well before the exact parameters of the project are known. This is a form of "overselling" in which managers promise clients a product or, in this case, a time line that is unrealistic for the staff on hand. Overselling happens in all kinds of professional services.[17] Another problem is that once a plan is made with the client, the plan often changes. Jonathon, the development manager who tries to protect family time but still feels overloaded, explains that his team may get partway through a project and then the clients "decide to cancel project A and move to project B." At that point, "they usually want it yesterday." Despite the hassle and chaos, Jonathon accepts this as just the way it is:

> We have to move at a fast pace to keep up with what the business wants. In a real, dynamic, and changing world, the key is flexibility.

Here Jonathon is expecting adaptability or flexibility *from employees* responding to "what the business wants" and not expecting flexibility *for employees* regarding when, where, how, or how much they work.

Tight time lines are particularly problematic for those later in the development cycle. When intermediate deadlines are missed, tasks that fall later in the cycle must be accomplished in less time than originally planned. Vanessa recognizes that missed deadlines early in the process cause stress later on but accepts that the release dates, scheduled a year in advance, do not change.

> Well, the business never meets their dates [for describing their needs]. So then the systems engineers can't meet their dates to get their work done on time. So then we can't meet our dates, and then we can't give our estimate back, saying how much the cost is in the time frame that we need to [meet]. So it's kind of like a trickling effect and then everything gets crunched at the end.

Yet Vanessa says pushing back is not done.

> But the [release] date doesn't move. You still have to figure out how to meet the date. . . . And we don't seem to have a lot of focus to push back to the business to say "Sorry, we're done. You know, we can't do this anymore."

So IT professionals absorb the pressure of working toward unrealistic deadlines, even when requirements change along the way or early delays create major strain later in the development process.

These professionals and managers are also dealing with a new set of tasks, including additional documentation requirements, without feeling there is adequate time to fit that work in. The firm had decided to pursue a specific set of "process changes" where these technical professionals are supposed to document their decisions and their workflow processes in great detail. The IT professionals are now asked to follow standardized steps and to use established templates to both diagnose and solve technical problems. Not surprisingly, many people dislike the additional documentation and feel their autonomy and creativity has been curtailed; some think the tools are helpful and help rationalize the firm's approach to software development. But everyone agrees that the new process involves new work.

Tanay, the development manager, believes the extra work required for this documentation has questionable value, particularly in the context of lean staffing:

> You talk about someone that has three jobs already and then you throw in this other thing about writing all these documents . . . So they end up being the victim of doing 80 hours of documentation for 10 hours of work.

McKenzie, a testing manager already facing intense demands and overload, believes the documentation has "gotten out of hand." She sees the push for the new processes as a distraction from their primary goals:

> I think the bottom line is you need to produce good quality code and that's why we're all here. I think we're all kind of lost and confused and I hope it doesn't kill us.

Her frustration is clear:

> And in the end, will we have produced better code? Will things be better? I don't even think we're measuring for that—I don't even think—we're just looking to see did we do the documents. And it's really a crying shame.

McKenzie claims that her employees will accept when "the work gets crazy"—when hours are long and demands high—but they are more frustrated when it is these new documentation tasks that are adding to their workload:

> They will consistently challenge me, "Why do I have to do that? Doesn't make any sense. Why am I doing this?" . . . They don't care if the work gets crazy. They do care if I'm asking them to do stuff that doesn't make sense.

IT projects are officially evaluated on three criteria: being on time, on budget, and of high quality. But unrealistic time lines mean employees and managers feel pushed to do their work quickly, even when that interferes with quality. Simeon says it is simple:

We have way too much work to do, and not enough time to do it. So it's as simple as that . . . We rush to get stuff done, and it ends up being not as good as it should be, not as complete, not as [pause] anything.

In a focus group, Jude explains that "all the management ever can see is whether we met our dates," and not whether problems were thoughtfully avoided.[18] Another coworker, Daren, expanded on that point:

As a software developer and as an architect and designer, I'm concerned about how I build it. [But] I don't get reinforced for building it well and avoiding crisis. And, as a culture, I wish we would pay more attention to that . . . I wish we were rewarded more for professionalism and given the time to do them too.

Daren brings up his professional identity (as a developer, architect and designer) to explain why he chafes at that approach, but:

We are under siege and doing the best we can, as best as we can, in making shortcuts.

His coworker, Marie, says that others will cheer when the team makes a deadline:

"Yay! We made it on time." But I know how we made it on time and I wouldn't be applauding that. [everybody laughs]

The tight time lines do not have as big a drag on quality as we might expect, though, because the IT professionals and managers try their best to do high-quality, professional work even if it means bending the rules. Kathleen, the development manager, has been emphasizing quality— "driving my team on the quality path"—but that has affected their time lines. The executives above her want her to give up on technical perfection ("go with the 80/20 rule") in order to meet the deadlines and stay within the budget, which is primarily driven by the hours her developers charge to this project. Kathleen is resisting that guidance because she values quality and because her clients "expect it to be perfect." But most managers do compromise and, within a year, Kathleen was moved to a different role—one that would likely be viewed as a demotion because it involved fewer employees and a lower-profile project.

The rules are sometimes bent by IT professionals who do hidden work; that is, they spend more hours on a project than they actually bill in the firm's time-tracking software. The IT professionals may decide that getting the project done well requires more time than managers have allocated to it. So they decide to pursue that quality and put in the time, but not bill the client to avoid "blowing the budget." (These employees and managers do not personally lose any money by reporting fewer hours in the system than they actually work because they are salaried and classified as exempt from overtime pay under the Fair Labor Standards Act.) But this practice encourages future overload because it creates false expectations about how long the technical work actually takes. As Georgia, a testing manager who works long days herself, explains:

> That's part of the reason it's hard to get the money we need for future projects. Because it looks like we were able to do all this work, you know, with less hours than it really took us to do it. So it gets to be a vicious circle.

Georgia instructs her staff to report their real hours for that reason. But she recognizes that senior managers and executives often do not see the long hours or exhaustion of a given team, so they may believe a project only took 1,000 hours (as officially reported and billed) when it actually took 1,200 hours.

While many managers saw the "vicious cycle" and encouraged accurate time reporting, others felt pressured to stay within budget even if that meant hiding hours. One salaried employee who said he is "compelled" to report 40 or just over 40 hours per week sees this as an ethical concern. He also expresses frustration that those long hours are not recognized:

> If I work 50 or 55 or 60 hours in a week, I should be able to tell you that and then you can level the workload appropriately, right? Because otherwise it just sends a mixed signal.

If I say "Gee, boss, I'm working like crazy. I'm on early in the morning. I'm on late and night" and then you see my time sheet and it says 41 hours, you're going to go "What the hell are you talking about?" And so it, it may appear to be a corporate myth that folks are really overloaded.

Despite this, the employee concludes that complying with these directions—hiding his own labor and effectively giving that labor away to clients without any compensation—is required to keep projects coming in.[19]

Unrealistic time lines also encourage IT professionals to skip or defer maintenance of systems and hardware and to underinvest in developing new tools. Jonathon lays out the consequences of setting aside maintenance because of time pressures:

> You pinch a penny here and you pay for it there. I can upgrade this server now or I can postpone that till later, you know. There's no free rides in this stuff.

Jonathon talks about having too little "bandwidth" or staff to have anyone spend time maintaining the current systems, even though he expects they will pay for it later when they face another crisis. But this point can be extended beyond maintaining existing systems to improving those systems—innovating either by developing new technological solutions or by creating better processes for learning across the organization. Management scholars Nelson Repenning and John Sterman describe this classic problem: management must decide whether to direct time toward making more of a given product using current processes or toward developing capabilities that will lead to improved quality or productivity *later on.* As the title of one of their articles (and the focus group participant we quoted earlier) reminds us, "Nobody ever gets credit for fixing problems that never happened." Furthermore, it is tempting to just push harder "because working harder and taking shortcuts produce more immediate gains and help solve today's problems," even though that decision creates vicious cycles and more problems in the middle- and longer term.[20]

Downsizing and Implications for Collaboration

Overload—the sense that there is too much work to do given the re-sources at hand—results directly from a decrease in "human resources," meaning employees. Time lines feel unrealistic in part because the de-mands or scope of a project often don't match up with the supply of professionals available to work on that project. TOMO cut its IT work-force by almost half in the decade before our study began, with some US staff replaced by offshore workers. Downsizing was routine enough that IT employees expected it in the same quarter of each year. And we know that downsizing has lingering effects for those who stay, as well as for those who leave the firm. A survey of employees in the United King-dom found that those who had survived a downsizing in the past three years were more likely to report having to work very hard, feeling more used up or burnt out by work, and having more difficulty unwinding after work.[21] Tanay, the development manager mentioned earlier (who is widely respected within the division), sees a clear challenge with low staffing levels and high workload:

> I would just say that it's the pure [fact of] too much work for the people. We're doubling the work and cutting the people.

Lean staffing within a team affects the quality of the work and the ability to maintain systems or innovate—as noted earlier—but lean staffing also means employees are not available to help other teams. So lean staffing makes it hard to sustain the kind of supportive, col-laborative culture that many value.[22] Joseph, a manager of about twenty employees, works about 55 hours per week routinely. He ex-plains that the project managers who report to him used to pitch in when another group was feeling overwhelmed, but he now advises them not to do so.

> My team's just as strapped for time as their team is. I mean, in the big picture, in the reality of it, this company has laid off and laid off and laid off and they have not stopped the amount of work that's coming to us . . .

So our workload [has] just gone up and up and up and individually for every person. So I don't have the bandwidth to do that [pitching in for the other organization].

Later in the interview, Joseph responds to a general question about how he would describe the company culture by sharing the depth of his frustration.

Don't apply for a job here. I don't mean to be so callous. But, I'll be very honest with you: the only reason I'm here is because it pays the bills. I used to love my job. I used to love to come here.

Joseph recalls that he used to look forward to coming to work, despite the long hours, but he thinks the culture has changed. His boss is often in a terrible mood, and he feels no one takes time to recognize each other or say thanks. Another important change is collaboration and support across teams:

People went out of their way to help each other. It was really truly a team-oriented effort, and not just within each little individual team but across groups, across organizations. 'Cause everybody was pitching in to help make it happen and help get it done.

The irony is that Joseph mourns the previous collaboration within the larger organization and yet as his earlier story reveals, he feels pitching in is just not feasible for his employees who now have more work than they can handle. Joseph's reflections are also illustrative of how love for the job most often came up in our interviews: in stories of how these IT professionals and managers *used to feel* about their work.

Collaboration and teamwork are also threatened by the fear of losing one's own job. We heard rumbles, in interviews and in other conversations, about employees who withheld information because they were worried about losing their jobs. One manager described a "fear-based" strategy where his subordinates were reluctant to ask others in their group to help, even when they were swamped. By completing the tasks on their own, even if those tasks were too big for one person to complete with a reasonable workload, these employees hoped that their contributions would be recognized and their boss would not choose them to lay off in the next round of downsizing. Employees who were now the only person who knew a given program or system well (often because their previous coworkers had been let go) were cautious about training others. For example, Hayward, a developer and dad who described a specific program he had written as "his baby," seemed to put up with very long hours and calls at any hour because being the sole expert on this program meant his job was protected. In our survey analysis of over 900 IT professionals and managers, we find that those who are more fearful of losing their jobs in the next year report that they help their coworkers less frequently. That scale is called "organizational citizenships behaviors," and this finding suggests that workers are less willing to go above and beyond, particularly to assist others, when they feel insecure in their jobs.[23]

Offshoring as a Labor Strategy with Practical and Emotional Implications

While the number of IT staff in the United States has been falling, TOMO has moved more and more work offshore. Many of the US employees and managers are now working closely with workers in India, coordinating with contractors officially employed by Indian IT consulting firms, with Indian employees of TOMO's subsidiary, or both. (While Indian IT outsourcing was dominant for many years, IT work is now often done in Eastern Europe and South America, as well as Vietnam, China, and other Asian countries.) This global labor chain has been made possible by new technologies—new options for data storage, new advances in computer processing, and new communications technologies, including more reliable phone and Internet service in other countries. Other technologies affect the future of work for IT professionals and managers via automation, robotics, and artificial intelligence (AI). Although those changes were just on the cusp when we were in TOMO, the possibility that white-collar knowledge workers will lose their jobs as some more routine tasks can be handled by AI is real.[24]

For the firm, there seem to be obvious cost-cutting benefits to offshoring (as well as anticipated savings from automation and AI). The salaries paid to IT workers in India are estimated at 10 percent to 25 percent of the salaries of IT employees in the United States.[25] Yet the professionals and managers we interviewed identified important costs to a global labor strategy, some of which are borne by the employees and their families and some of which affect the firm quite directly.

TOMO employees and managers are figuring out the practicalities of working closely with counterparts across the world. Hours are stretched to facilitate that coordination, with early and late calls; that is to be expected. What is often unrecognized are the additional tasks, such as reviewing work products and training new offshore staff, that fall to onshore employees because of this labor strategy.[26] Week after week, these additional tasks fall to the US-based professionals and managers, directly contributing to intensive work practices and overload. But because these professionals and managers are salaried (and their overtime hours do not increase their pay) and because they feel pressured to do whatever is asked of them in hopes of keeping their own jobs, the full cost of this labor strategy is not clear—or is known, but not explicitly accounted—to the firm's leadership.

Kathleen explains how this global coordination work has stretched her team's hours, describing a 10-hour day in the office and then calls "from 8 to midnight, sometimes past." We shared stories of the late-night and early morning availability before, but we did not emphasize that those stretched hours are due to routine coordination with offshore staff, not only from technical emergencies or the crunch just before a major deadline. Those in the technical lead role—who straddle doing the technical work and coaching others' technical work without an official management title—are on calls more often, with some leads "on calls every single night," Kathleen shares. Employees and managers in the quality assurance (QA) role also tend to coordinate closely with offshore staff; those testing tasks have increasingly moved offshore. (Testing is seen as critical but less technically complicated than software development or planning how IT systems will work together.) One QA manager told us that 80 percent of her testers were now offshore. And experienced workers may find these stretched hours to coordinate with offshore particularly challenging, as Saul explains:

They're being asked to you know to get on phone calls at 10 o'clock at night, stay on until midnight [or] one o'clock and do those hand-offs. And, you know, some of these folks have been on the job here for thirty years. That's a big mind shift from what they're used to doing.

These intensive work practices do not just require a mind shift but require physically pushing their bodies, disrupting their sleep, and routine intrusions into their family and personal time. The challenges may be more obvious for "folks [who] have been on the job here for thirty years" and are older, but they are felt by younger workers who have always been asked to be flexible and available late at night and early in the morning too.

While some coordination work is required just to keep the global labor chain going (e.g., sharing information on project progress and responding to questions), the employees and managers in the United States believe they need to train new offshore staff and monitor the work that is done offshore. TOMO is pursuing a very low-cost labor strategy in India, paying only enough to get the least experienced IT workers there. Training inexperienced people on TOMO's particular systems requires a lot of time and supervision from the US-based employees. This can feel inefficient and irrational. For example, Joni, a director over software development groups who is also the mother of three young children, explains that experienced staff in the United States have to write very detailed descriptions of what is needed for a given segment of code (requirements) so that the offshore, less experienced staff can then write that code itself. The highly skilled developers in the United States

> don't end up developing very much. Because they spend all their stink-ing time communicating with offshore.

Employees and managers question the rationality of distributing work this way. Saul, a director, says employees tell him, "You know, you'd be better off just hiring one person onshore that can do the work of what it's taking me to coordinate with three offshore people."[27]

Respondents recognize that there are different strategies for going off-shore and TOMO's low-cost strategy means they are still relying heavily on the expert labor of the US-based professionals and managers to set up the tasks and then review them. Given the booming demand for IT labor in India, TOMO's Indian pay rates are not high enough to recruit experienced IT professionals or to retain those people long enough so that they gain experience in these applications and projects. Joni, the director quoted earlier, explains that more experienced IT staff in India have many more choices. But,

> Because we don't pay well, we end up with people who come straight out of school, have a job for six months, and then leave. So we've always got these people who really just are very inexperienced, which makes it even worse.

Joni and other IT managers are careful not to seem resistant to offshoring generally, but they do sometimes question the firm's current strategy:

> We try to lower costs so much and, at some point, somebody just needs to say, "Hey, we get what we pay for."

But the reality is that TOMO is getting more than it pays for: the firm pays the experienced IT professionals in the United States the same salary and benefits whether they work 40 hours per week or 60 hours per week. These workers take on the new tasks of communication, coordination, training, and reviewing the work of less experienced IT professionals in a poorer country, without the firm having to pay anything more for the US-based workers' labor. The firm "compensates" the US employees by allowing them to keep their jobs rather than by increasing their salaries, bonuses, or benefits as their workload increases due to the global staffing strategy.

Even beyond the extra work, there is emotional strain tied to the offshore labor strategy. Working with offshore IT professionals who are paid so much less makes US TOMO employees feel anxious about the future of their jobs. Jonathon and his team work extensively with offshore staff because they "hand off problems" back and forth. If his team can't resolve a technical problem, they pass it to the India staff to work on it for eight to ten hours and then it is passed back with notes on what was tried. Jonathon says the language differences and cultural differences (such as how you recognize coworkers or coach people) create "incredible" challenges. Yet he knows,

> I have to make sure that my team here is partnering with their team there. And my team's been reduced and we're sending more and more work offshore. So, you know, there are morale issues around that. A lot of concerns, especially in this climate, as [to] "How secure is my job?"

Many, including Zach, seem resigned to this staffing strategy:

> Most people are frank about it: you've got to tolerate it to keep your job. But do you ever really welcome that arrangement? Probably not.

But that tolerance does not provide protection. Zach describes a meeting where a senior executive was "blunt" about the likelihood of further layoffs in the United States. As Zach recounts, the executive was asked what middle managers could do to meet their technical goals (i.e., how these teams could support IT systems with so few employees left).

> He said, "Well, the thing you can do is make sure your people are trained. So if or when they do lose their job, they have a better skill set to get another job outside of TOMO." And he kind of talked frankly [about] the situation.

Because of the global staffing strategy, the firm will not, and individual managers cannot, protect these jobs or add new ones in the United States. Instead, the executive implies that the responsible managerial action is to help prepare these workers for returning to the open labor market by offering some training and expanding their skill sets (which is difficult to do, given the time pressures they face).[28] Zach accepts this reality and then laughingly admits he expects to be laid off as well.

> I'm only half joking when I say if you guys [i.e., the interviewers] come back in eighteen months, that box down there [under my desk] is pretty much an empty box. When the day comes, I'll pack my box and go. [both laugh] No, I'm serious. I've been here seventeen years. It's a matter of time, you know, to be honest.

Insecurity Limits Dissent

Fear of losing one's job renders overload the lesser of two evils. Melissa, a testing or QA manager, explains these links:

> People are afraid to say no. And they'll take on extra work instead of saying no because they don't want to be the one that said no. And people are concerned because a lot of applications are being moved offshore and IT's being hit pretty hard by that.

Recall that the testing function has seen a dramatic shift to offshore jobs and downsizing in the United States, and that Melissa later tied that pressure and long hours to her own "blood pressure–induced" stroke and forced retirement. Other interview respondents repeatedly drew connections between the global labor strategy, increased insecurity, and real effects on stress and health. Yet they put up with these demands, seeing no alternatives. Marcia is a white married manager in her fifties who works at least 50 hours per week and has been with the firm over twenty years. She describes increased stress since the firm shifted to a global labor strategy:

> All that happened and then the workload went up and on top of that— the icing on the cake—was really the worry that no matter what you did, your number could be drawn tomorrow. And I think there was tremendous pressure on everyone.

The insecurity and lack of control over what happens with your job is palpable; Marcia talks about knowing that the next round of layoffs of US-based workers might include "your number" being "drawn," almost at random. Marcia sees the effects for herself and her team:

> And I know that it brought tons of stress to me personally and I think that's inevitable . . . I would swear on a stack of Bibles that there wasn't a single person that wasn't impacted by that.

Ethan too recognizes that "people, quite frankly, get scared" and worries that "one day, I'm the next one" to lose a job. But Ethan, like a substantial number of our interview respondents, is not resentful of top management.

Instead, he assumes that the business should be "market-driven" and believes the market demands this cost-cutting and the speed-up of work for those who still have their jobs.[29] Ethan explicitly links the unrealistic time lines for projects to the promises that upper management is making to financial markets (or Wall Street). He explains that executives are

> telling the Street, "Look, we're going to turn the corner on our revenue." Right. And to turn the corner on our revenue, we got to get these projects done.

Ethan expresses some sympathy for the stress that those executives face, but he also decries the unrealistic time lines and promises they have made.

Job insecurity is the emotional engine that motivates submission to a system of intensive work demands and continual overload. The insecurity tied to the global labor process is very evident, while passion for the work (and a related interest in proving one's commitment in order to move up the career ladder) takes a back seat. IT is on the forefront of the globalization of highly skilled knowledge work and the incorporation of advances in communications technology and automation that mean these workers may be replaced by cheaper labor or displaced by machines. We expect that more and more knowledge workers, including professionals and managers in a variety of contexts, will feel this insecurity in the coming years and be pushed to accept a speed-up and ramp-up in work demands as part of justifying the continuation of their jobs.[30]

Clarifying the Consequences for the Firm

Overloaded and exhausted professionals and managers often put in very long hours and work almost frantically to the detriment of their health, well-being, and personal lives. But is this system actually good for the company? We see two possible answers. On the one hand, the firm may maximize its profits by pushing this intensity and overload even though these work practices create problems for employees, families, and communities. Individuals, families, governments, and the broader public then bear the costs of related health problems that unfold over the longer run. Society also misses out on the contributions that these workers might have made to their communities. Still, companies like TOMO may well benefit from pushing these workers as hard as they can, partly because financial markets reward them for tightly managing labor costs.[31]

Alternatively, the current practices may be problematic for the firm, but the costs associated with intensive work and overload are just unrecognized or ignored. In that case, the long hours and high intensity that current management practices encourage do not actually maximize profits. That would mean there are other viable and indeed smart labor strategies that top management could pursue, if executives fully understood the costs of their current strategies.

Unfortunately, it is hard to evaluate these two possibilities conclusively. Firms do not have a counterfactual world that allows them to test whether performance is better or worse when the same projects are carried out under the sped-up, lean system or an alternative system that has more generous staffing and more job security for employees. We cannot say exactly how the costs of the current strategy stack up against the apparent benefits of cost-cutting—in part because payroll costs are tracked carefully, but also because other factors that influence firm performance over the longer term, including quality, collaboration, creativity, and innovation, are not as easy to measure.

But there are many costs to the current strategy, and we are getting better at documenting them. There is the cost of losing talented, experienced workers who have deep knowledge of particular systems and have decided they just will not work this way anymore. We see, in our survey of TOMO professionals and managers, that those who report subjective overload (saying there is not enough time to do their job) have significantly lower job satisfaction, are at greater risk of reporting burnout, and are more likely to be seriously considering leaving their job.[32] Those exits can lead to significant delays in projects and often to lower quality, at least until the new people develop expertise in particular programs or systems. Turnover has similar impacts in other contexts when the people who leave have deep knowledge of particular clients, vendors, systems, or product lines.

There is also the cost of reduced quality and a related dampening of innovation. IT professionals and managers—and indeed workers in any field—are unlikely to come up with particularly efficient, creative, or innovative solutions to thorny technical or business problems when they are run down and stretched thin. Quality suffers because employees are trying to do more than is feasible, at a faster pace and with a leaner team. For example, when TOMO IT professionals have less time away from work between workdays—when they work later one day or begin earlier the next day—they are more likely to forget tasks and meetings at work and to have trouble concentrating.[33] Long hours and overload contribute to mistakes and poor-quality work, which frustrate these professionals and managers. Our interviews reveal how they mourn the mediocre code they must turn in, dread the problems that are likely to arise down the road because steps have been skipped or maintenance has been deferred, and feel "under siege," to use a phrase from one focus group, in an organizational culture that has changed for the worse.

When these interrelated problems escalate, the firm compromises its future performance. Management scholars Hazhir Rahmandad and Nelson Repenning also studied IT software development work processes. We see striking similarities between our case and theirs. When faced with an unrealistic workload and fast pace, the struggling IT group they study begins what they call a "get the work done loop." Facing high stress, workers are distracted and take shortcuts, and they are more likely to be absent due to exhaustion or to quit. This means the remaining members of the team face even greater pressure to somehow still get everything done, and it is easy to fall into the "make more mistakes loop." This creates long-term problems. The software developers Rahmandad and Repenning studied, like those at TOMO, are often pulled back into a project to help fix bugs in the code. So teams that have made more mistakes in past projects then end up splitting their staff time between the new projects—which still have firm and unrealistic deadlines—and desperate efforts to correct old problems. The new projects are then completed under intense pressure and with shortcuts, and the cycle of "destructive firefighting" continues.[34]

Rahmandad and Repenning use systems dynamics methods to model the longer-term impacts of this out-of-kilter system, quantitatively summarizing the situation that we had identified in our qualitative interviews at TOMO. They point out how the capabilities to do excellent work erode within the organization because employees and teams are less likely to make the investments that will benefit the firm in the future. In the context of intense pressures and especially when there is also real fear about losing their jobs, employees are less likely to devote time and energy to learning new firm-specific skills or to building connections with coworkers or clients that could help them better address future challenges creatively.[35] We heard related stories about limited pitching in and collaboration, from Joseph and others, which affects the organizational culture and discourages creative exchanges between teams. Our interviews often revealed a sense of piling on—of multiple reasons that left respondents frustrated with their jobs and exhausted. Megan, for example, finds her job "very frustrating, very stressful," and ends by saying:

> I must say I come to work every day wondering what the hell do I do here?

A work culture that prompts those feelings very likely has negative consequences for the firm. Yet the resulting losses in productivity and quality are difficult to quantify, at least in the short term and in a way that management tracks. In contrast, the cost savings that arise from cutting staff based in the United States are regularly tracked by management and monitored by investors. Even if some in top management suspect their current practices reduce product quality and innovation, it is difficult to push back against the obvious financial savings of letting people go and pressing those who remain to do more.

Other Good Jobs and Overload

Feelings of overload are evident among professionals and managers well beyond the IT field, in many "good" jobs across many occupations and industries. In some cases, the situation is very similar to the one we have sketched here: faced with pressures to be as lean as possible, management trims staff but still expects the work to get done, creating unrealistic time lines, unreasonable workloads, or the expectation of always-on availability. After downsizing (or when those who retire or leave are not replaced), the remaining workers must do more with a smaller pool of co-workers. Those employees are asked to coordinate with contractors or other contingent workers—either in the United States or offshore—who have less security themselves, lower pay, and few, if any, benefits or protections.[36] And today offshoring is not the only threat; automation and AI "assistants" may eventually crowd out even more workers, or at least transform the work that professionals and managers do.

Manufacturing workers were first affected by globalization, of course. The growth in imports of goods produced in China and elsewhere occurred at the same time that US manufacturing employment declined by almost one-fifth.[37] But professional and technical services are now routinely performed offshore too. The legal profession provides an excellent example of increased risks to high-paying, high-status jobs in the United States that make it hard to resist escalating demands. The American legal services industry moved more and more work offshore in the last decade, driven in part by a ratio of pay for Indian as compared to US professionals that is similar to what we see in IT. Attorneys in the United States have seen increased instability, with more layoffs, bankruptcies of large firms, and reduced hiring, and a decline in jobs helps explain stagnant wages in the legal profession. Work processes are also changing in law. Work that was previously highly autonomous and directed by professionals (with the support of younger attorneys and paraprofessionals within the firm) is now divided into more routinized tasks that can be handed, as separate modules, to a contract attorney in the United States, a legal services firm in India, or even automated.[38]

In medicine and biotech industries, offshore workers are doing tasks like "reading X-rays, carrying out lab experiments for new drug discovery, developing engineering design, administering payroll for companies and preparing documents for filing patents."[39] This means that some medical specialties, some scientific and engineering jobs, and whole swathes of administrative work that were previously the purview of human resources specialists and clerical workers in the United States are now susceptible to being routinized, divided, and performed offshore. When that happens, the remaining workers in the United States do higher-skilled tasks—so they may not mind that some of the grunt work is no longer on their desks—but they perform the remaining work in the context of high insecurity and high pressure. Today, debates about what types of tasks and jobs are susceptible to offshoring are being eclipsed by similar debates about the types of work that can and will be automated in the near future. Whether the cause is offshore workers or automation, the perceived threat leaves these professionals and managers with limited leverage to push back. Indeed, rather than complaining about the extra work that they are now asked to do in a leaner team or the 24/7 coordination across the globe, these professionals and managers are expected to embrace change and proactively prove their value to the restructured firm in order to keep their jobs a bit longer. In our TOMO interviews and in other studies of job insecurity today, most people just accept that as the new reality.[40]

There are also industries and firms where the link between insecurity and overload is not as clear, but we still see that technology facilitates increasingly intensive and fast-paced professional work. In medicine, for example, physician burnout is now a major concern. Doctors in primary care clinics and registered nurses in nursing homes, along with other health care workers, feel overwhelmed by larger patient loads and additional documentation requirements implemented with electronic health records. That documentation is useful to patients (who benefit from the consolidated records), but it is also used by healthcare systems and insurance companies to decide whether the professionals are providing high-quality care. This technological advance is experienced as a new hassle, since these professionals need to spend time learning the new systems and often report that these tasks interfere with patient interactions. It also facilitates closer scrutiny of their professional work. Many healthcare providers feel they have less autonomy in how they will treat a given patient or how long they can meet with someone, given their closely monitored patient load. Here the issue is not worry about job loss, since an aging population and medical advances mean the demand for medical care is rising. But these professionals are worried about the transformation of the work, the decay of professional autonomy, and the possibility that high burnout will mean high turnover—with practitioners leaving the field after extensive and expensive training.[41]

Unrealistic time lines and workloads are also evident in rapidly growing firms. Start-up founders expect employees to take on massive amounts of work in support of launching these firms. Here executives often oversell (like the IT vice presidents did in TOMO) in order to get their funders excited or land their first major client. Then they turn to staff to somehow get it done by pushing harder and faster to meet unrealistic deadlines.[42] Management may be cautious about hiring additional staff, particularly if the funds supporting the fledgling venture need to go first to developing new products or technologies. Or the existing management team may simply be unable to bring in and train as people as quickly as needed. Often there is only one human resources manager, because the founding team prioritizes technical talent or marketing experts. Early employees, who still have their own (outsized) jobs to do, then train and informally manage whatever new people are hired. Similar pressures appear in established firms that are moving into new markets. When a company is opening an office in China or developing a new product line to reach a new group of customers, management also pushes the existing staff for more—more time, faster work, and constant availability— and motivates that with the need to enter and "win" these markets, to use the corporate jargon, before their competitors do.

Intensive work may feel exciting in these start-up or high growth situations because there is an aura of working together for the business's success. But the stress effects of burnout are real, and sometimes result in the loss of key people who just can't put up with the excessive hours and expectations. Here too, compliance is partially motivated by the threat of losing your job because everyone knows that if the key targets are not hit or the big client is not found, it will be harder to get the next round of funding and the start-up might fail.[43]

Even in these times of low unemployment rates, then, many American workers—including professionals and managers—feel acutely insecure. Even if a particular job seems likely to last for the next few years, there is a sense that it will probably be harder to find a good job, with good pay, good benefits, and prospects for security and advancement in the future. And it seems even more unrealistic to find a good job, in terms of pay and benefits, *that also has* reasonable hours, a realistic pace of work, and permission to turn off their devices and take time fully away from work. In the context of growing inequality and the sense that the United States is increasingly a winner-take-all society, even relatively privileged professionals and managers feel pressured to do whatever they are asked in hopes of being labeled a winner and keeping hold of what they have.[44]

Part II

A POTENTIAL SOLUTION

⌘

Chapter 4

⌘

DUAL-AGENDA
WORK REDESIGN

UNDERSTANDING STAR AT TOMO

This book isn't just about the problem of rising work intensity and corollary feelings of overload. It is also about what might change at work to address the unrealistic demands and unsustainable toll of working long hours and feeling always on. The previous chapters paint a dire picture of how management decisions, in conjunction with new technologies, produce work intensification and overload. While this is happening in all kinds of settings, the experiences of IT professionals and managers at TOMO are particularly striking because we can see how technology facilitates offshoring and automation and how survivors of repeated downsizings feel pressured to do whatever they are asked, just to try to keep their jobs.

Decaying job quality and a related increase in job insecurity is a national challenge that requires updated and more elaborated public safety nets, as we will discuss in the last chapter. But in addition to public policy changes, are there organizational changes that might help?

We conclude that overload is a tractable problem that corporate executives, senior managers, and even work teams can take on. As part of the larger Work, Family, and Health Network, we developed and rigorously tested a potential solution. This organizational change initiative, called STAR (for Support. Transform. Achieve. Results), invites employees and managers to consider how they can work more effectively and in more sustainable and sane ways.

STAR is one example of a *dual-agenda work redesign*.[1] Dual agenda refers to the fact that these changes address both organizational concerns (working effectively) and employee concerns (working in ways that are more sustainable and sane, that reflect their personal and family priorities and protect their health). Work redesign refers to the fact that the changes proposed are not simply policy changes written in some employee manual and do not set up individual accommodations or encourage individual workers to simply be more organized. Work redesign is an effort to construct a new normal, to reconsider and then revamp what is expected and what is done in a given team.

STAR aims to challenge and change the old rules of the game. More specifically, STAR questions the previously taken-for-granted expectations that good employees are working at standard workplaces, in the office, and standard schedules, at least 9 a.m. to 5 p.m., while *also* being expected to be always on, always available for work via new technologies.

STAR was developed and evaluated by the Work, Family, and Health Network, a large research team of sociologists, psychologists, economists, public health scholars, and family scholars from five universities and two not-for-profit research centers who were supported by the National Institutes of Health, the Centers for Disease Control, and several foundations.[2] The network's goal was to identify and rigorously test changes in workplace policies and practices that might improve public health, support families and children's development, and also do well by the companies implementing them. STAR is the change we decided to test, after promising pilots and with input from organizational development experts.

Our network implemented STAR as a randomized field experiment in the company we call TOMO. That means that some work units or teams received the "treatment" or "intervention" of STAR, while others (the control group) did not. This research design allows for strong conclusions about the effects of these changes for employees, their families, and the firm. We are comparing similar employees, doing similar work, in the same organization to see how their experiences change—or do not change—under the treatment or control conditions.[3] The next chapters turn to whether STAR worked or not, but first we explain what this workplace intervention is.

What We Are Trying to Change with STAR and Why

A fundamental premise of our approach is that we try to change the workplace, not the worker. This principle became the mantra of the Work, Family, and Health Network as we planned, implemented, and evaluated STAR and the pilot projects that preceded it. In the occupational health world, this is called a primary prevention approach because it focuses "on eliminating the work hazard in the work context before it impacts health."[4]

That strategy is quite different from the popular wellness initiatives that many employers now offer. Economists note that the "workplace wellness industry has more than tripled in size to $8 billion," and over 50 million US workers are covered by employer-based wellness initiatives.[5] These workplace wellness programs begin from the premise that the employees' unhealthy behaviors harm their health over the long term and that employers can encourage—and often incentivize—healthier behaviors. Employers hope to reduce healthcare costs and absences tied to sickness or chronic conditions by encouraging people to engage in healthier behaviors. Wellness programs target individual behavior change, providing coaching and accountability for quitting smoking or exercising more or teaching stress-reduction practices like meditation and yoga. Even corporate programs that aim to create a healthier work environment focus on healthy food in the company cafeteria and taking the stairs more often while at work.

These behavior changes may help people handle stress better and may encourage healthy behaviors,[6] but *corporate wellness programs take the problematic work conditions as a given*. Our perspective is different. We do not want to help overloaded employees and managers cope with stressful work conditions by nudging them to exercise or teaching them stress management techniques. We fear that wellness initiatives are Band-Aids that may provide a bit of relief for some employees but are unlikely to decrease overload, reduce burnout, or curb turnover. We want to change the stressful work conditions themselves.

STAR targets three specific work conditions in pursuit of the broad goals of improving well-being and making work more manageable over the longer term. STAR is designed to (1) increase employees' control over when and where they do their work; (2) promote social support for personal and family lives (including recognizing the need for time off from work); and (3) manage high work demands by focusing on results rather than time spent in the office or online and by reducing low-value work whenever possible. These targets are intertwined: if organizations evaluate employees on concrete accomplishments (results), it becomes less important to dictate exactly when, where, or how the work is done. Then workers are more likely to feel their outside commitments are respected and valued, along with their contributions on the job.

The Work, Family, and Health Network began to design STAR by drawing on social science theory.[7] We were influenced by the job strain model developed by Robert Karasek, an organizational scholar who pioneered studies of work and health. Karasek's claim was that the combination of high work demands and low control, including limited authority to decide how to do one's work and limited utilization of one's skills in that work, promotes stress and harms health. Karasek and Theorell later expanded this model to include social support, suggesting that workers with more support from their managers, coworkers, or others might be able to handle the strain of high demands and low control more effectively and therefore not suffer as many negative health consequences.[8]

Our Work, Family, and Health Network team drew on these well-established concepts of demands, control, and support at work, but we extended these ideas in important ways and conducted pilot studies that tried to actually change these work conditions. We saw that understanding job quality and the many ways work impacts health and well-being requires us to think *beyond the job*, to consider what work conditions are central to managing life at work *and* life outside of work.

The classic perspectives on work and health emphasize control over how work happens—called job control in Karasek and Theorell's model—such as being able to decide what to do on a given day or having a say in how you approach a project. We also consider workers' *control over when and where* they do their work. This concept of schedule control does not replace job control, nor is it folded into it.[9] Both matter. We found in a pilot study at Best Buy's corporate headquarters that both job control and schedule control affect people's well-being, their pursuit of healthy behaviors like adequate sleep and exercise, and their attitudes about their jobs.[10]

Just as we added a schedule control component to the broader concept of job control, Leslie Hammer and Ellen Ernst Kossek recognized that classic discussions of support at work needed expanding. Hammer, an occupational health psychologist, and Kossek, an organizational behavior scholar, worked together (and as part of the Work, Family, and Health Network) to study and empirically measure manager and coworker support for an employee's life outside of work. Supportive managers predict employees' job satisfaction, well-being, engagement, and commitment, but we have usually focused on how managers support employees' work performance, not considering *how managers support an employee's personal or family life*. In a pilot study in grocery stores, Kossek and Hammer developed new strategies for capturing "family-supportive supervisor behaviors"—the concrete things that managers do and say to convey their support for employees' personal or family life. They found that managers' support for personal or family life uniquely predicts job satisfaction, plans to leave a job, and levels of work–life conflict. Kossek and Hammer also developed training for frontline managers to encourage them to demonstrate support for employees' family and personal lives.[11]

The network's pilot studies also pointed to the value of moving from *focusing on time to focusing on results or concrete accomplishments* in the workplace. The language of "results orientation" and "results only" comes from Cali Ressler and Jody Thompson and their Results Only Work Environment (ROWE) initiative developed at the corporate headquarters of Best Buy Co., Inc. Gender scholars have long critiqued the assumption that an employee's performance or contributions can be measured by long work hours and especially face time in the office, visible busyness, and a willingness to prioritize the job over family and personal life. These markers of an "ideal worker" are an inappropriate measure of who gets work done well. The attention to long hours, face time, and availability for work also reproduces and reinforces gender inequality, because women and particularly mothers find it harder to live up to those ideal worker expectations.[12] Ressler and Thompson build on this critique of a time orientation to work and name the alternative as "results orientation"—a name that is likely to appeal to management. Our own pilot study at Best Buy demonstrated how employees benefited when they let go of evaluating commitment by hours worked or visible busyness and ask how all their tasks and activities actually contribute to the end goal or key result.[13]

Taken together, these pilot studies confirm that we can change the workplace with regard to schedule control and supervisor support for family life, and we can foster a results-oriented (vs. time-oriented) culture. These studies also suggest that those changes improve employees' health and well-being and benefit organizations through increased job satisfaction and reduced turnover. Building on that research plus valuable input from organizational development experts Cali Ressler and Jody Thompson and a small advisory group of TOMO employees and managers, the network designed the STAR initiative to target these three elements:

1. STAR empowers employees regarding when, where, and how they do their work on a day-to-day, operational basis, with the expectation that teams will work together to determine what is feasible for employees in specific roles. This shifts some control or latitude from managers to employees, although the basic parameters of what projects they are tasked with and what metrics they are trying to meet are still decided by management.

2. STAR recognizes and affirms that employees are people with responsibilities and interests outside of work. STAR facilitates team conversations about employees' and managers' wishes and goals for their personal and family life, claiming that it is

legitimate to keep those priorities in mind when planning work rather than simply fitting life in around the edges of an intensive job.

3. STAR encourages employees and managers to reduce low-value work—reflecting on whether particular activities are useful for achieving a certain result or are simply habitual, like regular meetings every Monday with no particular agenda. STAR provides a venue and script for teams to critique inefficient and time-consuming practices and to challenge expectations that the best employees put in long hours and are always available to work.

We did not explicitly design STAR to address how technologies are used but we see, in retrospect, that this is also an important element of this initiative. STAR training and related conversations encourage employees and managers to be more deliberate and thoughtful in the use of new communications technologies that are clearly central to their work lives. As we show in previous chapters, interrelated changes in technology and in firms' labor strategies create escalating demands for the remaining US employees who are now coordinating their work around the globe and around the clock. Many people—in our IT case but also in many other professional and managerial jobs—feel they cannot control when or how much they work because emails, texts, instant messages, and virtual meetings grab their attention and pull them away from their "real work" during their work time. And it is harder to get time fully away, meaning completely unplugged, from work too. Managers, coworkers, and clients or customers all know that the new technologies mean a professional or manager *can* be reached 24/7 and so many expect that they *should* be responsive almost 24/7.

With STAR and similar work redesign initiatives, though, professionals and managers can interact with these technologies differently. Rather than reacting immediately and automatically, workers and teams can become more deliberate about how they want to use the technologies for their own purposes and goals. Dual-agenda work redesigns prompt reflections on how technology tools are working or not working for getting the job done. Employees also reflect on taking care of personal and health needs by stepping away from their smart phones, email, text, and chat. In addition, these discussions may help professionals and managers stay focused on their real work by creating more protected, offline time while working too. It is challenging to resist the pressure to be always on and always available, but technologies can be tamed and used to workers' advantage if current practices are interrogated with an eye toward both what works for the company and what works for workers.[14]

These are the three targets of STAR, but how are those changes pursued? STAR pairs bottom-up changes implemented by teams of employees with structured training to promote managerial supportiveness. Specifically, STAR includes (1) supervisory training for managers on strategies to demonstrate support for employees' personal and family lives while also supporting employees' job performance; and (2) participatory training sessions where teams identify new work practices and processes that would increase employees' control over work time and help reduce low-value tasks.

As implemented in TOMO, STAR involves eight hours of participatory sessions for employees (with managers present) and an additional four hours of training for managers on their own, plus an activity where managers reflect on and track how they are interacting with their employees. STAR sessions are spread out over eight to twelve weeks so that managers and employees hear new ideas and then have time to process those, discuss them informally, and try out new behaviors between facilitated team trainings.[15]

Early in STAR, managers are encouraged to try out expressing more support for their subordinates' family and personal lives, as well as being sure they are offering encouragement and resources about work tasks and career goals. This part of STAR focuses on increasing managers' explicit support for their employees; it begins by recognizing that managers often feel they are supportive, but that they may not convey that support to their employees. Building on Hammer and Kossek's pilot, we gave managers an app that reminded them, a couple times each day for a week at a time, to either connect with an employee to express their support or to track any supportive interactions they had already had that day. The idea is to encourage managers to see supportive interactions as a relevant goal and to create new habits by reminding managers to act in more explicitly supportive ways.

Employees and managers also attend participatory training where they discuss the organization's expectations of workers, everyday practices, and company policies, and then identify new ways of working where employees have more say in when, where, and how they work and where support for others' personal obligations is more consistently expressed. Sessions are structured, yet very interactive. The first session is intended to signal top management's support for changes associated with STAR; the vice president for that work unit is often present or, at a minimum, the facilitator mentions the executive's support for STAR. Subsequent sessions then prompt discussions such as how much work at home is feasible for different jobs and how teams can communicate and coordinate effectively without as many meetings or calls. Employees and managers discuss inefficiencies and frustrations with old work patterns and imagine how working differently may benefit their productivity as well as their personal and family lives.

STAR versus Flexibility as Accommodation

Work redesign initiatives like STAR differ in important ways from the more common flexibility policies, even though the common arrangements also involve changes in work schedules and work location. Company policies may allow flextime (shifting work hours occasionally or regularly), telecommuting (working from home on an occasional or regular basis), and perhaps shifting to a part-time schedule in a job that is usually full time. A study of over 1,000 US employers with at least fifty employees reports that 81 percent allow at least some employees to periodically change the times they start and stop work and 67 percent allow occasional work at home or telecommuting.[16]

But the devil is in the details. Individuals can ask for a flexible work arrangement, but managers generally have blanket authority to approve or deny a request for flexibility. That is the situation when there is a formal company policy (because managers' approval is written into the policy) and when there is no written policy, as in many smaller work-places. We call this approach *flexibility as accommodation*.[17] An individual employee negotiates with a manager, and the dynamic is often one of "Mother, may I?" or "Father, may I?" Ideally, the manager's decision is based on whether it is feasible to make the requested changes in this job, and ideally the employee is supported by a company culture that conveys broad support for flexibility. But the whole discussion is approached as an individual, personal need that the employer will address or accommodate if it seems possible to do so. In practice, then, many workers—even professionals and managers—have limited access to flexible work options.[18]

One story from TOMO illustrates the dynamics of flexibility as accommodation. In the years before STAR, a man we call Hayward requested permission to work at home between two and four days per week. Working at home seemed feasible because 90 percent of Hayward's interactions consisted of calls, IM chats, and emails with clients or other IT teams using the application he had developed and now supported. Few of those interactions were with people who worked in the same building. Hayward's manager, Lachlan, approved the arrangement and referenced it positively when we interviewed him. Hayward reported "no worries, no hassles from managers." Working at home regularly also worked well for Hayward and his family, including his wife, who works as an IT professional in another firm, and his two young children. If Hayward worked late one night, he could easily shift his hours to start later the next morning and take the kids to school:

> I tell my wife, you just get yourself to work and I will do the morning. I can do that because I don't have to be in [the office] at 8 a.m.

These arrangements changed, though, when the IT division was reorganized—again before STAR—and teams were shuffled to report to new managers. Hayward reports that his new manager, Rhonda, "doesn't like to work that way. So I had to start coming to the office five days a week." From Hayward's perspective, what he does in the office ("getting on the phone, doing emails and IMs") is just the same as what he would have done at home, except:

Now I've spent two hours commuting. And I'm signing my kids in and out [of the after-school program], saying "God, they spent 10 hours here" . . . You come home, you're cooking dinner and it is 7 p.m. You are thinking, "Something has to change. This isn't working."

Rhonda wasn't comfortable with regular work at home, even though there were no practical problems with Hayward's work patterns (we interviewed her as well). She doesn't give a practical reason for requiring five days per week in the office—and, in this accommodation framework, she doesn't need to. Flexible work options like regular work at home can be approved or denied, at the manager's discretion.

In Hayward's story, we see that flexibility as accommodation is valued and appreciated by those individuals who successfully negotiate it, and we also see how little control employees have over whether they win or keep a flexible work arrangement.[19] There are also real equity concerns when flexibility is doled out in these ways. Workers who are not professionals and managers are more likely to be in place-bound jobs or have rigid shifts (for those in hourly service jobs in retail, restaurants, or hospitality). And there are many administrative and clerical workers who could work more flexibly—especially given current technologies—but are not allowed to do so. Workers who earn more, who have more education, or who seem to have more options for finding another good job are more likely to have their needs accommodated when flexibility is negotiated in these ways.[20]

Even for those who win flexibility, using flexible work arrangements like flextime or work-at-home options is risky. A growing base of research shows that these arrangements often trigger "flexibility stigma." When these options are treated as accommodations and seen as deviations from the norm, employees are expected to trade off promotion opportunities or wage increases in exchange for being able to work in these ways. Those who are allowed to shift their schedules or work at home may be viewed as less committed to their work and evaluated as less suitable for advancement.[21]

The career risks tied to using flexibility policies may, ironically, reinforce gender inequality. We say this is ironic because US firms adopted flexibility policies in part to respond to women's and particularly white, middle-class mothers' movement into professional and managerial jobs in the 1980s and 1990s. Women may be more likely to seek these arrangements because their family caregiving loads are often larger. And mothers may accept the attendant career penalties because there is cultural support and even pressure for mothers to prioritize family over work. Men may seek out informal avenues for flexibility and work at home, changing their work routines under the radar without using the formal, and stigmatized, flexibility policies. For example, Erin Reid's study of management consultants found that about a third of the men (and about 10% of women) "passed" as ideal workers. These consultants limited their work hours and their travel, as compared to their peers working very long hours, *without using the company's official flex policy.* Those who passed had performance ratings that were "significantly better than those who revealed their deviance" by seeking out formal flexible work arrangements. In Reid's study, women were more likely to seek out the formal flexible work options, to feel marginalized or penalized for doing so, and to leave the firm in frustration.[22]

There is one more risk of flexibility as accommodation: it distracts from the real problems of intensive work, overload, and instability and offers a solution that is not on track for solving those problems.[23] We have been studying work and family concerns for over twenty years—and we have been examining companies' work–life policies for most of that time. But our thinking has evolved in recent years. We now see that the core concern for professionals and managers is not how to balance work and the rest of life (or work and family caregiving, more narrowly) but how to manage all that one is asked to do at work. The root problem is not how work and family come together, but intensified work. This means flexible work arrangements that are understood as an optional accommodation for the personal needs of particular workers send us down the wrong track.

STAR as Institutional Work and Institutional Change

In contrast to the more common flexibility as accommodation, STAR and related dual-agenda work redesign initiatives have deeper goals, a broader reach, and a different process. Let's look at the deeper goals first. *STAR tries to create a new normal, to rewrite the rules of the game* in this work organization. Scholars use the term "institutions" to refer to the rules of the game that guide people's behavior in a given social setting.[24] In workplaces (and other organizations such as schools and community groups), rules and policies formally guide behavior by laying out what is allowed and what is not. But people are also guided by informal norms that become deeply embedded in the way that people work together and that affect how people are judged by others and by themselves, and how they are rewarded.[25]

As it relates to overload, the central rules of the game are those determining when, where, and how work is done, who has control over those decisions, and whether it is legitimate to organize one's work time and work practices around personal and family life. Things like the working full days from Monday to Friday (regardless how much work was done over the weekend), working on-site during certain hours of the day, responding immediately to any text from a manager, and even starting meetings five minutes after the official meeting time on the calendar are taken for granted and often unnoticed—unless someone does not comply with those expectations.

When people try to establish new rules of the game, when they challenge the current rules of the game, and when they work to expand, enforce, or avoid those rules of the game, they are doing what organizational scholars call institutional work.[26] STAR is a sustained example of institutional work because the initiative prompts employees and managers to look critically at the way they work, aiming to disrupt the institutionalized rules of the game by pointing out all the problems they create for individuals, teams, and organizations. STAR then encourages employees and managers to identify new ways of working that can benefit them personally while also achieving organizational goals.

Changing the institutionalized rules of the game requires a multifaceted and multilevel approach. To illustrate what we mean by multilevel changes, consider two specific behaviors that are central to STAR: working at home and shifting work hours. Individual behaviors can and do change in STAR, but this work redesign approach involves more than just beginning to work at home or shifting schedules for personal and family reasons. STAR aims to change how people understand their roles (as employees, as managers, as dedicated members of their families) and what is accepted and expected in everyday interactions and practices. In STAR, the individual behaviors of working at home or varying one's schedule are not viewed as an accommodation that is granted, sometimes, by a manager.

Instead, in STAR, people may work different schedules and work at home more but, as importantly, *employees and managers have different assumptions about who legitimately decides when, where, and how work is done* and what these work practices signal to others. They also interact differently based on these new understandings and decision rules; a manager would no longer expect an employee to ask if she can work at home one afternoon, for example, and the employee may not tell anyone at all where she is working. Of course, management still makes a key decision— the decision to initiate STAR or a similar work redesign initiative—and this type of initiative may involve policy changes that need executives' approval. But STAR simultaneously involves frontline workers and managers, talking together and as teams, grappling with the way they do their work and how they interact with each other.[27] This means STAR is much more than a policy change approved by top executives and then rolled out to subordinates.

It is vital that *STAR and related work redesign initiatives are implemented through a collective process.* A whole team moves into STAR in TOMO; in other organizations, a whole department, division, or even the whole firm may do the work redesign. The team or work group collectively discusses how best to accomplish their objectives. They discuss the needs and preferences of individual members, covering both what is required to get a given person's job done but also what the employee or manager hopes to do with regard to their health, personal life, or family life. The collective process of STAR training is key for the institutional work of reinterpreting existing beliefs and practices and then legitimating the new ways of working.

The collective experience also means we avoid a common problem with flexibility as accommodation: the assumption that working in different ways is only needed by some subgroups, such as mothers, women with other caregiving responsibilities, and perhaps men who are unusually committed to family time. STAR is not about some people asking for something special (like permission to work at home or to be offline on Thursday afternoons) but about everyone reflecting together on current practices and possible improvements.

The dual-agenda framing means this type of work redesign looks for changes that are valuable to the firm *and* to employees.[28] As we show in the following sections, employees in STAR readily see what is in it for them if their team succeeds in supporting everyone's freedom to work when and where they choose. But the personal benefits are balanced by the anticipated company benefits. This is important because family-friendly initiatives are so often understood as women's issues. In dual-agenda work redesigns, the "work smarter" goals may make it easier for men to get on board without necessarily admitting that they, too, care about personal and family commitments. Supporting STAR can be consistent with masculine expectations of being fully committed to work—because STAR is about improving workplace effectiveness as well as other (previously questionable) personal goals.[29]

What STAR Looks Like: Illustrating Institutional Work

STAR provides an unusual opportunity for employees and managers to reflect together on the way work is done and how individuals, teams, and the larger organization can function more effectively while also supporting employees' health, well-being, and personal commitments. Two central messages in STAR are that employees are free to work when, where, and how they choose, although they must still get their work done and be part of their team, and that it is perfectly appropriate to discuss and prioritize family and personal life alongside work responsibilities. But how are these messages conveyed so that the rules of the game might actually change?

This kind of change requires *a space where employees and managers can set aside their regular tasks to take the time to reflect and experiment.* STAR training sessions are both temporally bounded and symbolically bounded or set apart from the usual tasks and rhythm of the day. Employees and managers are asked to set aside their usual work for this time of talking as a team about how they work, and the company is providing permission to pursue these changes by providing this time.[30] This kind of change also requires *guides who will lead and model the process of questioning the old rules of the game and articulating new ones.* In TOMO, these changes were guided by expert facilitators, especially Jody Thompson and Cali Ressler.[31] Those promoting work redesign—whether they are external facilitators or internal change agents—need to deftly employ multiple strategies to help this collective process work, always reading the room and adjusting their delivery to create enough disorientation to prompt learning without pushing so hard that they create a panic.[32]

Motivating Change: Establish a Broad Need or Desire for Change

Facilitators motivate participants' interest in STAR by showing that the current ways of working are not working well for many people at TOMO. Facilitators first ask people how the work gets done in their group or team. Then the facilitators ask: "Given the way things are today, how do you feel?" Participants were asked that simple question and then invited to write one to three words on a white board (without comments from others at this point). In Figure 4.1, we see responses from ten training sessions where over twenty-five teams of employees and their managers responded. The larger words were offered as answers more frequently, and we have marked words with a positive valence in a cursive font and those conveying negative feelings in an upright font.[33] Not surprisingly, the feelings here reflect the stories and insights we shared in previous chapters. For example, Randall (whose frustration with long hours and evening meetings was described in chapter 2) responded to the question of "how do you feel today" with the word "dread," while his boss, Jonathon, wrote "bitter" on the white board.

Notice that work–family challenges or parents' or caregivers' needs are not understood as the primary problem to be solved—although they are treated as legitimate concerns when participants share them in STAR training. When all employees and managers are invited to reflect on the

FIGURE 4.1 Responses from employees and managers from 25 teams participating in 10 separate STAR Sessions at TOMO to the question "Given the way things are today, how do you feel?"

culture of the organization, it is not only mothers or parents who describe negative feelings. Most feelings are focused on the employees' experiences *at work or while working*, not only how work fits with the rest of life. STAR addresses the way everyone works, calling out the inefficiencies and inconsistencies in the routine ways of working and suggesting there are smarter practices that will benefit employees—of all genders and all life stages—as well as benefiting the organization.

There is a powerful message in this collective opening to the STAR training sessions, where insiders make the case that change is needed. Individuals know they are stressed, unhappy, and frustrated and they may realize that they are not working in the most efficient, effective, productive, or sustainable ways. But the breadth of frustration expressed in these sessions suggests that the status quo is not working for the organization as a whole. Hearing so many of your coworkers and even managers acknowledge their dissatisfaction makes it harder to argue against the need for *some* change—even for those who are skeptical about STAR specifically.

Deinstitutionalizing: Prompt Critique of Current Practices and Assumptions

Facilitators then set up opportunities for critical reflections on the current ways of working. Organizational scholars call this *deinstitutionalization*—challenging what was previously accepted and perhaps even unnoticed or taken for granted. The old practices and beliefs are called out and made visible, no longer assumed to be legitimate or reasonable or just the way it has to be.[34]

Facilitators raise questions about current practices with regard to (1) how flexible work is approved; (2) how work tasks and meetings are prioritized and managed; (3) how communication norms function; and (4) how rewards are distributed.[35] While facilitators are clearly encouraging critical reflections, the participants articulate the critiques. Some TOMO professionals and managers disagree with the critiques but then they hear from their peers, who may be more convincing to them than the outside facilitators would be. This dialogue helps individuals in the organization take ownership of the changes offered via STAR.[36]

One important critique presented in STAR is that flexibility is doled out to employees inconsistently and unpredictably. Before STAR, TOMO operated with flexibility as accommodation: an employee who wanted to work at home or shift their hours on a given day or even skip a meeting to meet a more important deadline needed a manager's permission. (Recall the story of Hayward.) Some managers approved such requests routinely and a few of the most supportive managers told employees to just do whatever they needed—though employees were sometimes told to keep those arrangements quiet. But other managers did not approve these flexible work practices (as we saw with Rhonda requiring Hayward to come back into the office full time) or expressed annoyance, leading employees to worry they might pay a price for such arrangements in their performance evaluations or future prospects.

Facilitators suggest that this uneven playing field reveals a lack of trust from managers, regardless of managers' statements or intentions. As one facilitator explained in a training session, when flexible work arrangements are "doled out one by one" there is often "hostility and resentment, not the inclusive environment" that TOMO wants. One facilitator said she had learned from focus groups at TOMO that "flexible work programs are a 'who you know program' . . . if your manager is willing, you can do it. But if you have a less willing manager, you are not able to do much about it."[37] The two top managers in the room nodded in agreement at this description. In contrast, the facilitator explains that in STAR, "no permission is needed to do what you need to do at any time."

A second critique is that there is too much low-value work—and especially too much time wasted in meetings that these technical professionals do not see as their real work. It is proposed that overload can be addressed, at least partially, by setting aside some tasks and by blocking out more time for the technical work. In a session with one of the first groups moving into STAR, lead facilitator Cali Ressler asked the participants how productive meetings were. (Again, this type of questioning and crowd-sourcing encourages insiders' acceptance of the emerging diagnosis of the problem.) An employee stated that only about 5 percent of the meetings she attends are productive, and most of her coworkers in the room agreed. Other teams (responding to the same question in other sessions) put the proportion of worthwhile meetings higher—but every group said that some meetings were unproductive and unnecessary. For example, an employee says to her peers and managers:

> We can spend at least an hour or two–three hours at a minimum in status meetings and keeping the tools up to date . . . We spin constantly.

Facilitators do not dictate how low-value work, including specific meetings, could be trimmed or revamped, but urge teams to consider this together.

Facilitators also ask professionals and managers whether they actually need to be constantly available to handle work questions. Here they are critiquing flexibility as always-on availability (without using that language). Facilitators note that TOMO has developed a culture of instant responsiveness, where people expect that others will reply to IM or emails immediately or pick up their phones for any work-related call at any time.

Participants are invited to reconsider when quick responses are actually required and when they are habitual or perhaps reinforced by formal and informal rewards. Facilitator Cali Ressler argues, in one training session, that

> There is a *sense* of urgency and there are things that *are* urgent. You need to determine which things, in your estimation, are [truly] urgent.

Melissa, whose experiences are detailed in chapter 3, admits in a STAR session that her team has "fanned the flames" of the "fire drills" and then says, "This is a culture we need to break."

Employees in other jobs and companies also fall prey to treating everything as urgent, expecting immediate responses, and pushing for near constant availability. Leslie Perlow, in her study of management consultants, lays out this "cycle of responsiveness" within teams that leads to "sleeping with your smartphone" (and then introduces a dual-agenda work redesign that we will discuss later). Kate Kellogg's study of very long hours in surgical units in hospitals considers how different units responded to a regulation limiting residents' work hours. In resistant units, the assumption was that having residents there—either on the floor or sleeping in the hospital—was essential for coordinating patient care effectively. In other units, though, teams found new tools and routines to share information effectively and take good care of their patients while also trimming residents' hours. While the old practices relied on residents' constant presence, that was not the only plausible way to meet the goals of providing good care.[38]

Employees and managers in the STAR team training see the personal costs of being always on and treating every query and task as urgent. Still, the facilitators' argument that they can be offline more—not available on IM or email—is sometimes a hard sell for TOMO professionals and managers. A critical part of the IT role, within business organizations, is to keep systems up and running 24/7. That need for constant surveillance and tending of the IT systems is accepted as a given across many groups and for many roles, even though it is actually a relatively small group of IT professionals who respond to problems in launched systems and applications at TOMO.[39] Ironically, the production support teams who are officially on the hook for quickly solving technical problems in live systems tend to be well prepared for STAR. These teams are already deliberate about sharing the burden of being on call (with rotating "pager duty" routed through their phones), and they recognize it is important to deliberately structure some time fully off work. These teams have established protocols for handling technical emergencies, so they had already discussed what was truly urgent and what was not. STAR aims to encourage that kind of deliberate reflection and team coordination in other groups and across all roles.

The next step in the critique is to ask how the reward systems work in this organization: Are people recognized and rewarded for long hours, quick responses, and always-on availability, or for their actual contributions to a project? Facilitators propose that managers and employees often focus on face time or visibility in the office (and quick responses online during the evening, night, and weekends). We heard about this in interviews, like Kathleen's quote earlier, where people paid attention to when their bosses were in the office and tried to be sure to stay until they left. Comments about how long people are working, when they come in, or whether they are available on IM are labeled "sludge," a term developed by Jody Thompson and Cali Ressler in their Results Only Work Environment (ROWE) initiative.[40] Facilitators point out that sludge and the self-justifying responses to those comments reinforce the old rules of the game. For example, suppose a person comes into the office at 10 a.m. and a coworker says, "Just coming in? Wish I had your hours." This one comment reveals the assumptions that the employee was not working (earlier or perhaps late the previous night), that work needs to happen in the office for it to count, and that adherence to specific schedules will be noticed more than the actual work tasks that are accomplished.

Because work time, work location, and always-on availability are not accurate indicators of productivity or dedication, facilitators claim, they should not be the focus of managers' or others' evaluations. This critique helps participants accept that employees can appropriately decide when they work (with appropriate coordination across the team), where they work (with appropriate consideration of what types of tasks are easiest face-to-face), and when they are away from work to concentrate on other parts of life.

But if hours and adherence to old norms isn't going to be rewarded, what is? The idea is that being clear on an employee's goals and evaluating actual results helps managers and other employees avoid the temptation to evaluate performance based on hours, face time or visibility in the office, or always-on availability. Yet in STAR sessions, we sometimes heard frustration about vague goals and unclear priorities. For example, when Judd said "I need a clear assignment," other TOMO employees in the room suggested he go to his manager to push for clarity on his goals and priorities. This illustrates how STAR discussions go far beyond what is usually seen as flexible work arrangements to encourage reflection on current work processes and management practices, including setting clear goals and being thoughtful about the metrics that are used to measure performance.

Proposing and Framing New Practices: Align New Ways of Working with the Organization's and Managers' Interests

Once the old routines and expectations have been critiqued, new ways of working need to be proposed and sold as appropriate and worthwhile. Facilitators need to show how employees and managers can both be good members of TOMO and be excited about STAR. Three claims align the new initiative with the firm's interests and managers' valued identities.

First, the language of professionalism is deployed to argue that STAR's focus on autonomy is appropriate for this particular workforce. Facilitators suggest that professionals—including the IT developers, testers, analysts, and managers at TOMO—are ready and able to work differently. Because these professionals are already trusted to make technical decisions and to work hard to achieve their work goals, it is sensible and even smart to trust them with managing their own work time and work processes as well.[41]

Second, facilitators contrast STAR's understanding of managers as supportive coaches with managers' previous scrutiny of employees' work schedules, work location, attendance at particular meetings, and the like. The old ways are critiqued (usually by other participants responding to facilitators' questions) as "micromanagement" or monitoring "butts in seats." In one session, a facilitator explicitly compares young adults' experiences of being trusted in college with their experience on the job— which implies that managers are inappropriately treating employees like children. She says that college "kids" are trusted to get their work done, with resources offered to support them but no monitoring by "mom and dad."

> Then they graduate and go to work and get a cube assignment and they are told to be there [in the office] from 8–5, Monday to Friday with a certain time for breaks and lunch. How do we know if that person is productive just because they are at their desk? . . . People just want to be trusted.

Many managers welcome this analysis, suggesting that STAR matches the way they would like to manage. They want to think of themselves as "managing the work and not the worker," to use a phrase from training. Wyatt, a manager who supervises about forty people working in multiple locations, declared:

> I view my direct reports as professionals. They know what needs to be done more than I know what needs to be done. For the results, they are up at 3 a.m. working. They do not need to come in at 8 a.m. They know what they do.

Wyatt assumes that his employees will do what is needed, even if that means long or odd hours, so he does not need to direct their work schedules. He uses the term "professionals" at the same time he describes his employees' knowledge and dedication as the rationale for not having rigid schedules.

Facilitators lay out the shift in control and a shift in decision rights (without using that language). Cali Ressler explains how work redesign "flips" the pattern of "decision-making and autonomy" in the organization:

> In every organization, there is a hierarchy. There are people at the top and everyone has a role. So when we think about it in STAR, instead of vertical, the hierarchy sits horizontally. People still have the same positions [i.e., job titles] but decision-making and autonomy are all level. There will be no more asking about when and where to do things.

A manager responds to this point by saying, in an approving tone:

> It sounds like we're moving out of the way and empowering [them].

We contend that STAR was so well received in TOMO because existing identities as professionals could be leveraged to legitimate the new ways of working and new ways of managing. Many of these middle managers identify as *IT managers*, meaning they think of themselves as technical professionals who are now in managerial roles. IT managers often report that their job is to support the work of their team and "remove roadblocks" and barriers to the technical professionals doing their best work. When facilitators say that managers no longer need to be "hallway monitors" but instead can be "coaches," that appeals to many of these IT managers who feel affinity with and genuine respect for most of their employees.[42]

This tie to professionalism means that similar initiatives may be more difficult to implement in organizations where frontline employees are not cast as professionals and where operational autonomy—control over how the work is accomplished—is limited at the start. Implementing work redesign initiatives like STAR may be more difficult in lower-wage jobs that are viewed as "less skilled" or as attracting individuals with "bad work ethics." We might expect more resistance from frontline managers in these settings too. That is an important hypothesis to explore in future research and change initiatives. The Work, Family, and Health Network conducted a parallel study involving a customized version of STAR implemented in nursing homes. Our findings there are complex, though some are positive.[43] Managers and administrators in the nursing homes may have been more cautious about accepting the changes suggested by nursing assistants, for example, because they doubted some of those workers' professionalism, work ethic, or expertise.[44]

Even in the context of TOMO and its IT professionals, managers raise questions about less trustworthy employees who are likely to "slack off" when they have more freedom. In response to these concerns, facilitators float the question: "How do you know they are working now?" Because frontline managers are not able to carefully watch exactly what their employees are doing in the office (because they are swamped themselves and because they have large teams and often have employees in multiple locations), it becomes clear that judging employees by their time in the office is unwise. Managers seem to appreciate that point, repeating the question in our interviews and in their conversations with each other, long after the STAR training.

Facilitators also suggest that STAR actually prompts better management—that managers will now be able to focus more easily on who is performing their work well and then follow through with the company's performance management processes for those who are not performing as expected. In a session where managers were being introduced to STAR, Tanay (a highly respected software development manager seen in chapter 3) volunteered to share his positive experiences with STAR.

> Our group is embracing STAR. People have said there's a big difference. We had a big deliverable in March and we wouldn't have been able to do it without STAR.

Then a peer manager in the room, Kunwar, asked Tanay about the possibility of "abuse" by some employees, noting:

> This is an exciting opportunity but for managers, this can be easily abused.

Tanay's response is that managers already know who is likely to try to take advantage of STAR. He says STAR prompts more active coaching on the specific work outcome they expect and argues that

> STAR forces managers to be more clear. I would find it funny if I heard myself [say this in the past].

With this last comment, Tanay reassures the group that he too had these worries previously, but he now supports STAR.

Third, facilitators point out that work practices have changed significantly in recent years as technologies have changed, but the institutionalized rules of the game (as expressed by company policies and culture) have not. Facilitators claim that technology and related changes have left many employees stressed, "because they are trying to figure out how to live life while always connected to work." Without using our language of always-on availability, the facilitators are pointing out that employees are exhausted by their constant connections to work.

Facilitators share photos that show a typing pool in a large open room with supervisors roaming, then add cube walls to the room, and then replace the typewriters with laptops. This is described as "the 1950s colliding with the twenty-first century," and contrasted with photos of people working apparently effectively and happily on a couch at home and in other locations. The point is that the technological tools were already in place, in this knowledge-work organization, to reduce commute time, to be more available to family (or friends, neighbors, or pets) during the workday, or to work away from the office for any reason. But a work redesign intervention was needed to change the *social meaning* so that new ways of working (such as remote work, variable schedules, and a shift in control or decision-making) are legitimate and logical rather than questionable or deviant.

The technologies do not disrupt or transform the organizational culture on their own and, in fact, contribute to overload and intensive work. It takes a deliberate effort to tame these technologies—so that they can be used by employees and frontline managers in ways that work for them, rather just creating more demands and pressure.

Defusing Early Resistance: Hear Concerns but Encourage Experimentation

The STAR initiative is participatory—meaning insiders need to be part of diagnosing the problems in this organization and need to get excited about making changes. But there are invariably insiders who are less enthusiastic. In STAR, facilitators listen to the concerns expressed by skeptical employees and managers but simultaneously push for people to begin experimenting (in the sense of trying things out, not in our sense of a research design with treatment and control groups). The expectation is that early changes will be successful and will create escalating commitment to STAR as people get a taste of working in new ways. The remaining skeptics can then be convinced by their peers' positive experiences and can be coached by a supportive HR manager or peer if needed. To get the organizational change moving, facilitators work to defuse defensiveness, provide opportunities to practice new interactions and actions in the training sessions and outside of sessions, frame anxiety as natural, and turn to local champions.

The critique of current ways of working can easily be experienced as personal critique, particularly for managers who have enforced the old expectations and practices. Facilitators try to minimize defensiveness on the part of these managers. They present the old rules of the game as a holdover from the 1950s, suggesting that the firm is simply behind the times, rather than calling out particular managers' deliberate decisions. One exchange was particularly telling because a manager who had been blamed for specific decisions was publicly accepted as a proponent of change. About two years before STAR was introduced, a well-known vice president, Marilyn, had decided to require the hundreds of employees who worked under her to be in the office five days a week. This decision had prompted criticism from employees and frontline managers; her unit's poor scores on the company's employee survey were the topic of executive and HR discussions. In one of the first STAR training sessions, Marilyn acknowledges her previous decision and attempts to convince her subordinates she supports STAR. She mentions that her previous decision "caused a big stir," then claims that she is fully on board with STAR and sees it as an exciting change. The facilitators welcome this expression of support for STAR and do not question her openness to the new organizational change. (In sessions where Marilyn is not present, the facilitators get questions about her actual support for STAR, and employees repeatedly ask their managers directly if "leadership," and Marilyn specifically, is really on board.)[45]

Depersonalization also occurs when someone questions the emerging critique. For example, if someone says that their team or manager is already supportive, flexible, or focused on results and so they do not need STAR, the facilitator will say that "focus groups at TOMO" or "our experience with other teams at TOMO" suggests there is a real need for change. The facilitator may even step back to say that this is an issue in corporate America more generally. The claim that "we are already doing this" is not directly challenged, even though we (as researchers) often saw a difference between the limited flexibility a manager previously allowed and STAR. The facilitators did not push that point, instead suggesting that these individuals' positive experiences in the current culture can be an example for others moving forward.

The STAR sessions also provide many opportunities for participants to practice new ways of interacting, often through role-plays and quizzes. For example, "sludge" role-plays prompt employees to say (politely and with a smile), "Is there something you need?" in response to questions about where they were, why they are coming in "late," or when they will next be in the office. Facilitators explain that the phrase "Is there something you need?" helps to refocus interactions on work tasks or goals and how the people in that conversation can work together effectively, rather than allowing the interaction to focus on when or where work occurs. These exchanges may feel false, unfamiliar, or even insubordinate to those in the room—particularly if their team had strict norms about work time and work location previously—so it is useful to practice the new interactions that disrupt the old culture.[46]

In a later STAR session, facilitators set up a quiz game where two temporary teams answer questions such as, "How should you notify people when you are not working in the office?" The "correct" STAR answer is that you do not need to notify people when working offsite. Your coworkers should already know how to reach you (by several different means if there is a possibility you would be needed for a true emergency like an IT outage), and your team should have discussed how quickly responses are needed for specific types of issues. As the players discuss their answers, the facilitator can easily check on participants' acceptance of key STAR ideas. Furthermore, those who have the "right" answers can offer their perspective so that everyone hears peers, not just the facilitator, advocating for the new way of doing things. We often observed coworkers playfully calling each other out and people laughing as they saw how they were still falling back into old ways or giving inconsistent answers across questions. Engagement is often high—with minimal eyerolling, even though the game is admittedly silly—because participants want to get clear on what is allowed and accepted as their teams begin to implement new ways of working.

Facilitators also minimize opposition by framing anxiety as natural and expected while encouraging early experimentation. The anxiety was often palpable in the first session where managers talk on their own, without their subordinates in the room.[47] Senior executives are invited to the session and asked to express their own support for STAR. While this occasionally backfired if an executive expressed his or her own anxiety, a supportive executive encourages managers to move forward despite their worries. For example, Jason, a vice president, urged his managers to move forward despite their discomfort:

> I'm going to have to leave here soon but I did want to tell my team [he turns to face the group] that I think it will be more change than what you perceive right now. You will have different levels of comfort with this . . . I do believe it's a change that is worth taking. You have to be open.

Jason is acting as an institutional entrepreneur—openly advocating for the change and using his authority, as a boss, to push the process forward—and his support is key for his subordinates. As with other changes in organizations, middle managers' anxiety can stall changes but can be countered by the combination of top management support and bottom-up enthusiasm from employees.

Early experimentation is built into the STAR training. Each person is asked to choose two specific actions that they will try in the next week. These actions include individual changes like grocery shopping on a weekday before 3 p.m., questioning a meeting where the intended outcome is not clear (with the idea that you would either clarify why your input is needed at the meeting or you would decline the meeting), or committing to promote STAR within the team. Facilitators encourage teams to discuss what they learn from the experiments, offering questions for team meetings like, "What did I try? How did I feel? How did it work for me? How did it work for others? What can we do to do that better?" Here facilitators are exploiting an organizational change strategy of pushing people to go ahead and try small experiments even if they do not feel comfortable with the larger change. They expect to capitalize on peers' "small wins" to encourage further implementation of the intended changes.[48]

At this point, facilitators describe employees and managers as "pioneers" who are leading these changes in TOMO and in the corporate world more broadly. Sometimes that is not reassuring, as when an employee stated, "Most of the pioneers died" and many people in the room chuckled. But this is another example where anxiety is reframed as expected but not a barrier to moving ahead.

Finally, turning to local champions helps defuse early resistance. Certainly, senior managers and executives are encouraged to express their support for STAR to their subordinates, but it is also valuable to hear from those outside of the official chain of command. Tanay, the director mentioned earlier who discussed the risk of "abuse" under STAR, had volunteered to talk with managers in other units about the initiative. He describes himself as a skeptic who thought facilitators "were from another planet."

> [At first] I dug my heels in, trying to find things [to show STAR] wouldn't fit. I was a skeptic and in some cases, still am. But the change in my team is too dramatic to go unnoticed.

Tanay's enthusiasm reassures those who have questions and concerns that they may get excited about STAR along the way too. Insider support is a convincing rhetorical tool. Testimonies from insiders encourage those who are most skeptical, including those who question whether a model developed outside of this firm can actually work here, to be willing to try out STAR ideas and practices.[49]

What STAR Looks Like: Concerns that Come Up

The initial response to STAR was largely positive, with some cautious or skeptical reactions and little overt resistance. But professionals and managers did have questions about STAR and share their concerns in the sessions, in team conversations, and in our interviews.

Is It Wise to Pursue These Changes?

IT professionals and frontline managers raise concerns about whether it is wise for their careers to embrace STAR and implement the changes suggested in the training. In particular, participants ask about top management's support for STAR—and they often express skepticism about that. These questions sometimes point to worries about how those above them in the company hierarchy will evaluate their performance if they make these changes. In one team that has been through several training sessions and has been given official permission to go live with STAR, for example, multiple people bring up management support:

> WOMAN 1: STAR concepts have made upper management very nervous.
>
> WOMAN 2: We are making upper management nervous . . .
>
> MAN 1 [seconding the comment]: I have been told that by middle management . . .
>
> WOMAN 3: [There is] fear with [regard to] the leadership chain and people are living with a lot of fear but are doing [STAR anyway].

Discussions about senior managers' support for STAR are most explicit and prolonged in the second managers-only training session where frontline managers are with their peers (without their subordinates or bosses in the room).[50] Jonathon, Melissa, and Tanay—managers we have already introduced—repeatedly raise questions about upper management support when they are together in one of these private forums. Melissa explains that she is trying new things herself, moving "out of my comfort zone." But she believes that the managers above her are "freaking out" because they have been playing by the old rules and now they are being told that long hours, visible busyness, and instant responsiveness "doesn't mean anything" (or will not be rewarded). Melissa asks the facilitator directly whether upper management supports STAR. Jonathon says he "can't believe" two specific executives support it, but then reminds the group that one of those executives voiced his support in the video embedded in the managers' training and that the other executive had come to an early STAR training to express his support. Melissa isn't convinced, asking a third time in five minutes whether top management is on board. Tanay—who later became a STAR champion who visited other manager sessions to reassure them—says directly to the facilitator:

> You're not stupid. You can fully see we don't believe [upper management supports this].

They continue discussing how Vanessa (the director to whom several managers report) has not yet adapted to STAR; she is asking them why they had missed particular meetings or where they were at certain times, when they now see those decisions as their own. But these middle managers are motivated to work through their worries because they see potential benefits for their teams and for themselves. Jonathon asks his peers to be "courageous" in implementing STAR, and they agree to support each other in pushing change forward.

Are These Changes Going to Address Our Problems?

Participants also sometimes ask whether the changes suggested by STAR will actually benefit the IT professionals and managers. These questions come in two related forms. First, are these new ways of working feasible given the realities of IT work and, in particular, the current context of running lean after repeated rounds of downsizing plus offshoring? In other words, if employees have more control over when, where, and how they do their work, if they feel their personal and family lives are recognized and supported, and if they can trim some low-value work from their responsibilities, will that be enough to counterbalance the high demands and unrealistic time lines? Can STAR bring relief if it does not directly challenge the sheer quantity of work that is requested of the remaining TOMO staff or the staffing strategies that create more work by requiring coordination with offshore workers? This is a critical question and one that was central for our own analysis, too. The obvious fix, from the perspective of employees and frontline managers, would be to hire more skilled staff or take on fewer projects. Facilitators knew this was off the table for top management but sometimes participants probed this possibility, asking whether STAR can truly help if it does not directly address lean staffing.[51]

Second, given the current context, will focusing on results mean these IT professionals and managers work even longer and feel even more strain? This is the more personally focused version of this concern. The worry is that unrealistic targets set by management will lead people to work even more once their hours are less important as an indicator of effort or productivity. As Ewan, a software developer, explained in a STAR training session, if the company no longer pays attention to work hours, how will anyone know that they have done enough and can stop for the week? He explains that if he is "continually in a triage situation where I can't accomplish all my objectives," he might put in 50 hours and then stop, even though he is still behind on critical tasks. Once STAR has launched, he wonders, will anyone ever feel it is legitimate to stop working? There might be pressure to work even longer if IT professionals believe they will not get credit for working hard and doing quite a bit—but not getting to the end result in the specified (but unrealistic) time—under STAR. This, too, is a concern that we had; one of our primary worries, all along, was that initiatives like STAR might unintentionally create additional pressures to work long hours and intensively. We will see how this played out in the next chapter.

Will These Changes Last?

The question about the sustainability of STAR was especially salient because a merger was announced during the rollout of STAR—to the surprise of both the research team and those inside TOMO. TOMO's acquisition by a firm we call ZZT was announced while we were in the thick of data collection and facilitators were delivering STAR training sessions. Worries about job loss spiked after the announcement; 45 percent of those surveyed after the merger announcement said that it was "fairly likely" or "very likely" they would lose their job or be laid off in the next twelve months as compared to 25 percent of those surveyed in the months just before the merger announcement.[52] Yet we learned, from our fieldwork and interviews conducted during this period, that many TOMO professionals and managers tried to adopt a wait-and-see attitude. Many had been through a merger before, and they also realized it would take at least two years before the merger was final, the reorganization of the combined IT division was complete, and the two companies' policies were integrated.

In the STAR training sessions, the TOMO professionals and managers raised two related questions: Would STAR survive the merger? And how did this initiative fit with the culture of the acquiring firm? Discussions of STAR being sustained after the merger prompted HR managers to try to reassure participants in the training sessions. Our field notes say that participants were very attentive, "really wide-eyed" and focused during these discussions. There were soon rumors that the ZZT culture was very traditional regarding when and where work was done. For example, in a discussion after the merger was legally finalized and IT was being reorganized to incorporate employees from both companies, a manager shared that

> The people we're working with on the other side [i.e., the ZZT employees his group is coordinating with as they prepare for the merger] are in the strictest culture. And they are told to be there [in the office] every day 8–5, Monday through Friday.

In chapter 7 we describe these worries and the eventual decisions about STAR in more detail, but the general anxiety about job loss, the question of leadership shifts with the merger, and the view that ZZT was too conservative to accept STAR were all evident in STAR training sessions soon after the merger announcement.

Are There Gender Differences in Concerns?

We have argued that with its dual-agenda approach, STAR skirts a tight association between flexibility and family. Rather than tying the initiative to family responsibilities, which are often assumed to be primarily women's concerns, STAR portrays new ways of working as reasonable and appealing for almost everyone. That raises the question of whether men and women react differently to STAR. In this IT workforce, women and men seem to be supportive or skeptical of STAR in equal proportions. We see very few gender differences in responses to the change initiative—and very little overt resistance to it during the training sessions themselves. When facilitators, our research team, and the TOMO employees participating in STAR training identify the apparent skeptics, they are both women and men, with women managers' commitment to STAR questioned as often as men managers' openness to the change.

Our own pilot study of ROWE, a related work redesign, at the corporate headquarters of Best Buy found something different. We saw notable gender differences in responses to the work redesign initiative in that setting. In both initiatives the messages were gender neutral and some of the facilitators were the same people, with parts of the STAR training pulled from ROWE training. At Best Buy, we found that women in their thirties and forties, who were presumably more likely to have children at home and extensive family and household responsibilities, were particularly enthusiastic during the ROWE training sessions. Both men and younger women at Best Buy seemed more cautious about the initiative, and the (limited) overt resistance to ROWE that we observed was voiced by a few senior male managers.[53]

There are two differences between Best Buy and TOMO that may explain why gender seemed more salient for employees' responses to a similar work redesign initiative in one setting. First, TOMO employees were older, on average, than the employees going through ROWE at Best Buy. The TOMO workforce includes many people in the middle-aged and arguably most overloaded period of their lives—more people who are providing childcare, care for older adults, or both. And more of these middle-aged workers are also recognizing the limitations of their own bodies. Established ways of working, including the always-on

expectations, were causing problems across the board, with many men at
TOMO discussing their exhaustion and health concerns as well as their
children's and spouses' frustrations with their work lives. Second, these
IT professionals and managers are in a fairly flat organization where the
common identity of being IT professionals is central. Status is demonstrated by technical prowess as well as by job title and rank. And the
reality is that there are not many spaces higher in the hierarchy to which
people can be promoted. In contrast, the workforce at the Best Buy corporate headquarters included more relatively young men and women
who presumably hoped to move up the management ranks. Embracing
a work redesign initiative might have seemed riskier for these young
people's careers. It would be useful to see, in other studies, whether
work redesign initiatives (and other strategies for increasing flexibility
or taming overload) take root more easily depending on the demo-
graphics of the workforce and the career structure of the organization,
meaning how people expect to prove themselves and get ahead there.

Changing the rules of the game is exciting, but also hard. It raises anxiety for those few people who are happy with the status quo and also for
those who are excited about the possibilities of change but unsure how
it will unfold. The facilitators providing STAR training address these worries by depersonalizing the critiques of old ways of working, framing
anxiety as reasonable and encouraging experimentation; by leading
people through role-plays and games where they can try out new interaction patterns and see others willing to move forward; and by relying
on local champions who are known and respected by TOMO insiders.
These strategies seem to work rather effectively to address the concerns
about whether it is safe, in terms of job security and career progression,
to embrace the new ways of working and whether these changes will help
overloaded professionals and managers. But facilitators could not as effectively manage concerns about the unexpected merger. No one—not
top TOMO executives or middle managers, much less STAR facilitators
or we researchers—knew what would happen next.

Despite this ambiguity, STAR was a success. Uncertainty about the
future tempered some changes but the STAR redesign had clear benefits
for employees, families, and the company. What worked? And why? The
positive story of STAR successes begins next.

Chapter 5

⌘

THE BUSINESS IMPACTS
OF WORK REDESIGN

A Turning Point for Sherwin

Recall Sherwin, the talented and respected IT professional we met at the beginning of the book. Although he loves working with smart people on TOMO's technical challenges, a heart attack (in his fifties) helped him see that something had to change in his work life.

STAR came along soon after his health crisis, and Sherwin uses it to fashion work patterns that support his health and help him work more efficiently as well. Sherwin is working many fewer hours with STAR, in contrast to the "60-, sometimes 70-hour weeks" that had been routine for him. By trimming his hours, "I'm able to actually stay more focused." Deadlines continue to cause some stress, and Sherwin still works longer hours some weeks. But "with the STAR program, it allows you to be able to have more control over it . . . I'm constantly busy. I stay busy. But I don't feel overwhelmed. So that's huge."

Sherwin now gets to bed at a decent hour most nights. He says, "I won't rob myself of sleep anymore," and he is up early to ride his exercise bike and read ("personal reading, not work-related reading") most mornings. He has been able to meet his goal of exercising at least thirty minutes a day for over a year.

For Sherwin, STAR is not primarily about working at home—although he is pleased he can do so in the summer, when his young teen daughters' day camp ends mid-afternoon, without feeling guilty. Instead, Sherwin emphasizes how STAR helps him work more efficiently, including cutting back on "status calls" where his input is not really necessary. He describes greater efficiency and focus, partly because he no longer attends some meetings that he finds "worthless." The STAR way of working now seems normal. Sherwin amplifies,

> It seems like common sense. But for years we worked in environments where there was so much red tape and "you have to do this." And you just waste a lot of time, when you can be more efficient without the red tape.

Sherwin notes that the changes involved in STAR are also internal, in terms of his sense of what it means to be a dedicated worker and a good employee. STAR prompted him to re-evaluate his assumption that he should be in the office certain hours and that long hours signal dedication. He continues by reflecting on the perception that

> people [who are] online later at night, those people must be working harder and they must be better employees.
>   Well, no. That's not necessarily the case, right? . . . So your work can speak for itself without having to work long hours . . . The work that gets done here is what really should be judged, and how you get it done is really up to you.

Because his team has discussed their new work patterns, communication hasn't suffered. Sherwin says, "I've never had any problems contacting fellow workers" and "they don't have any problems getting ahold of me." What *has* changed is "the guilt" that came from working at home when others assumed that if "you're not here between 8 and 5, [then] you must not be working."

These changes have clearly brought relief to this previously overloaded employee:

> From a year ago now [when STAR started], it's a hundred percent less stress on me than where I was even a year ago . . . Being able to get the work done, being able to deal with the important things in life as they come up, emergencies with your kids or your mom or something else. It's priceless, to have that off of your plate . . .
>   I feel sad for people in other companies that still work in that [pre-STAR] environment.

The Broader Questions and
How We Can Answer Them

For Sherwin, STAR is a success—both "common sense" and "priceless." But do work redesign initiatives that acknowledge both work effectiveness and personal life (like STAR) help professionals and managers who are overloaded? And if they do in fact work, who benefits? Does this work for employees only or for both employees and the firm? We use the case of STAR at TOMO to illustrate that dual-agenda work redesign innovations bring benefits to organizations that embrace these new ways of working *and* their overloaded employees.

TOMO invited our research team into their organization because of concerns that their employees were burned out, exhausted, and looking to leave the company at the first possible moment. IT executives and HR professionals alike recognized the overload that had come with repeated downsizings and the need to coordinate with offshore counterparts. New technologies undergird those management practices and contribute to an always-on, always-working culture. STAR might—they hoped—reduce burnout, increase job satisfaction, and help the company retain valued employees.

Our field experiment with over a thousand participants demonstrates that *STAR succeeded on all these measures* that were important to senior leadership in the firm. How do we know this? Research on workplace policies or other management innovations usually compares workers across many different organizations and investigates whether those who are exposed to a certain HR policy (like the availability of a telecommuting policy) or work condition (like reporting to a more supportive or creative manager) look similar or different to other workers. But workers who are lucky enough to land in a more generous company and have a more supportive manager may well be lucky or smart or strategic in several other ways. Is it the policy or work condition that is driving their experience, or those other unmeasured factors? Social scientists use statistical models to adjust for as many other influences as we can, but those study designs still leave us with many questions and messy comparisons. The vast majority of research on work and workplace policies uses those imperfect study designs.

The Work, Family, and Health Study, in contrast, is designed as a rigorous field experiment studying *change* in people's work environments, not comparisons across different organizations. Experiments allow us to know, with a great deal of confidence, whether a certain organizational policy or innovation (the treatment or intervention) has a positive, negative, or neutral (null) effect on a specific outcome. Our group-randomized field experiment took fifty-six work units or departments within TOMO's IT division and basically flipped a coin to see whether each group would receive the STAR work redesign (serving as our treatment group) or continue on following the company's existing policies (and serve as our usual-practice control group). We are comparing apples to apples by comparing employees in TOMO who went through STAR with employees who did not, with roughly equal numbers of employees in the STAR treatment and the control conditions, no self-selection because people do not choose whether they are assigned to STAR or not, and the same company and industry context for both groups. We investigate both groups as they change or fail to change over time. Because the participants in the two conditions are extremely similar at baseline, we can be confident that any differences between the two conditions later on are truly an effect of the work redesign treatment.[1]

For us, it is also very important to be in the field watching how the intervention is delivered and received (which was the focus of the last chapter) and hearing how changes are unfolding on the ground. Our in-depth interviews and observations reveal the mechanisms behind any positive or negative effects identified in the experiment. In other words, the field experiment data tell us *whether* STAR has an effect, and the interview and ethnographic data tell us *how* this work redesign innovation works to bring these benefits.

We use both types of data to examine the effects of STAR for the business outcomes that senior leadership was concerned about. Did this work redesign reduce burnout, increase job satisfaction, and limit voluntary turnover? Digging deeper, we look at what actually changed on the ground. How did teams and individuals implement STAR? Are there tangible productivity or performance benefits for the firm? What can be learned from this case for other organizations that desire similar benefits?

Changes in Burnout, Overload, and Job Satisfaction

We heard over and over in interviews conducted after teams moved into STAR that people are less overwhelmed and happier, even though their jobs continue to be both intense and somewhat insecure. So even though these IT professionals and managers are still working hard to meet their deadlines, coordinating with coworkers and contractors around the world, and feeling uncertain about their futures, they are doing better while facing those challenges.

Recall that burnout refers to the sense that work is wearing you down. It is troubling for the firm because burnout very often leads to reduced engagement and effort. *Both our quantitative (survey) and qualitative (interview) data demonstrate that burnout declines as a result of the STAR redesign.* From an interview with Ursula, who is a manager and single woman in her fifties, we hear that:

> My energy level is very high. I find myself to be able to not get as overwhelmed with the meetings and questions since I've been able to schedule my days like that. STAR has allowed me to do [my work with more] flexibility.

This is surprising: Ursula's workload has actually increased recently, because she has added people from ZZT (the acquiring firm) to her team of TOMO employees and offshore contractors. She also has a new boss—who did not go through the STAR training himself—but Ursula still reports "a huge improvement in my overall outlook for work."

> I'm not stressed, I'm not overly anxious; I used to be . . . I was always in a fast-pace mode. And now I've gone into a more normal-state mode where I don't feel, "Oh, I've got to go to this and then I've got to log onto work and then I've got that meeting and then I have to run downtown and then Ahh!" I don't feel that anymore. I mean that. The anxiety has really gone.

Employees and managers repeatedly told us that they love STAR. Jonathon, one of the overloaded managers we quoted earlier in the book, reports:

I have been going through performance reviews I have been asking them, "What do you think about STAR?" And the feedback I have been getting is: I love it. I love STAR. I love that the company trusts me to get my work done when I feel like I need to get it done, instead of defining a specific window for me to get my work done.

Jonathon's employees are also quite positive. From Randall—the single man who said he felt "owned" by the company before STAR and who resented the evening meetings he was pulled into—we hear:

STAR has been such a benefit to us. I've gotten so much of my life back that if you call me on a Saturday and say I want to suck up four hours of your Saturday . . . I'm not that bitter about it . . . I've gotten so much time back already that, comparatively, it's not that bad.

Randall also shares a story about realizing that he and his team are no longer burned out when he interacts with a team that is not in STAR. Randall's team met with another group to ask for an estimate for a service that was within their normal work domain.

And they were really pissy. They were angry, they were uptight, they were oh, defensive and it was just a horrible meeting.

Randall's team chatted about the meeting afterward and realized that the other group was overloaded, just as they had been a year earlier. Randall's team remembers snapping at requests then:

I can't sleep and now you're asking me for this?

Randall says he doesn't see that attitude as often anymore.

You don't really realize it—until you see the extreme—that people are a little happier.

Survey evidence from the field experiment also identifies the benefits of STAR for burnout and job satisfaction. Recall that STAR and control groups are very similar at baseline and neither individual employees nor their managers get to choose whether they are moving into STAR or not. Yet when we look at the surveys one year in, we see that those in STAR report significantly lower levels of burnout and higher job satisfaction than their control counterparts. Employees and frontline managers in STAR are still working hard and facing high demands, but they less frequently feel "emotionally drained" by work, "used up at the end of the workday," or agree that they feel "burned out."[2] Reduced burnout means that employees and managers can continue to contribute to the firm, doing good work without having to give too much. Job satisfaction increases significantly as well, with especially large improvements for the nonsupervisory employees.[3] These are exciting changes to document because job duties do not change—the work that they are asked to do is the same—but the work is less draining and the job is more attractive after STAR.

One unexpected complication for our clean experimental design is that the merger was announced and unfolding at this same time. The changes in job satisfaction and burnout are much larger and clearer among the employees entering STAR before the merger was announced. We know, from our interviews and observations, that employees and managers who began the STAR process after the merger was announced were also pleased and excited about the changes. Additionally, our survey data shows that those who moved into STAR after the merger announcement changed their schedules and patterns of working at home when the initiative allowed them to do so. But that later group moving into STAR after the merger was announced is also quite aware that the changes might not last.[4] Their behaviors change, but they do not sink into the new ways of working with as much confidence. We believe that is why the benefits of STAR regarding job satisfaction and burnout are weaker for those who started later.

Changes in Turnover and Turnover Intentions

Employees who have been through the work redesign process with STAR are more committed to staying with the firm than their control group counterparts. Our repeated survey reveals that employees who are *not* in STAR have an *increased* interest in leaving the company as the merger plans proceed, while turnover intentions did not jump up for those in STAR. Using HR records, we find that employees in STAR are significantly less likely to voluntarily leave the firm than their counter-parts. Over the ensuing three years, voluntary exits are 40 percent lower for employees in STAR.[5]

Our interviews echo these findings and also show the close connections between improved job satisfaction and reduced turnover as employees gain control over when, where, and how they work and feel more supported. Hazel, a technical lead in her forties and a married Latina woman, responds to a question about how STAR has impacted her by saying:

> It just made me happier [laughs]. I just have so much more time. I don't have to get up at 5:00 in the morning to get here by 6:00 in the morning. I don't feel the stress of having to get a certain amount of things done by a certain time because I have to get on the road [to avoid] traffic . . . It prevents me from looking outside the company for a job. It just has alleviated a lot of stress.

The benefit of STAR with regard to retention is intertwined, in Hazel's mind, with her new schedule, her increased ability to work at home, her reduced stress, and (as she mentions later in the interview) the ability to walk her dog and exercise more regularly. McKenzie, a manager of a software development group with fifteen employees plus additional contractors, notes that her days working at home are quite productive for finishing various tasks while her days in the office are filled with interactions. This mix works well for her and for the team.

> If I didn't do STAR the way I felt I needed to do it, then I would be miserable. And I'd have to get a new job.

McKenzie feels that she's good at managing, that her subordinates choose to stay in their jobs because "they like to be on my team," and that their increased satisfaction benefits the company.

Isaac, a manager of a team of IT project managers, also believes STAR is key to retention and that is especially true after the merger.

> Nine out of 10 people that are on my team—the only reason that they're still working for this company is because of STAR. We talk

about it all the time . . . It is a huge, huge retention [tool] right now. And I just don't think management sees it.

Isaac goes on to explain the dismay that he and his subordinates are feeling as the merger unfolds, pointing to worries about whether they will keep their jobs, who they will work with and for, and how compensation and especially bonuses will change. Isaac was himself reorganized into a management position that is no longer eligible for a bonus. Still, control over when and where he works is crucial:

> The person [from ZZT] that took my job will get my bonus. I'm not happy about that. And even though I'm not happy about it, I can sit here and say, I get to work from home. I get to spend my day how it makes sense. I'm allowed to go get my kids from school and not have anybody asking me when I'm coming back.

Others worry that dissatisfaction with the merged company's policies and benefits will spiral if STAR is rescinded. Marsha, a married white manager with two children, explains that her employees are upset about changes in bonuses, vacation policies, and more.

> It's just been awful and the biggest concern people have is "Will I lose STAR? I can't lose STAR. If I lose STAR, I'm leaving the company." That's the last straw . . . Take my vacation; don't take my STAR. That's very telling.

STAR helps the company retain especially experienced workers. With almost 300 baby boomers in our TOMO survey sample, we could investigate whether professionals and managers ages fifty to sixty-four described their plans for retirement differently if they have been through the dual-agenda work redesign. We find that boomers who moved into STAR plan to stay with the firm longer than boomers in the control group.[6] Those in STAR are 18 percent more likely to say it is very likely they will continue working in the company until age sixty-five or later. Plans for doing any work (like part-time consulting or an "encore job") at older ages do not differ across the two groups, but STAR makes it more appealing for these older employees to stay in their current positions. As

Heidi, a manager in her fifties who has several boomers reporting to her, explains:

> I think it helps the employee retention, which our company has trouble with because of the age of our workforce. Especially with the merger, you know? There's some people with their foot out the door. If it weren't for STAR, they would probably be gone . . . due to their age and issues they have.

Heidi notes that these employees appreciate how easy it is to go to the doctor and says that a "rigid work schedule" is unappealing for those with more "aches and pains." She concludes:

> They have so much knowledge and the company doesn't want them to leave. I just think that it's a win–win situation.

What Actually Changes, on the Ground?

So what changes in work patterns, in interactions, in social life within teams and within the company to produce these improvements in burnout, job satisfaction, and turnover? Our work redesign approach is complex by design, because it aims to change the rules of game with regard to when, where, and how work is done and who makes those decisions. The IT professionals we study adopt more customized, flexible schedules and work at home much more—but that is not all that is involved.

This multifaceted understanding of dual-agenda work redesign is conveyed by Jonathon, the manager we heard from early on, when the interviewer asks him a general question about his team's performance and whether it has changed.[7] Jonathon first says that there is a STAR effect on their morale, tied to lower stress. He then explains, forcefully, that STAR is more than flexible hours or remote work:

> It's not just working from home, you know. It's trying to encourage people to push back against unnecessary meetings, trying to empower them a bit more to take control of their deliverables. Look at it with a more critical eye in terms of "This what I'm doing. Am I adding value?" . . . We are trying to change the status quo.

Changing Where and When Work Is Done

Although STAR involves more than changing when and where work happens, as Jonathon explains, those changes are an important part of the work redesign initiative. The role of new technologies is particularly evident at TOMO, because these employees and managers are part of a global labor chain where the technical work and associated documentation happens in many time zones and countries. The same technologies were not consistently put to use to support and facilitates employees' chosen work practices before STAR, though; instead, there were expectations that employees and managers were always on, always available, *and* working in the office during traditional hours. With STAR, employees and managers are able to decide themselves when and where they work. Holden, a project manager in his fifties, loved STAR and said with a laugh that it came "twenty-five years late." He recognizes that STAR is multifaceted but especially appreciates working from home. Skipping his long commutes on some days means work is

> less stressful for me. And I know it's less stressful because I've been going to the doctor for regular checkups and my blood pressure has come down.

Kunwar, a South Asian woman who manages a quality assurance and testing team (and who previously shared that her work stress had led her to lash out at family), appreciates that STAR allows her to skip the commute time. She ties the commute to starting her workday feeling behind.

> By the time you reach work its 9:15, 9:30—you're already like almost two hours behind, especially for [the coworkers and clients who] are two hours ahead of you. You're frantically trying to catch up. Before you know it, you have to leave to drive all the way back to pick up your child. There's a lot of stress going on then. If you feel like you're constantly playing catch up, you don't have enough time to do quality work.

Many people told us that working at home increased their focus and allowed them to move through their work more quickly. For example,

Tori (a development manager who supervises many offshore employees) notes that "at first, it felt odd" to change her work routines. But she finds it worthwhile:

> I'll just say when I work at home and not the office, I feel like I get a ton more done because there's less distraction. My phone is not ringing.

Even though Tori keeps the chat application (IM) turned on so her staff can reach her easily, she finds working at home less disruptive than "yakking" with coworkers in the office.

> If I'm at home, there's nobody to talk to and I get a lot done. So for me personally, it's more productive to work from home.

Working at home and offsite was common at TOMO even before STAR, but those in the work redesign initiative increased their remote work significantly compared to their peers. At our baseline survey, almost everyone did some work at home and employees worked remotely for, on average, about 23 percent of their total weekly hours. Once STAR had launched, STAR employees and managers began working 41 percent of their weekly hours at home, on average, and continued to increase to 51 percent remote hours about a year later (by the time of our fourth survey).[8] Clearly, these IT professionals and managers were interested in the possibility of working at home more. But it took a work redesign initiative that welcomed that as a reasonable and perhaps wise strategy—rather than framing flexibility as accommodation—before those changes took off.[9] Importantly, the changes are evident not just for parents but for employees who do not have children at home as well. Under STAR work at home becomes a normal option, but not one that is forced on anyone.[10]

Other research also demonstrates that a work redesign approach reassures employees and managers that remote work is legitimate and appropriate, encouraging broader take-up than we see with other flexibility policies. A quasi-experimental study called New Ways of Working was unfolding in a large Dutch financial company at the same time as our STAR intervention at TOMO. That workplace change is similar in that it was a collective change (rather than individually negotiated flexibility), involved workshops to discuss new ways of working, and was supposed to encourage "time and place-independent working" with a focus on the work that was performed rather than hours or work location.[11] About ten months after the initiative was launched, Dutch employees in the New Ways of Working intervention were working at home about 35 percent of their hours as compared to about 18 percent of hours worked at home for employees in their reference group.[12]

Of course, some employees and managers decide to work in the office almost every day, and this is perfectly acceptable in STAR and similar work redesign efforts. Jayden, an IT analyst who now works about 90 percent of his time at home (and is partnered, with no children), explains:

> Of my peers, it seems like the only ones who come to the office are the ones who want to. I even have a developer peer who comes to the office every day. Part of it is he likes to go out to lunch with his coworker friends. But he [also] doesn't like merging the home world and the work world. It's very important for him to leave work at work.

Here Jayden refers to what scholars call a preference for segmentation, as opposed to integration, of work and nonwork activities and spaces. The coworker he mentions is a clear segmenter, while Jayden is a hard-core integrator who loves his home office and the possibility of fitting in a few chores during the day or meeting his brother for a quick lunch nearby.[13] He continues:

> That's the whole thing about STAR though, is you have the choice, the flexibility.

Many interview respondents described how both remote work and flexible schedules allowed them to seamlessly fit in personal commitments such as taking kids to school, taking an afternoon break (after logging in quite early in the morning) to run errands or mow the lawn or stop by an elderly parent's house, or taking a few hours to go to medical appointments with loved ones or to supervise children's or grandchildren's activities just before dinner. That work still had to be done, of course, but many employees and frontline managers appreciated that they could return to their work later in the evening or shift some work to weekends, without asking for permission or reporting their plans to anyone.

Other employees did not use STAR to flow between work and personal tasks but instead used the work redesign to set boundaries, so that work was more contained and personal time was protected. This was a minority of those we interviewed, but some individuals made it clear that they would not be checking email or chat in the evenings. They wanted to be called for a true emergency (like a systems outage), but reminded their teams they would not be responding immediately otherwise. STAR prompted team discussions about how people preferred to be reached and clarified expected response times for common issues—relieving anxiety that availability was always expected and quick responses would be rewarded.

Even when professionals and managers chose to work in the office almost exclusively, many found STAR useful. For example, Elise, who is a married software development engineer in her early sixties, describes how she shifts her work hours but not her workspace.

> I just prefer [working in the office] because I feel like I get more done here rather than at home or rather than at Starbucks or rather than anywhere. But the flexibility is something I just like. I come in late, I come in early, I come in on Saturday. I do what I want because I know what I have to do.

Elise works closely with contractors who work Tuesday through Saturday in another country. She sometimes shifts her schedule to work with them on Saturday and then takes a Monday off or uses that quieter day to catch up on other work.

For some teams or individual employees, the ability to shift schedules and do so in a forthright way allows them to do the extensive coordination with the offshore staff (in India) without trying to *also* work regular days. Joseph explains that his project management team began closely coordinating with an offshore team in the last year. Their hours shifted to mostly nights and the employees were able to take time off during the day, rather than working in the office during US day hours and also working with the offshore team at night. Joseph believed that the shifts they made in schedules should have been made even in the absence of STAR, because his staff had stepped into this global coordination role that necessarily involved many nights of work. But he sees that

> STAR helped us get there—not because we were able to throw it in anyone's face and say "This is STAR" or anything like that. But we had more background and more ammunition to explain to people why we had to do it this way and why it would work this way without jeopardizing the project . . . We had better tools from STAR to explain that this is what we needed to do to make this work.

Our survey evidence shows changes in employees' and managers' schedules too. We asked people to choose the schedule they usually worked with an option to say a variable or rotating schedule, rather than a regular day, regular evening, or regular night shift. With STAR, those reporting a variable or rotating schedule jumped from 22 percent to almost 40 percent (at six months after baseline). We then see a decline to 35 percent and then 30 percent reporting a variable schedule as their usual schedules over the next year. That decline over time might reflect the fact that these employees and managers settle into a new schedule that works well for them, or perhaps the unfolding merger means some employees revert to a regular daytime schedule in response to new managers' or coworkers' expectations.[14] Our interviews provide ample evidence, however, that many in STAR continued to shift and flex their schedules for both personal reasons and around specific meetings or work deadlines for several years after the work redesign initiative began.

Changing Roles and Decision Rights

There are deeper changes too, which go beyond behavioral changes in work schedules and work location. With STAR, employees come to understand that *they can decide* on when, where, and how they work—in dialogue and consultation with their team and those who rely on their work product—and *they feel more supported* by the firm and by management in making these decisions themselves. These are inter-twined benefits, as one employee's comment makes clear:

> I'm just happy. I love the flexibility . . . but also the way our managers have supported it. They're respecting us and letting us do it and not questioning it.

When we asked, in surveys, about control over when and where work is done, those who moved through the STAR work redesign report significantly greater choice over their starting and stopping times, taking a few hours off during the day, and working at home. These differences between the STAR and control group are evident immediately and continue through the four follow-up surveys.[15]

Our work redesign approach involves a shift in decision rights regarding everyday work practices. Rather than assuming that managers will approve working at home or a shift in work hours (or withhold their approval), employees in STAR make these decisions themselves. Even for those who had worked at home extensively before STAR, this represents an important shift. Recall the story of Hayward, a developer and father who had negotiated with one manager to work at home routinely and then lost that arrangement when he began reporting to a different manager. In contrast to flexibility as accommodation, where a manager can grant or deny flexible work arrangements as she or he sees fit, Hayward describes STAR as

> a huge change for middle management, particularly for those used to watching over people, saying "What are you doing, what are you doing, what are you doing?"

Hayward points to the suggestion from the STAR training that employees redirect questions about where they are or when they are working by asking, "Is there something you need?" Hayward recognizes the shift in control (from manager to employee) that comes from these changes. In an interview soon after the training, he points out that he doesn't work on a production line ("making widgets") that obviously requires him to do the work in a certain place. So asking his manager what she needs from him refocuses their conversation on the work process or product—not on where he chooses to work.

The ability to say that is quite powerful. I don't know if people realize that yet.

When employees have more say in when, where, and how they do their work, they may share less with their peers or managers about those decisions. The decisions are theirs, the work gets done, and coordination across the team needs to happen, but the specific reasons for working different hours or working at home do not need to be discussed.[16] In STAR training, employees were encouraged *not* to explain the reasons behind their work practices because that reinforces or "justifies" the "sludge" of monitoring when and where people work.[17] Randall explains that the role-playing in the training sessions (where people practiced responding differently) felt "silly," but was important for getting people to live out the new norms after training. Randall reports that a very few people he interacts with don't follow STAR, and it is now their explanations about where they are or when they are working that seem unreasonable. Laughing with the interviewer, Randall says:

> If they have a dentist appointment, they explain it for five minutes in front of thirty people on the call. It's like "Well, I really can't and blah blah." Will you stop? You know? The rest of us are over this.

One would think managers might resist these changes that cede their control over employees' work patterns, but we do not see much evidence of that. Instead, many managers see the shift in control as sensible.[18] Joseph supervises project managers and analysts who interface between the business clients and the development teams who write the code. He tells us about one employee, whom he calls his "STAR poster child." As they were chatting, the employee shared that he had worked the previous week from New Mexico. The project manager had gone with his wife, who had business in New Mexico, so he could do his work during the day and enjoy the trip with her otherwise. Joseph says, with delight:

> I had no clue. The business had no clue. The development team had no clue and the program managers had no clue.

Joseph saw this as a perfect example of how these changes can work even when the employee has a coordinating role:[19]

Everything went off without a hitch. So I think that's just a really good example, in our industry, of how well STAR can work.

Kunwar, a manager who appreciates working from home more herself, says that these changes have helped her "lighten up" as a manager. Before, she allowed people to work at home occasionally on an "as needed" basis (which they needed to explain to her), but now her team makes those decisions themselves. She feels she has become "more trusting." She also plans meetings with more advance notice, recognizing that deciding at 2:00 to have a 2:30 p.m. call may not work for everyone.

> We've learned to become more flexible. But for the most part it has taught me to lighten up.

Even managers who had been much looser about remote work appreciate STAR because it sets up new norms. Kenny notes that it creates "a paradigm" so that all managers are more likely to recognize employees' individual lives, needs, and preferences.

Our survey measured employees' perceptions of their own manager's support for their personal and family lives, with a scale developed by Leslie Hammer and Ellen Kossek. We see significant differences in employees' assessments of manager support, as compared to their peers, at the first follow-up survey. Fathers, in particular, feel that their STAR managers have become more supportive of their personal lives and employees who rated their supervisors as less supportive initially also see bigger jumps after STAR launches.[20]

Changing Meetings and Other Coordination Practices

This work redesign approach also encourages employees to take more control over how they do their work, including how they coordinate as a project team and how meetings fit into that coordination work. Randall explains that his group has questioned their regular meetings.

> After STAR came into existence, people would ask, "Is anyone getting anything out of this repetitive meeting? Do we still have to hold it or can we just cancel it?" . . . And after STAR we canceled them.

He has regained many productive hours—varying by week and the stage of the project, but sometimes up to twenty hours per week—because of the reconsideration of meetings.

Questioning meetings does not necessarily mean people skip the meeting or do not contribute to the coordination of a project. Some employees now ask for an agenda or ask about specific questions they can weigh in on, before deciding whether or not to participate in the meeting. Others provide information in advance and decline the meeting, but promise to be available on IM if any questions come up. The previous practice was to multitask on conference calls—so people were often apparently present at the meeting but not focusing on the project fully. STAR prompts employees and managers to recognize that the old practices were not working well and opens the door for these new practices around meetings.

New communication routines need to be developed to replace the assumed coordination via meetings. Joseph, a manager who supported multiple process changes within his group of project managers and analysts, explains that his team has cut a recurring meeting because they realized there were twenty-five people on the call, but most only cared about a particular five minutes of the call. Instead, STAR inspired them to create a new "dashboard" for status updates and also review existing reporting templates to make them easier and more effective, which Joseph describes as getting "the nonsense and noise out of them." Again, technologies facilitate these new coordination practices, but it took the work redesign experience for employees and managers to see how they could use technologies for *their* purposes. Joseph appreciates that STAR has "given us all an opportunity to look at meetings" and be more thoughtful about when they occur and who needs to be there.

This shift in work practices reveals the power of the previous norm that one should accept and attend meetings when invited, even if the value of the meeting or one's role in the meeting was unclear. Katya says she is making progress in changing her old habits:

I'm a little bit more brave in choosing what meetings to accept . . . I have kind of old-school mind, so it's kind of hard. If I'm invited, I have to be there.

> But then if I think it will be total waste of my time. So I'm starting thinking in terms of me—my time, my work, how do I help others? And I think the company supports me a lot.

This mental shift feels challenging (requiring her to be brave) despite the fact that Katya accepts the critique of unnecessary meetings, saying that she thinks about 75 percent of the meetings "can be skipped" or dramatically shortened.

And there is sometimes a reaction against the new approach taken by employees and managers who have been through the STAR work redesign. Kenny, a white manager in his fifties who supervises a team of almost twenty developers and offshore contractors, reports that he turned to his director, Joni, for help negotiating about a meeting. He and his team received "a nasty-gram" or hostile email about not attending a recurring meeting; the person sending the email had not been through STAR. The organizer had declared "there [are] no excuses for you to not be at this meeting," but Kenny went to Joni and asked why fifteen people from her unit were being told to attend this meeting when they were not sure why they were needed. Joni turned to her peer who had called the meetings and asked, "How can this be cost justifiable?" (according to Kenny). With her prodding, a new expectation was laid out: you should attend this meeting in weeks when you were the person who found a problem or you were the person who did the initial work with an identified problem. For this team, that meant a couple testers and a couple developers would attend the meeting each week. Others on the team did not need to come.

> So that's an example of how we need to get better, get smarter. And STAR brings about more consciousness around those things and the need to fix them.

Changing Instant Availability and Assumed Urgency

Productivity gurus advocate protecting work time to do concentrated, high-quality work, rather than being pulled into quick queries by chat or email or agreeing to every meeting or call that is proposed.[21] Some people—like CEOs and tenured professors—can do that by declaring that their heads-down time for planning or writing is a priority and simply refusing other requests for that time. But for many people in professional and managerial jobs, it is taboo to be unavailable or to respond slowly to an email, text, chat message, or phone call from a boss, client, or even coworker. And making oneself unavailable to tend to a personal appointment or prioritize a health commitment, like regular exercise or volunteering in a child's classroom, would be even less acceptable. Yet with this dual-agenda work redesign, the expectations for being always on, always available are challenged. Employees and managers are allowed and encouraged to protect blocks of time—either for concentrated work time or for personal time.

There is variation in the extent to which teams use the work redesign initiative to think about how they do their work, in addition to reflecting on when and where they do their work. The fullest implementation of STAR involves proactive conversations about how each person on the team can work effectively and how the team can coordinate seamlessly, even though people are working differently. In addition to questioning meetings, some teams discussed whether and how to tame the chat systems that so often interrupt them. Some individuals are eager to get off of their internal chat application (IM or, for many companies today, Slack) for some period of each workday. They desperately want to work without interruptions for a few hours. That change seems to go smoothly when teams talk through exactly how to reach each other (for questions at different levels of urgency) when coworkers are offline. People often have questions for each other and want—and sometimes feel they need—an answer immediately. Of course, sometimes the urgency is imagined and not real. Joseph, the development manager whose team cut a recurring meeting from their schedule, said he has changed his thinking by "understanding that people aren't always going to be on IM." He now asks himself whether information is actually needed immediately. Joseph talks through a hypothetical example where a question filters down from his vice president, Mehal, but the project manager who can answer the question is not online right then. Joseph says previously he would get nervous about not responding to Mehal right away. But now he realizes he could ask his boss:

> "Mehal, do you need to know this right now or can it wait until tomorrow?" And when you start thinking in that way and learning how to push back appropriately (because you have to learn how to push back appropriately), then they start getting it too.

A key role for managers in STAR and with similar work redesign approaches is to model being comfortable with less-than-immediate responses. These managers need to avoid panicking if an executive or another manager asks them why an employee has not responded immediately. Instead, supportive managers either step in to address the question themselves or reassure the other party that the employee will respond soon. Ideally, managers begin to retrain the other parties, what Joseph calls pushing back appropriately to reset expectations about instant responsiveness and constant availability.

Turning off IM, Slack, or other connectivity technologies are the high-tech version of work redesign and teaming initiatives that have been around a long time. Leslie Perlow, a Harvard Business School professor, studied software developers in the 1990s and found them to be overloaded, strung out, and frustrated with their packed days. With her guidance, a team implemented "library hours" during the regular workday, where no meetings were scheduled for a two- or three-hour period. Technical professionals could then do their real work (like writing the code) during the day, rather than leaving it to late at night.[22] Other companies have experimented with "no meeting Wednesdays" or similar practices. Like those initiatives, STAR prompts employees and managers to reflect on how their scattered and interrupted work practices are causing problems—for the quality of their work as well as for the families and friends who put up with their stretched and long hours. What has changed since Perlow's study of those software developers, though, is the new communication technologies and global work process. Interruptions are coming in electronically and immediately, from across the globe as well as from those in the same office. A work redesign approach like STAR encourages employees and managers to be more thoughtful and deliberate about how they deal with those interruptions and how they can take control over the technologies, rather than being controlled by them. The benefit is finding concentrated time to do their work or to attend fully to their personal and family lives. In contrast, a simple work-at-home policy may allow people to work away from the office but not help them work smarter by being offline. Work-at-home policies that do not question the current practices and culture may instead create a technology tether and pressure to work at all times and any time.[23]

Coordination routines need to become more explicit and deliberate when chat and IM are not used universally and when employees are working from multiple locations. Those new routines vary by team and by function. Tori's development team agreed that if a person needs concentrated time (for a work task or for personal reasons), they should not open the IM program at all so they are not tempted to respond when they are marked "red" or unavailable. They also agreed on a protocol for reaching out to each other if there was an urgent question while the person was off IM. Tori had just called an employee at home in that situation because he had listed calling his home phone as his preferred way to be reached when he was off IM—even though calling an employee at home would have felt intrusive to Tori before STAR. Felicia, a maintenance and production support with around thirty subordinates, explained that she has shifted from routine IM to more emails. She tries to be more explicit about time lines when she makes a request of her employees and also tells people, proactively, that there is no rush for a certain piece of information when that is the case.

> And the fire drills have reduced, that sense of urgency [has decreased]. And I think that that has helped to lessen the stress for people because everything's not urgent all the time.

New norms and practices are taking hold—through experimentation, dialogue, and with support from frontline managers.

There are some teams in TOMO that did not come to consensus about getting off IM, and there was sometimes frustration when individuals changed their practices without an explicit effort to develop new team norms. Bridget, a systems engineer and married white woman in her forties, reports she has mostly turned off IM because it distracts and annoys her so much.

> I've had some people say, "Well, we never see you online anymore. Are you working?" And then others say they feel like I'm more available because they are getting [work back from me] throughout the day.

Bridget believes she is doing better work because she concentrates better when she is offline, and she responds fully and carefully to her emails rather than constantly jumping in and out of conversations on IM. She believes that this initial frustration from others has been resolved:

> But we worked it all out. And they're fine with that because I do respond to the emails and they can always get a hold of me. So they've learned to be O.K. with my not being on IM.

It seems wise, though, for teams to take the time to reset their norms collectively and to check back in on how new work practices and patterns are working for everyone. Experimentation and continued collective reflection are intended, and important, steps in STAR.[24]

Changes in Engagement, Collaboration, and Reflection

We heard, in some interviews, that the changes prompted by STAR result in greater engagement in the work, more deliberate reflection on work processes and possible improvements, and better or different collaboration. These stories are intriguing—even though we did not hear them across the board, and our analysis of survey measures of pitching in and doing more (as measured by survey questions on "organizational citizenship behaviors") did not show significant differences between employees in STAR and those in the control group. We see these reports as reflecting the possibilities of work redesign when it is implemented fully and thoughtfully.

Chuck, a software engineer who is the team lead coordinating the work of a number of developers and engineers, proposed a virtual "job jar" where he and others on the team could identify small and medium-sized tasks that needed to be done but were not obviously linked to a particular person's expertise. If someone on the team had a bit of free time, they could claim a job jar task and work on it (with any lingering tasks eventually assigned to someone specific). Teamwork increased, overloaded employees felt supported because they could put a task into the job jar, and cross-training was also encouraged by this practice.

Peggy, a software developer on a different team, said that she has always met her deadlines but now she is open to checking with coworkers to see if she can help with their tasks. Before STAR, she reports feeling that she would do her work and her colleagues would do theirs. But now, she says, she is more likely to have the time to help others and she doesn't mind that. She is feeling better generally, and she specifically feels better about her interactions with her coworkers.[25]

In addition to improved teamwork, other work processes could change with STAR. Ursula, a manager who described feeling increased energy, less anxiety, and "a very happy mood" under STAR, also believes she's become "more innovative" as a manager. She now fits in an evening "check-out" time where she will journal about anything that came up that day. She considers what is happening with her full team and all their projects, and journaling gives her ideas for what they might do differently. In this sped-up and lean environment, it is rare for a manager to take concentrated time to reflect on the team's performance and possible process changes, but STAR has allowed her to prioritize that.

Managers also sometimes report that STAR has affected the way they interact with and direct their subordinates—prompting the managers to ask the employees to be more reflective or innovative themselves. Elijah, a development manager in his fifties, explains that he now leaves more decisions to his employees regarding "time, due dates, deliverables." Allowing employees to determine when and where work is done led Elijah to counter his inclination to jump in immediately to solve problems about *how* the work is done too.

So, as a manager, what I've found is it helps me hand over that responsibility to folks. And instead of solving issues and problems and figuring out the best way to do things for a particular individual, now I'm more inclined to say "How about you take some time try to figure that out? If you have a hard time, then come back for me."

Ursula, for one, believes that changes in how her employees work together have improved her team's performance. She reports:

Their communication—and my communication—skills have improved immensely . . . I see my team more focused, if they're wanting to share something about an issue or concern, to bring value to the company than before.

Ursula tells a story about her boss asking her team to investigate whether a reported problem with one application arose from something the users were doing or something else. Frank, an employee on her team, summarized some of the issues he had noticed about this application—going beyond the stated question and concluding that the application "is not bringing any value to the company." Ursula was delighted that Frank had approached the analysis so thoughtfully. She explained to us that Frank had worked on his summary notes at 2:00 a.m., after he had gotten his baby back to sleep and was wide awake himself. She saw this story as reflecting the "empowerment" that STAR had fostered in her employees with regard to both work schedules and taking an expansive view of their work roles.

The STAR program has allowed them to think outside of the box and not be so structured, if that makes sense.

What Might Have Changed, But Didn't?

While these interviews point to positive changes in individuals' and teams' performance and both interviews and survey evidence demonstrate benefits to the firm with regard to burnout, overload, job satisfaction, and turnover, did this work redesign approach affect productivity? That is a hard question to answer because measuring productivity in knowledge work is notoriously difficult, but we investigate this in several ways.

Hours

Hours might have increased, decreased, or stayed stable with the STAR work redesign. All of those changes are plausible. The firm may have wanted to get even more hours out of these salaried employees (assuming that additional hours were productive and did not prompt burnout or turnover). From our perspective, we worried that hours might increase. Our Work, Family, and Health Network research team did not want to encourage working longer hours—with less time for family, less time to take care of oneself, and less time for recovery from work stress and strain—even inadvertently. And research suggests that there is a real risk that working a varied schedule and especially working at home may increase work hours.[26]

Permission to work whenever and wherever you want could turn into pressure to work all the time and everywhere. In an analysis of a nationally representative survey, sociologists Jennifer Glass and Mary Noonan claim that "the capacity to work from home mostly extends the workday and encroaches into what was formerly home and family time" because "the ability of employees to work at home may actually allow employers to raise expectations for work availability during evenings and weekends and foster longer workdays and workweeks."[27] In fact, flexibility as always-on availability was the norm for many IT professionals and managers in TOMO when we began our study. We hoped we had designed STAR so it would not further intensify work by increasing work hours. This work redesign initiative is unusual—as the previous chapters laid out—in its collective critique of the assumption that long hours, availability, and instant responsiveness necessarily yield good work. We hoped those elements of our dual-agenda work redesign approach would counter the risks of increasing hours, but we knew that further intensification and additional hours were a real risk.

What our field experiment shows, though, is a null effect on work hours. STAR did not increase or decrease work hours, on average. There

are no significant differences in work hours between the IT professionals and managers who moved into STAR and their counterparts in the
control group.[28] We do find that *parents* who were randomized to the
STAR condition had a slight decrease of about one hour per week, though
these parents still averaged more than 40 hours of work per week.[29]

The qualitative interviews provide a richer picture of the various situations behind these null effects. Some IT professionals and managers
report that their hours have decreased—as we saw with Sherwin's reduced hours (from a high of 60 or 70 hours) and Randall's reclaiming
of time when meetings were cut. Many employees also cut their commuting time significantly because they began working at home much more,
and so they found extra time on a daily or weekly basis. Some employees believe that the company now gets more out of them, because part
of the time saved in their reduced commutes goes into work tasks. So
there is a mix of people who have cut their total work hours and people
who have increased their work hours a bit. But even without dramatic
decreases in work hours, employees and managers consistently tell us that
the work feels more manageable.

Ava, a software engineer and team lead in her thirties who is a married white woman (with no children), explains how she appreciates the
changes that have come with STAR even though she believes it may have
increased her work hours a bit. She brings up the option to grocery shop
more quickly during a week day, the freedom to have lunch on her "beau-
tiful deck" at home, the time saved by not dressing for work and driving
into the city each day, the ease of fitting in more exercise (as suggested
by her doctor and leading to weight loss), and the ability to avoid "political games" by not being in the office every day. She reports STAR is
"great for my stress levels." While Ava thinks she may work longer at
home, she says:

> But I'm happier when I'm at home versus in the office. I have my own
> office. I'm happier there. It doesn't matter if you know if I am working
> those longer hours—I'm in a more comfortable chair. I'm in my slip-
> pers. The dogs can sit there. I can pet the one ear as I'm working. It's
> very soothing.

Ava goes on to reflect, with some ambivalence, on the broader changes in work and the increased permeability between work and nonwork time that is evident in so many jobs and organizations. She knows that work is "more fluid," and there are fewer boundaries or rules that separate work and nonwork today. In fact, she thinks the current corporate message is that employees should be always on, always available. Ava sees STAR as a valuable counterbalance to those expectations.

> The thing is that companies are expecting us to be available 24/7 or work longer hours sometimes. This gives us a little bit of the balance back.

Would STAR be needed, she wonders, if the workday was still bounded as it was in the old days?

> If you were still saying 8 to 5 [and then] at 5 we would shut down? [pause] We wouldn't ever have to take work home, we wouldn't ever have to do pagers, we wouldn't ever have to carry our cell phones with us? Then I wouldn't have an issue with it. . . . But if you're going to ask your employees to do that, then you have to give them some of the flexibility back.

Productivity and Performance Measures

Just as hours might have gone up, gone down, or stayed the same, STAR might have made the TOMO employees and teams more productive, less productive, or had no net impact on productivity. Working with the IT executives in TOMO, we identified several productivity and performance metrics that the firm collected in the course of doing business. The company and the Work, Family, and Health research team worked hard to fairly assess whether STAR positively or negatively affected productivity and performance.[30] In the end, all we could say was that the company metrics showed no dramatic improvements or declines over time and no clear differences by condition. STAR neither helped nor hurt productivity or performance as measured by company data. Given the benefits we do see on other measures (reviewed earlier and in the next chapter), we take this finding of no negative effects on productivity or performance as good news.

To complement the analysis of the company's own data, we also asked a series of questions in the survey that calculate absenteeism, presenteeism, and productivity. These self-reported performance measures have obvious limitations, since people tend to think they are themselves above average. But they represent the best scale available for these topics. We found no significant differences between the STAR and control groups in the productivity measures through the eighteen-month follow-up period. The only significant difference was in the hours that employees reported they were expected to work, which declined about one hour per week for those in STAR. Note that hours worked did not decline significantly (when reported as usual hours or as hours worked in the last seven days).[31]

In interviews, some managers reported that specific employees had improved their performance and a few identified concrete improvements in how quickly their teams moved through their work. But the null effects on productivity are also reported in many interviews—in part because documenting these changes is challenging. Felicia, the production support manager, notes this when she says:

> Can you quantify the productivity [changes with STAR]? Not at this point. I think especially in our space [that is hard to do].

Yet Felicia sees valuable changes:

> Overall communication has increased, morale has increased because of that. People are taking more accountability than they were before, I think, for their jobs because they have the flexibility to do what they want to do when they want to do it . . . So yeah, I think it's a great program and I hope we continue it.

Other research also finds it is hard to determine, with confidence, the effects of workplace flexibility on productivity and performance. This is partly because different types of flexibility and different approaches to these changes make it hard to compare across studies.[32] As we described in chapter 4's discussion of flexibility as accommodation, limited and individually negotiated flexible work arrangements may not bring the benefits—to employees or to firms—that a broader and more substantial change like STAR does. It would be no surprise to us if firms that allowed employees to make just modest adjustments in their work hours or to work at home a day or two each week, with their manager's permission but with worries about whether these work patterns were actually supported, saw no benefits. These "Mother, may I?" arrangements may not prompt a sense of greater control and greater support that lead employees to be more satisfied, more engaged, and more committed.

But two recent studies with rigorous designs do find positive effects of initiatives where employees have substantial control over when or where work is done. Stanford economist Nicholas Bloom and his colleagues also ran a true field experiment, but did so in a Chinese call center where half of the interested employees were randomized to work at home (exclusively).[33] Those who worked at home had superior performance, both because they had fewer absences and took shorter breaks and because they could handle more calls in the quieter environment. Employees working at home also reported significantly higher job satisfaction and lower turnover rates. When the company later opened up the work-at-home option for all employees and allowed everyone in the call centers to choose where to work, the performance benefits were even greater (moving from 13% to 22% improvement). Some employees who had been at home returned to work because they realized they preferred to be in an office, while others headed home (and presumably people could mix up their work location as well). These findings demonstrate that allowing employees to make these decisions themselves—as is the case in our work redesign approach—brings the greatest benefits to the firm. More research is needed, but it is interesting to see these documented performance benefits in a setting where the work product is more easily measured and tracked.

Another study takes advantage of a longitudinal panel of German workplaces to see how moving to "trust-based working hours" affects the firms' performance with regard to innovation specifically. This form of flexibility also gives substantial control to employees, although there is no expectation that teams will have the conversations and reflections that are central to a dual-agenda work redesign approach. Olivier Godart and colleagues compare firms that adopt trust-based working hours to similar firms (using a matching strategy) and find that companies with the broader flexibility strategy are 12–15 percent more likely to innovate with regard to their products and 6–7 percent more likely to innovate with regard to work processes in the years just after this change. The researchers find these benefits even when controlling for a more limited type of workplace flexibility and conclude that "innovation seems to be driven by the degree of employee control and self-management over working time, rather than by merely allowing working-time flexibility."[34]

Returning to our study: we also calculated the return on investment of the STAR initiative at TOMO to compare the benefits of these changes—for the firm—to the costs. Economist Carolina Barbosa and a larger team of Work, Family, and Health researchers "micro-costed" everything involved in bringing this work redesign initiative to the company. This included adding up all the wages for staff time and contract costs for consultants' work that went into customizing the initiative for the firm and preparing training materials and delivering the trainings, plus the wages associated with employees' time participating in training sessions and even the cost of the company conference rooms used for training. Then potential benefits were examined, including the possibility of reduced absenteeism, reduced presenteeism (which refers to lower performance on days when working), lower medical costs, and reduced turnover. While the evidence regarding the first three benefits to the firm is limited, the effects on turnover were clear, as we have noted. And turnover has real costs to companies, estimated at 1.5 times the employee's total annual compensation, due to the staff time needed to hire a new employee and the lower productivity of that employee as he or she is learning the ropes. The estimated return on investment was 1.68, meaning that "on average organizational costs fell by $1.68 for every $1.00 spent on STAR."[35]

What have we learned so far? These changes are not only feasible—but the best evidence available demonstrates they bring benefits to the firm as well as to overloaded employees and managers. With STAR, the company experienced increased job satisfaction, reduced burnout (which means more sustained engagement), employees who are less interested in finding another job, and fewer people choosing to leave the company. The dual-agenda work redesign facilitates a set of interrelated changes, with more flexibility in when work is done, more acceptance of regularly working at home, more employee control over those decisions, more deliberate coordination practices including fewer meetings in many teams, and a willingness to question whether everything is urgent and whether being always on and available for work is actually productive or wise. These changes become common sense, as Sherwin described, for many teams and they bring some relief and sanity to daily life as well.

Chapter 6

⌘

WORK REDESIGN BENEFITS FOR HEALTH, WELL-BEING, AND PERSONAL LIFE

We have seen that a work redesign innovation brings benefits in terms of burnout, overload, job satisfaction, turnover, and more. But our research team is called the Work, *Family*, and *Health* Network, and so we are also interested in the question of whether work redesign affects health and well-being and family or personal life. Improvements in health—both physical and mental health—are important to individuals, families, and society in their own right. Improvements in health are also of interest to firms that care about reducing health-related productivity losses (such as absenteeism or reduced effort) and minimizing healthcare costs.[1]

The Work, Family, and Health Network built on some of the strongest evidence on work and health when designing STAR. What we know is that a sense of control and support at work are critical resources for managing work stress and high demands. Since the 1970s social epidemiologists, sociologists, and organizational scholars have found that workers who have less control in their jobs are at higher risk of heart disease (partly explained by higher blood pressure, cholesterol, and smoking) and also face higher mortality rates and worse mental health. The basic idea is that not having control over how your work unfolds is stressful, resulting in both heightened arousal that is physiologically taxing and a sense of helplessness that reduces motivation.[2] Extending that rich research base on job control, our work redesign initiative attempted to increase employees' and managers' sense of control by giving them a greater say in their schedules, work location, and everyday processes for completing and coordinating their work.

The second critical factor is social support. Feeling connected and respected matters enormously for health, and the support an employee receives from their manager is particularly salient.[3] Our work redesign initiative also promotes support for employees' personal and family lives and especially targets managers' support for life outside of work. STAR increases employees' sense of control and their feelings of being supported by their managers (as we described in the last chapter), and we theorized it would bring benefits to employees with regard to their health, well-being, families, and personal lives.

But it is always an open question whether work redesigns like STAR will succeed. A review of over sixty studies found that employees' control over when and where they work consistently predicts a sense of work–life balance and positive attitudes about the job—but concluded, at that time, that there was "no consistent evidence" regarding its' impacts on health and well-being.[4] Fortunately, our rigorous assessment of this work redesign initiative, along with other research in a variety of occupations and industries, provides important evidence that changes at work can succeed in improving workers' lives and health.[5]

Subjective Well-Being and Mental Health

Our interviews reveal important benefits to mental health or subjective well-being. The stories we heard about burnout, job satisfaction, and more include repeated references to reduced stress, as does Sherwin's claim that STAR has created "100 percent less stress" for him and for others. While employees and managers routinely, repeatedly told us about benefits to their subjective well-being, we also use the survey evidence to investigate whether STAR reduced perceived stress and psychological distress. Stress is assessed with survey questions about feeling difficulties "piling up so high that you could not overcome them," as well as rarely feeling that "things were going your way." The psychological distress scale captures feeling hopeless, worthless, nervous, fidgety, and more, where the symptoms are not necessarily severe enough to warrant a clinical diagnosis of depression or anxiety but are still troubling.[6]

We find that STAR significantly reduces stress and psychological distress—but only for employees and managers who entered STAR before the announcement of the upcoming merger of TOMO and ZZT.[7] When people move into STAR believing that their organization's leadership supports these changes and that the initiative has a good chance of becoming their new normal, then their stress and psychological distress decrease. In contrast, there is no significant change in stress and psychological distress for those who encounter the work redesign initiative in the context of the merger, even though this later group sees other benefits like an increased sense of control and is able to engage in more work at home. As we mentioned in describing the burnout and job satisfaction effects, employees and managers quickly began questioning whether these changes would last through the merger. Not surprisingly, other studies also find that major organizational changes such as mergers, acquisitions, or dramatic rounds of downsizing offset the benefits of positive organizational changes like STAR.[8]

The second nuance is that the benefits of STAR for stress and psychological distress are clearer for women than men. By the twelve-month follow-up survey, women randomized to STAR have significantly lower levels of stress and psychological distress than women randomized to the control group. And it is not mothers who see the greatest declines but women without children at home (who tend to be older and are more likely to be single and to have adult caregiving responsibilities). Men in STAR look just like their control group counterparts with regard to stress and psychological distress, according to the survey. These men also report less stress and psychological distress than women at baseline—and men's stress is lower than women's in many other studies too. It may be that the mental health effects of work redesign initiatives like STAR are most evident when employees and managers are starting from a high level of stress or psychological distress.[9] It is interesting to note that men and women are similar in terms of STAR increasing job satisfaction and reducing burnout, intention to leave their jobs, and actual exits from the company.

Stress declines because this work redesign allows employees and managers to choose when, where, and how they work more generally and to trim what they call low-value work, meaning tasks (like some meetings) that they see as less necessary for getting the job done. Peggy, a software developer who discussed feeling able to pitch in with her coworkers more in STAR, also talks about feeling less frantic and scattered. The reduced stress helps her respond differently to challenges at work:

> I deal with that better than I used to. Before, I just pretty much beat myself up but now I'm liking me quite a bit [laughs] and beating me up less. So I'm thankful that the STAR program came along.

Our interviews are also clear that one important driver of these improvements in stress, burnout, and other well-being measures is the fact that people no longer feel guilty organizing their workdays around their personal lives, family commitments, and health priorities. Hala, a younger South Asian father of two and a software developer, shares that simply being able to take his daughter to school regularly has been "really nice." He continues:

> It's a sack of guilt [that] was taken off my shoulders. Because I don't feel guilty [now].

Hala still has quite a bit of work in his intense job but it is acceptable—to him, his boss, and his peers—to rearrange his workday to fit with the rest of his life. Kunwar is a South Asian manager and mother who previously described her long hours and split attention at home. She now feels better when she prioritizes a personal commitment:

> I found that working weekends, working nights still happens. But now if I do take a two-hour lunch with my mom, I feel great. I don't have to rush back.

Kunwar also sees that her employees feel less guilty when they work at home—even though she had tried to be supportive previously. Her employees have shared that STAR has removed the guilt factor. They don't feel guilty anymore about having to work maybe two or three times from home, and the same applies to me as well.

We also find that STAR changes employees' physiological functioning in beneficial ways. Penn State professor David Almeida and other Work, Family, and Health Network colleagues collected informative data on daily fluctuations in cortisol from 100 TOMO employees who were also parents.[10] These employees gave us saliva samples repeatedly over four consecutive days, at baseline and then a year later, so we could assess their daily patterns of cortisol. Cortisol is a hormone whose secretion generally follows a pattern of sharply rising upon wakening and then declining over the course of the day. This cortisol pattern indicates the body's ability to mobilize energy, so a blunted or flat pattern suggests fatigue or burnout. Employees in STAR saw significant increases in their cortisol awakening pattern on non-workdays—which points to better recovery among these STAR employees on weekends. Previous studies of work stress and cortisol patterns have compared employees who are in different workplaces and jobs, but we look at how changes in the organization of work affect the same individuals' cortisol pattern. This is the first evidence that a work redesign initiative like STAR affects employees' stress physiology—that these changes are actually getting under the skin.

Taking Good Care of Yourself

Do these shifts in stress and guilt also affect how people take care of themselves and their physical health over the long run? We all know that sleep, exercise, and healthy eating are behaviors that promote our long-term physical health as well as contributing to mental health. A dual-agenda work redesign gives employees the opportunity to make healthier choices—although it certainly does not guarantee they will do so.

Orfeu Buxton, the primary sleep scholar on the Work, Family, and Health Network team and a professor at Penn State, led us in investigating how specific work conditions and exposure to STAR affect these IT professionals' sleep. We measure employees' sleep using objectively measured sleep—with actigraphy watches that function like a FitBit but provide very detailed sleep data—as well as survey questions about feeling rested after sleep and how well you slept. Before STAR, employees' sense of being pulled between work and personal life affected feeling rested, sleep quality, and sleep duration. And there is a reciprocal relationship, where challenges one day affect sleep and poor sleep affects the next day's challenges. On days when an employee reports that work is interfering with the rest of their life or feels they do not have enough time for self-care (like exercise) or family connections, that employee is more likely to report that it takes longer to fall asleep. In the other direction, in the day following a night with shorter sleep time than usual or poorer sleep quality than usual, employees are more likely to experience work–family challenges or feel particularly time-squeezed.[11]

Using the field experiment to look at whether changes tied to the work redesign affect sleep, we find that employees moving into STAR see greater increases in their sleep as compared to their peers in the control group. (The differences are statistically significant, meaning they are not due to chance, but they are admittedly small. Employees average about 8 to 13 minutes per day additional sleep, depending on which wave of follow-up data we consider.) Employees in STAR are also significantly more likely to feel rested upon waking than their peers in the control group.[12] What's more, the changes in sleep stay steady over the eighteen months of follow-up, so the benefits of STAR for sleep quality did not fade over time

Improving sleep is important because chronic sleep deficiency is associated with important health risks including obesity, diabetes, hypertension, cardiovascular disease, and early mortality. Healthy sleep is measured in several ways. In addition to the duration of sleep, sleep apnea—a common sleep disorder where a person repeatedly stops and then starts breathing again while asleep—is an important indicator of unhealthy sleep. Using our TOMO data and parallel data from a long-term care workforce, Buxton and colleagues find that workers with more sleep apnea symptoms have higher cardiometabolic risk scores, meaning they score higher on a set of biomarkers that predict the risk of a cardiovascular event, such as a heart attack, over a ten-year period.[13] Among TOMO employees, those with both sleep apnea and shorter sleep duration face even greater cardiometabolic risks. STAR does not increase sleep duration dramatically for most of these employees but it does increase sleep duration and quality in a sustained way. These effects are found even though the STAR training does not directly promote healthy sleep.

We also did not ask about sleep directly in our interviews, but employees and managers brought it up in about one out of five cases. These stories illustrate *how* STAR encourages more sleep, and they document employees' and managers' appreciation of these changes. Sylvia, for example, is a white woman in her sixties who manages a team of software developers and lives about an hour from the TOMO office. Because of traffic on her commute, she had previously set the alarm for 4:30 a.m. to leave the house early enough to miss the worst of it. With STAR she works at home two or three days per week, so those nights she has at least eight hours of sleep rather than the five hours or so that she reports on commuting days.

> I'm not as tired as I used to be . . . That's been extremely beneficial to me, in that I do get more sleep than I've had in years.

Others share that STAR and working at home allowed them to manage minor illnesses easily, getting the sleep they need to recover quickly. Elise, a white married woman in her sixties, reports that she had recently been sick.

> I didn't come in until after lunch because I slept late that morning. I just felt like I needed to sleep. So, no problem. I just did it on my own. No problem at all with anybody.

When asked how she would have handled that situation previously, Elise says:

> Oh, I would have gotten the early bus and gone downtown. I would have, definitely, definitely. But I just feel like the flexibility allows you a few choices.

We also hear that sleep lost in late-night calls is sometimes reclaimed by employees who can shift their working hours with STAR. Kara, a white woman with two children, manages a production support team that is on call 24/7. When there is an outage or problem with their application, she and her employees are pulled into an urgent conference call at any hour and often for many hours:

> We get all the experts together and try to figure it out across India, Washington, Colorado, Nebraska, Virginia, Florida. It can be a very long night. So having the flexibility of STAR, [to] be able to sleep in a bit and catch a rest and then log on when you need to, it's a good thing.

Adjusting one's work schedule to reflect a late-night meeting is completely sensible—but it was not viewed as appropriate or allowed before STAR.

In addition to sleep, some employees tell us that they are now fitting in more exercise or having more success with weight loss. The changes in health behaviors are subtle for some people and dramatic for others. Duncan, a white married father who is an IT systems engineer, is delighted to share that he has lost over forty pounds, is managing his chronic health condition (Crohn's disease) much better, and feels less stressed and happier at home. Duncan now regularly puts exercise down on his calendar as an early-morning meeting, and his reduced commute supports his new habits in the gym and at home.

> So I feel 100 percent better. I'm not worried about having a heart attack or keeling over from Crohn's. I'm a much happier, better person and I want this to keep going. [laughs]

Denzell (also a middle-aged white man) describes a dramatic improvement in his heart condition. He attributes the changes to medication, exercise, and diet but also explains that he knows his healthy habits are easier to maintain because his workdays are more flexible and less stressful. He regularly finds time to use the exercise bike on days he works at home. In contrast, he remembers that after very long days in the office, he would come home and just want to sit.

Employees and managers who were already quite committed to exercise and healthy eating also appreciate how STAR supports their health goals. One man who serves in the National Guard finds it easier to prepare for his periodic military physical and endurance test because he can fit in workouts more easily. Patsy, an IT professional and mom in her forties, shared at the end of a phone interview that she had been cycling on her recumbent bike during the whole conversation. She had always tried to work out regularly but now that she is working at home more, she set up a laptop shelf to create a new "pedaling desk." Riding during some of her conference calls has increased her stamina and leaves her feeling energized.

Changes in stress and in healthy behaviors could well affect physical health over time. Harvard professor Lisa Berkman led our Work, Family, and Health Network team in combining the biomarker data we collected from TOMO employees (including blood pressure, body mass index, a prediabetes marker evident in blood, and more) to create a cardiometabolic risk score. This risk score predicts the likelihood of a cardiovascular event, like a heart attack or stroke, in the next ten years and has been validated in studies following people over many years. We find that employees who had higher risk scores at baseline see significantly greater improvements (declines in their risk score) in STAR, as compared to the changes for high-risk employees in the control group. We do not follow TOMO employees for decades—but this is exciting evidence that work redesign innovations can reduce the risk of serious health problems later on.[14]

Personal Time and Work–Life Conflicts

A dual agenda—where employees are encouraged to pay attention to both their professional and personal lives—is an essential part of the work redesign approach that we study. STAR prompts people to think about their work's impact on their lives outside of work and also consider how they can support coworkers professionally and personally. The message is clear that rearranging work to address personal or family priorities and commitments is acceptable. And the hope is that these new work practices will help people find more time for personal and family activities and feel less conflicted or pulled in different directions by their work and the rest of their lives. This approach brings broad benefits—helping those who have kids at home, those with caregiving responsibilities for adults, and those with fewer family ties.

Our survey asks about how often work demands interfere with personal or family life and whether time spent on the job makes it difficult to fulfill personal and family responsibilities (which scholars call work-to-nonwork conflict). We also asked about how personal and family life interferes with or crowds out work (measuring nonwork-to-work conflict).[15] Employees in STAR see significantly greater declines in perceived conflicts than their counterparts in the control group. Work-to-nonwork conflicts decline a bit and this is a marginally significant difference, while nonwork-to-work conflicts decline significantly in our analysis of the full sample of employees.[16]

Additionally, using a survey question about having enough time to spend with family, we find that employees in STAR have improved time adequacy as compared to the control group. And perceived time adequacy—or feeling less squeezed for time—matters for other outcomes. Our previous research in a different white-collar workforce demonstrated that employees with higher time adequacy also had more energy, a greater sense of mastery (or being able to solve the problems you face), better health overall, and more life satisfaction, as well as lower burnout and fewer physical aches and pains. What's more, following employees over time, we see that increased time adequacy over six months also predicts improvements in many of these measures of health and well-being.[17]

STAR helps level the playing field between employees who had "won the boss lottery" by reporting to someone who was quite flexible before the initiative and those who had not.[18] Our Work, Family, and Health Network collaborators Leslie Hammer and Ellen Kossek have developed new measures of supervisors' emotional and practical support for their employees' lives beyond work. Employees who initially reported that their supervisors were less supportive (at baseline, before STAR begins) see much larger changes in work-to-nonwork conflicts with STAR than those with a more supportive supervisor. Another analysis using data from TOMO also confirms that work-to-nonwork conflict and supervisor support are connected. Employees who have a supportive supervisor are less affected—as indicated by their cortisol patterns and by their reports of negative mood—by work-to-nonwork conflicts. So work redesign initiatives that increase supervisors' support for employees' personal and family life also make it easier for employees to bear the work-to-nonwork conflicts that remain.[19]

The interviews provide many stories of employees rearranging work to fit in more of the things they value. Randall—who is single and in his thirties and appeared in earlier chapters expressing his frustration with crazy schedules and overload—now has more time for the other activities in his life. Since STAR began he misses fewer recreational hockey games, which he says improves his social life. He is also able to make progress on renovating his house, because he is less tired with fewer long days in the office with a long commute after work.

> Now I'm going to go change my clothes and pick up a hammer or a paintbrush or whatever? You just have more energy [now].

Elise occasionally meets up with friends who have already retired for lunch, and she appreciates being able to go visit someone in the hospital during the day as well. She summarizes:

> I feel like I have a little more ownership of my time to do other things besides work and go home, work and go home, work and go home . . . Nobody asks questions, which is wonderful. They respect your time.

And Isaac finds that with STAR, he is able to volunteer in his community more. He is currently on the board of a nonprofit athletic organization for kids, and he is an assistant coach for a youth football team.

> Again, being able to set my schedule—the flexibility that STAR provides—allows me to give back to my community in a way that before [was trickier].

He recounts the stress, before STAR, of trying to leave the office at 5:00 p.m. to be at the practice field by 6:00 when "you had eighteen kids waiting for you," but the traffic was unpredictable. Now he is more likely to work at home on days that have an evening practice, and he says:

> I can come back and my day is not over. If I still have things to take care of, I still take care of [them]. But I've given back to my community. I've given something.

Time for Children and Related Benefits for Health and Well-Being

These benefits are clearly not limited to parents, but STAR facilitates important shifts in family time for both mothers and fathers. Chuck, a production support engineer, describes how his increased work at home allows him to spend more time with his children. He now takes his older child to horseback riding lessons once a week. The lessons, Chuck tells us, are scheduled

> 1:00 to 4:00, so right in the middle of the day. I would do that and later that evening, if I needed to, I would work a little bit or just work [more] on Friday if I needed to catch up.

Chuck is also arranging his work to spend some time with his infant daughter and support his wife while she is on family leave. Chuck took three weeks of vacation time just after the birth and then began working at home almost exclusively.[20] He often blocks an hour away from work tasks to care for the baby while his wife runs an errand or takes a break. Chuck reports that it has taken some experimentation to be able to focus with an infant and his wife at home, but they have an effective routine. With this increased control and support, employees can also shift their work routines easily as family needs change. In our next interview Chuck's wife is back at work, the baby is in child care, and Chuck regularly starts work at 6 a.m. so he can pick his older daughter up early from summer camp two days each week. Both Chuck and his daughter enjoy their afternoons together, and he is able to get the job done well, too.

Patsy, the developer who was cycling in her home office during one interview, lives with her husband and two children almost an hour away from the office. Working at home more affects her family's mornings and her time with her children.

> I'm definitely more engaged in the morning routine now, which I was never before . . . I actually see them get out of bed and I get to kiss them goodbye, which is a big thing.

Patsy's husband had previously handled breakfast, packing snacks and lunches, and making sure the kids left with their homework, permission slips, and jackets. Since STAR began, they divide the week so each of them handles some mornings. Patsy explains that the morning time is precious to her because her children have always had an earlier bedtime.

> We sit down to dinner and then it's homework and then it's bath and then they want to watch something. Or we have a game night now on Thursday and we'll play one quick game and then bedtime. So I get to actually see my kids [in the mornings now], which is nice.

The new ways of working (with greater control on the part of employees and support from coworkers and managers) also allow parents to pursue connections to their children's lives outside of school. In our next interview with Patsy, we hear that she is beginning to volunteer in her daughter's classroom regularly. She now works at the school most Friday mornings to fill the folders that students take home.

> I haven't really done a whole lot of volunteering before, just the one-off. And my daughter is now in 4th grade, so I feel like this is good. I can go in and get in there and I'm working on folders, but I get to hear how the teacher works with the kids and hear how my daughter does. [laughs] I feel like the fly on the wall.

Later in the interview, Patsy shares that she had "struggled with" not feeling able to volunteer regularly before but now she realizes:

> I could actually be a part of my child's education maybe, more than I was before . . . . It makes me feel good. And I know it makes my daughter feel good. She likes to see me in there when she comes in from recess.

Patsy works full time (and has since her children were born), has impressive technical skills, and feels a real commitment to her job and her team. With STAR, she can continue doing that work well while also connecting with her children and their school in a different way.

Children's time with parents is critical for healthy development, so we wanted to see whether STAR encourages that. Kelly Chandler, a family scholar now at Oregon State, led the Work, Family, and Health Network team analyzing data from almost 100 TOMO employees who were parents of an adolescent.[21] Parents complete "daily diary" interviews on eight consecutive days where they report on how much time they spent with that child in the last day. These interviews are conducted at baseline, before any of the parents moved into STAR, and then again one year later.

STAR facilitates time with children ages 9 to 17—even though work hours do not change for the full sample and parents' work hours only decrease by an average of one hour per week (as we reported in the discussion of work hours). For TOMO parents in the control group, the time spent with a child decreases over the year, with an average decrease of 24 minutes per day. This type of decline from year to year is actually expected among teens. Most fifteen-year-olds prefer to spend less time with parents than they did when they were younger, and adolescents often do more independent activities—including jobs, sports, or school clubs, as well as time with friends. (One of us is currently adjusting to how little she gets to see her teen these days!) But among parents in STAR, the decline in parent–child shared time did not happen. In fact, we see a significant increase in shared time. By the follow-up survey one year after baseline, employees in STAR average about three hours spent with their child as compared to just under two hours per day among parents in the control group. Digging deeper into the data, we find that the effects of STAR were more evident for mothers; fathers' time with kids is more stable for both the treatment and control groups. We also see that it is time with daughters, as compared to sons, that differs the most when we compare STAR with control group families. The stronger effects for mothers and for daughters are consistent with other research that finds mother–daughter pairs tend to report being closer and spend more time together in adolescence than do mothers and sons.[22] Patsy's story of spending more time with her children in the morning is quite consistent with the patterns we see in this quantitative analysis.

While the survey findings show a more dramatic effect for mothers' time with children than fathers' time, several fathers also use STAR to spend more time with their children and families. In addition to Hala, Isaac, and Chuck, Hayward reports that his family life is "much happier." His son is able to come home after school most days and either work on homework—in a desk right next to Hayward's—or play on the cul-de-sac. Their neighborhood is full of kids, so Hayward's son enjoys this time outside with friends and Hayward can check in on him as needed. Some days, Hayward picks up his preschooler around 4 p.m. and starts dinner then; he can finish up a little work after the meal if needed. Hayward's wife works full time (as an IT professional too, but not for TOMO). In a later interview, we learn that both children are now at the same school and Hayward's wife handles the morning drop-off. This allows Hayward to work from 7 a.m. to 3 p.m.—mostly at home—and then pick up the kids in time to make an early dinner. That evening time is important to Hayward, who had shared his frustration with his TOMO schedule before STAR and worried then about the long hours his children spent away from home in school or after-school programs.

Kunwar cried in an early interview when she described how work stress sometimes erupted into yelling at her daughter, but after STAR began, her daughter's week unfolds differently and Kunwar's mood is more relaxed. Because both Kunwar and her husband (who both work at TOMO in STAR groups) work at home some days, their middle-school daughter now comes home after school. Kunwar sees positive changes "in the quality of her life and her health" because she has a healthy snack, more time for homework, and more time for evening play. Kunwar also feels free to stay home when there is bad weather or to take her daughter to the doctor when there is a school release day. And she feels less stressed on regular days because she can end work early if she began work early and turn to cooking or other chores:

That way I'm not stressed out in the evening and not yelling and screaming at my daughter.

Kunwar's family shows the potential for both direct and indirect effects on children's well-being as parents put their work and family lives together differently. The direct effects come from increased time at home (for the parents and the children), while the indirect effects come from feeling less stressed, minimizing yelling and frustration.[23]

These quotes describe positive *spillover*—where changes in work bring positive changes in health, well-being, or family life for the employees and managers who move into STAR. This is a within-person link across work and nonwork domains. For example, as Kunwar's work stress declines, her mood at home improves. But we also investigate *crossover*—whether changes happening for the TOMO employees also bring changes for other people, and specifically for members of their families. Continuing that example, we would ask whether there is evidence that changes in Kunwar's situation at work affect her daughter's mood or other measures of well-being.[24]

Katie Lawson, a developmental psychologist in the Work, Family, and Health Network, led our analysis to consider these crossover questions using data from about 100 youth in the daily diary study.[25] Youth well-being is indicated by positive mood, negative mood, and how these young people react to everyday challenges (or "affective reactivity" to "daily stressors," using the scholarly jargon).[26] We ask: Do parents' work situations affect how happy or sad these kids and teens feel? Do parents' work situations affect how well kids and teens fare in the face of everyday challenges like an argument with a friend or family member or a problem at school? Because we interview the youth for eight consecutive days at baseline and then again a year later, we can compare how the youth do on days when they face one of those situations as compared to days when they do not, as well as comparing the changes over one year for the treatment and control groups more broadly.

Other developmental research finds a general trend in which older children and teens report less positive moods and more negative moods as they age. We see this expected decline in emotional well-being for the control group, specifically. But for youth with a parent in STAR, there is a significant increase in the frequency of positive feelings a year after baseline, and negative moods stay stable. For example, on days when a child with a parent in the control group has a daily stressor like a disagreement with a parent, we see bigger hits to their positive mood and bigger increases in their negative mood as compared to their reactions to that type of challenge a year before. For those with a parent in STAR, though, there is no change in positive or negative reactions over the course of the year.

We also investigate how parents' exposure to STAR affects children's healthy behaviors—specifically their sleep patterns. Again, previous research finds that healthy sleep deteriorates in the adolescent years. Penn State professor Susan McHale and Work, Family, and Health colleagues examine whether having a parent in the STAR initiative affects adolescents' sleep.[27] Sleep *duration* stays stable over one year for the youth in our study, with no differences for parents in STAR versus control group. But youth with a parent in the control group had significantly less regular sleep patterns (i.e., increased variation from night to night in sleep duration), reported worse quality sleep, and took longer to fall asleep at the follow-up survey then they had at baseline. For youth with a parent in STAR, though, there were no significant declines in sleep health.

As they move into and through the teen years, adolescents tend to feel more negative emotions and fewer positive emotions, to become more emotionally responsive to everyday challenges, and to sleep worse. What we learn here is that a work redesign initiative like STAR can be a buffer that protects children and youth from the usual declines in well-being and sleep. There is more research to be done to fully understand this type of crossover from parents' work experiences to children's lives.[28] But we see that many of the parents who moved into STAR at TOMO rearrange their work tasks to spend more time with their kids and, because they work at home more and can shift their schedules easily, become more available to their children even if their kids are busy with activities or not at home. Children and teens may feel less stressed knowing that they can turn to a parent more easily. And as parents feel less stressed and strung out, their interactions with others in their family may be more relaxed and positive. These are all plausible pathways—and all suggested by our interviews—for understanding how changes in a parent's experiences at work cross over to affect children's health and well-being.

Time for Other Family Members

Children and teens aren't the only family members who benefit from the redesigned work patterns and reduced stress. We consistently heard stories of ways that STAR facilitates employees' support of spouses, parents, and other adult family and friends who had health concerns. Georgia, a quality assurance manager, shares that three of her employees are men whose wives are pregnant for the first time. These men are all taking time to attend prenatal appointments, and Georgia knows they are "getting into the family thing a little bit more" while still getting their work done. Georgia is genuinely excited for these employees and supportive of their family transitions. Before STAR, Georgia probably felt supportive but her employees—the new fathers in this case—may not have been comfortable *openly prioritizing* these family commitments. Erin Reid's study of management consultants, for example, documents that men in professional and managerial roles sometimes take care of family and personal responsibilities but hide that from their coworkers and bosses, quietly "passing" as ideal workers who live up to the firm's expectations that they are always available for work.[29]

With STAR, men who previously feared it would be unwise to openly share their family commitments hear that it is legitimate and appropriate for *everyone* to rearrange work for personal reasons. Fathers' ratings of their manager's support for personal and family life increased *more* than mothers' ratings when STAR launched.[30] That may reflect changes as more managers realize that men's family and personal lives need to be recognized too. Additionally, some managers, like Georgia, just get more explicit about the support they had always meant to provide. Women benefit too, of course. Ava, an IT analyst we meet when she is pregnant with twins, has several doctors' appointments each week and sometimes needs to rest during the day. Without STAR, she does not think she would still be in this job—or, indeed, any job. With STAR, Ava continues to work for TOMO after the babies arrive, choosing to work at home most days while using a nanny and later childcare in her neighborhood.

STAR also helps employees and managers when their loved ones are facing health problems. Before STAR, Frederick, a quality assurance tester in his late fifties, took all his vacation time for his wife's intensive cancer treatment. Since STAR launched, he goes to his wife's follow-up appointments without worrying about whether he will have enough holiday time off later in the year. He feels completely comfortable doing that and appreciates that he can be part of her treatment. Frederick works later the day before that appointment to stay caught up and he says, more generally,

> If I take off time during the actual workday, then I certainly make that up. I'm accountable to myself and to my boss and to our projects and to the company. But at the same time, I'm more accountable here at home.

Frederick appreciates the "much more relaxed atmosphere" even though there is still a lot to do with both work and family commitments.

Katya provides an interesting example of daily involvement in her elderly parents' lives, as well as the stretched hours that some workers face when their technical work connects the offshore workers to the US-led projects. Asked whether and how STAR had changed her work, Katya offers to walk us through her typical day:

> I have a series of meetings with my offshore teams, because I work with more than one. So my meetings start around 5:30 a.m. every morning. So I get up in the morning, I do my meetings, I get my tasks for today from the guys I work with.
>
> Then I don't have to worry if I need to go to the office. If I need to, I'll go. If not—you know, nobody can tell me I need to be at the office. So I can take a couple of hours of do my stuff around the house. Because I live with my elderly parents. I need to take care of them . . .
>
> If I need to take a break during the day, then I don't feel bad about it at all. If I need to stay late, then [I will]. About 10, 10:30 p.m., I have another series of meetings [laughs].

Katya's day is quite stretched—and that was true before STAR—but now she is less concerned about rushing into the office at a certain time or even being online continuously from 9 a.m. to 3 p.m. She takes time to handle her family and home responsibilities, whenever those are pressing, and is reassured that she is still available to her coworkers. She may not be sitting in front of her computer, but she knows that everyone will contact her by phone if they need her.

The flexibility of working outside of the office also benefits employees and managers who are dealing with a family crisis. Gideon, for example, is a systems engineer and a divorced man in his fifties. He recently spent a couple months doing his job at his father's house (which was not in the same city as his TOMO office) as his father's health declined. At the time of his father's death, Gideon took some time fully off work but he also appreciates that he could work remotely while caregiving and working on his father's estate. This story first comes up in response to our interview question about whether STAR affected Gideon's work performance—positively, negatively, or not at all. He reports that his work probably would have suffered as he was dealing with his father's illness, death, and the work to take care of his father's estate. But, Gideon says,

It *didn't* have noticeable impact . . . and that's probably due to STAR.

Others shared stories of working remotely from a parent's or a sibling's home as that person recovered from surgery or needed support for another reason. For example, one woman spent two weeks at her mother-in-law's home to provide some company in the period after her father-in-law's death. She set up a home office there and feels that it all worked very smoothly. These decisions seem completely sensible in STAR—but those actions were not necessarily allowed before. What's more, employees may not even have explored the possibility of remote work periods previously because it seemed risky to share one's personal and family commitments.

We see broad and varied benefits of redesigning work. STAR benefits employees and the organization on the work front. Employees feel less worn down, view their jobs more positively, and are more likely to stay with the company. Frontline managers report either no concerns or an improved sense of collaboration and ownership among those they supervise. While hours stay similar overall, employees and managers find ways to work smarter and cut down on tasks they do not value (including commutes). STAR benefits employees and their families on the home front too. Parents find a bit more time with their children and the older children and adolescents in our sample fare better, in terms of mood and sleep, when they have a parent in STAR as compared to the control group. We also see that the benefits for personal life, health, and community connections extend well beyond those who have caregiving responsibilities for kids or other family members. This is a case where everyone seems to win.

And yet there is a challenge looming in the background. After the merger announcement, the employees and managers moving into STAR do so with less confidence and see smaller changes in their well-being. As the merger is completed and the new firm begins operating as one organization, the question of whether STAR will last comes to the fore. Patsy, the developer who fits in more exercise, more time with her kids in the morning, and new volunteer contributions, frames it this way:

> I feel a little bit like we're riding a gravy train right now with this. And I'm going to use it while it's there—because I do worry that it's probably all going to go away.

Patsy clarifies that there is a small chance that her position will be cut after the merger integration is done. But even if she keeps her job, STAR may be lost:

> I don't know if it's going to last with the new company. I just don't know.

Part III

LOOKING AHEAD
⌘

Chapter 7

⌘

TWO STEPS FORWARD, ONE STEP BACK

Nothing happens in a vacuum, at least not in the real world. We carefully designed our study as an experiment to identify the effects of a dual-agenda work redesign, STAR, but this was an experiment taking place in the field, not in a lab. These IT professionals and managers had to respond both to STAR and to unexpected—and very consequential—changes unfolding in their company at the same time. As we have discussed, TOMO merged with another technology firm that we call ZZT during the course of our study. Even though leadership proclaimed it to be a merger of equals, ZZT was the acquiring firm and the top management team of the integrated firm soon included more executives from ZZT than from TOMO.

These changes in ownership and leadership put the STAR initiative at risk. In the three years after the merger was finalized, executives in the IT division first pulled away from STAR without explaining what would come next, then considered a new policy some described as "modified STAR" and "STAR 2.0," then reverted to a more traditional management policy with each vice president setting his or her own expectations for work schedules and work location. Finally, after our study had officially ended, the firm announced that the entire IT division was going to follow the quite restrictive ZZT policy regarding work schedules and locations—"working at work," as it were. In terms of official policy that endorsed flexible, supportive, and self-directed work patterns, the IT professionals and managers we studied were now back at the starting line.

But we learned that the expectations and perspectives that had developed under STAR often continued.

The leadership of the merged firm ended STAR, even though the initiative was seen as a success by those who had been involved. When we surveyed IT professionals and managers who had been part of STAR, we learned that 95 percent of employees and 82 percent of managers said STAR had been "very successful" or "somewhat successful" for them personally.[1] These reports come from a survey conducted almost a year *after* the official end of STAR, in the period where it was not clear what the company would do next. Employees and middle managers might have believed that the firm's decision to end STAR was driven by real problems with the initiative elsewhere in the organization. In other words, they might have assumed executives were responding to problems with STAR even though they felt it worked very well for them and their teams. But 86 percent of employees and 72 percent of managers also believed STAR had been very successful or somewhat successful *for the organization as a whole.* So STAR was deemed successful by insiders, even after it ended.

Support for STAR was evident among some executives too. One TOMO vice president[2] described STAR as a "good concept" that produced real benefits for employees' and managers' "morale, happiness, and work–life balance." According to the executive, employees reported feeling trusted and appreciated that "managers aren't babysitting me" under STAR. Even when pushed to describe any concerns with STAR, this vice president said:

> STAR did not appear to have any downside, from a productivity standpoint either . . . No concerns bubbled up to me.

Another vice president expressed some concerns (and we will explore them in detail later) but concluded: "The way I look at it, STAR as a program—it worked."

Why, then, did the company move away from STAR? And what does the revocation of STAR say about the promise and feasibility of redesigning the ways we work? We detect a common story: organizational changes such as mergers, acquisitions, or major restructuring bring new leadership to power. New leaders make changes in company policy and management practices based on their previous experiences, their interpretation of what the firm needs now, and their desire to make their mark. Those decisions often don't make sense to the rank-and-file within the company, but employees and middle managers find it risky to complain too loudly or too long.

The Merger and the Official End of STAR

STAR was a casualty of the merger of TOMO and ZZT. During STAR trainings employees expressed worries that the merger would mean the end of STAR, and we know teams discussed that later as well. The threat to STAR posed by the merger was clear early on to employees and managers—and they were right.

Employees and managers recognized that the executives making the decision on how to integrate TOMO's and ZZT's human resources policies and management practices might be swayed by other concerns. Joseph, a frontline manager who primarily supervises project managers and analysts, hoped STAR would continue in the merged company. But, he noted,

> We're not going to make those decisions. You and I probably don't have any influence on who is gonna make those decisions. It would be nice if we did, but . . .

He fades off, implying that no one knows who will actually decide on the future of STAR. As it turned out, executives from both companies officially signed off on ending STAR—but the acquiring firm's leadership seemed to be calling the shots by the time that happened. Asked about STAR's sustainability soon after the merger, Holden, a senior project manager, said it has been successful and that ending STAR "would be a step backwards." But he noted that ZZT "isn't doing this stuff" and that management decisions "get to be these little, these political games." So Holden was not optimistic about STAR surviving the merger.

> I'm just enjoying it while it lasts. Let's put it that way.

Some executives also framed the merger as the principle cause of the revocation of STAR. The same vice president who noted that STAR had no downsides also concluded, once the merged firm was operating as one, that "the culture of this company isn't ready for the concept." The reality, according to this executive, was that "ZZT is in a different place and has a different paradigm."

> Their concern is this: we are used to having everyone in the office, to running down the hall to ask a question, to talking to people in the halls. That is the company culture, talking to each other, seeing each other in cafeteria, walking down the hall to talk through a question.

It was difficult to champion something that "goes so much against how ZZT operates," we were told, even when executives had seen the benefits to their teams in TOMO. Indeed, this vice president and others whom we knew to be quite enthusiastic about STAR quietly went along with the decisions to pull back from STAR and eventually agreed to reassert a quite conservative policy.[3]

We could interpret the decision to drop STAR and the eventual push for traditional, inflexible work patterns as a reflection of two different organizational cultures. TOMO was open to flexibility and its managers were ready to shift some of the control over everyday decisions to the IT professionals they supervised. ZZT, in contrast, emphasized a close-knit company culture, and its managers assumed that they should direct their subordinates with regard to work location and schedules. These two philosophies came together and—not surprisingly—the firm buying out the other one promoted its own culture.

But it is also important to note that the two cultures reflected the different staffing strategies the two organizations had pursued in recent years. Because TOMO had IT project teams working in several different locations (both in the United States and elsewhere), TOMO management had already been pushed to worry less about where and when work was performed. STAR seemed like a hopeful next step for working more effectively within the new reality of a globally distributed workforce. In contrast, ZZT had very limited experience with offshore staffing, so it prioritized working together, in the same location, with frequent chats in the halls and the cafeteria. TOMO employees and managers saw that the ZZT culture did not actually work well with the reality of a global organization and geographically distributed teams—but it is not clear that ZZT managers and executives recognized that fully. As Stewart, a director, explained:

> For them, face-to-face time matters deeply there. Going to the cafeteria to talk through a problem is something they value. The TOMO folks, we're used to dealing with people in India. We have figured out how to do the work remotely. In my staff meetings, I have people calling in from three or four cities.

Some legacy TOMO employees and managers described ZZT as "backwards" or less sophisticated—technically and in terms of management practices—than TOMO. Jonathon, the development manager we have quoted before, noted that ZZT closes the company for Good Friday, a Christian holiday just before Easter. Jonathon saw this as consistent with ZZT's "small-town culture" but odd for a global, diverse firm. He described ZZT managers and executives by saying:

> Their management style is a little bit different. They do want to manage people by walking around—looking to see who's in their desk and who is not and [questioning the] people who aren't there.

Jonathon reminded us at this point that he has subordinates in four US time zones as well as people he works with in India.

The ZZT management practices were no longer sensible to Jonathon—and his STAR approach was likely foreign to them too. These different assumptions caused frustration. Jonathon shares that his ZZT peers "get mad if you schedule a meeting at noon Central time" because that is lunchtime at the ZZT headquarters. But Jonathon's team would have to avoid meetings from 10 a.m. to 2 p.m. to avoid lunch breaks in the various US time zones where they work. He—and others—resented the assumptions made by ZZT managers and leadership:

> They think about things in context of their own little world. They don't think about a company as big as we are, as diversified as we are . . . They aren't used to that.

Pointing to ZZT's small-town culture and what they called "old-school leadership" style helped TOMO professionals and managers reconcile what could have been a big puzzle: Why was the company deciding to end STAR when it seems to be working well—from the perspective of employees, middle managers, and many of the TOMO vice presidents? Hazel, an IT analyst, said in an interview soon after the merger that she did not expect STAR to survive because ZZT is "stuck back in the '90s maybe" (and she laughs). Because of this, she expected ZZT leadership to just say, "We're not doing this [STAR] any more . . . Ding! It's going to get taken away." Peyton, a respected IT architect who was a fan of STAR, explained the end of STAR by saying:

> The assumption was that we were now part of ZZT and ZZT is head-quartered in [city removed]. And they don't agree with that sort of, you know, East Coast liberal namby-pamby, you know, workers get authority crap. That was my impression. And it was never actually said outright until I just said it.

Peyton clarified that "they didn't say why," but just said STAR was over.

So we all have to draw our own conclusions and draw we did.

Others also noted that ZZT executives did not see a need to change their management practices. They found the old status quo comfortable and they had the power, particularly after several of the early champions of STAR left the company, to end STAR—at least officially.

Alternative Explanations and Justifications for Ending STAR

Leadership of the newly merged firm never explained STAR's revocation to rank-and-file employees. Recall Peyton's comment that the new leadership didn't say why STAR ended. The lack of an explanation was feasible because those working under STAR constituted less than half of the merged IT workforce. Those with direct experiences of STAR were outnumbered by those in the control group, plus the legacy ZZT IT professionals and managers. Additionally, STAR had always been framed as a pilot.[4] Pilots often have an expected end date, and a decision not to turn a pilot practice into usual operating procedure may not garner as much attention as changing an established policy.

Even so, executives had to offer some explanation to middle managers—if not directly to employees—because there were many supporters and even champions of STAR among the managers and directors who participated in the initiative, plus others who had watched their peers thrive under STAR (and hoped or expected that a full rollout would pull their teams into STAR). We review three explanations for the end of STAR—one that is plausible but was not actually heard in TOMO, and two explanations that were actively offered by executives.

In the research literature and in popular discussions about why organizational changes fail, we often hear that middle managers resist change by stalling or by promoting the old ways as the best ways. We might have expected this for STAR, in particular, because this work redesign asked managers to give up some control to employees.[5] But middle managers did not actively resist or lobby for a return to old policies, as far as we saw or heard in our years inside the company. In fact, in what seemed to be an effort to root out middle manager concerns that would justify the decision to end STAR, the top senior executive within IT requested that human resources do its own poll of managers. We had reported evidence of manager support from our survey and interviews but the executive wanted his human resources staff to survey everyone again, just in case the managers had different things to say to senior leadership when the research team was out of the picture. Those poll results were also extremely positive (and all the managers responded, since the request came directly from their boss). So the executives could not claim that middle managers had discovered STAR just did not work. Of course, there were a few managers who were part of STAR and had been less enthusiastic, but even they had few concrete problems to share.

Still, executives kept referring to problems, and so we dutifully tried again to investigate these. In one conversation, Erin asked two HR professionals for more specifics about the problems the executives had apparently identified; we wanted to be sure that the new survey we were planning would capture the right topics so we could fully explore their concerns.[6] The HR professionals said that was a good question and asked the experienced manager who was sitting with us, Felicia, what she thought the root problem was. Felicia turned to them and said flatly, "There is no problem." Over and over, we saw this mismatch between what we heard on the ground from employees and frontline managers and what was discussed by the executives and HR professionals who were deciding the future of STAR. This conversation was striking because everyone at the table could see the gap between frontline managers' take and the executives' concerns quite clearly.

So what explanations or justifications for ending STAR were provided by the executives? The executives' explanations centered on anecdotes of "abuse," which was their term for purportedly unreasonable changes that a few individuals made under STAR, and worries that collaboration would suffer with new ways of working.

Anecdotes of Abuse

A few stock stories were told repeatedly in discussions about why STAR was ending—even when no one in the conversation had actually observed these "abuses" or knew the details of what had happened. Executives from ZZT treated these stories as clear evidence that STAR was a foolish or even nonsensical approach to management. Several TOMO vice presidents seemed to be swayed by these stories of abuse as well, and interpreted them as evidence that STAR should be either revamped or revoked.[7]

One abuse story that popped up repeatedly—and that executives mentioned in public discussions about the end of STAR—revolved around an employee who began to homeschool his child and supposedly refused to come into the office because of that. The actual situation was much more nuanced than the anecdote implied. Peyton, a single father who had partial custody of his older daughter, prioritized working at home when she was staying at his house, and that routine worked well for over a year. Peyton was widely respected, worked over 45 hours per week, and reported that his gifted daughter required very little supervision as she worked through her curriculum independently. What's more, when

Peyton got a new manager who wanted him in the office, he complied with that request. He began coming in to his local office, even though the group was spread across four US states plus India. With frustration, Peyton said that being in that office did not affect collaboration. He thought the manager's real reason was just a desire to walk past his subordinates' desks and see them working.

But these details were not shared when the homeschooler was mentioned as evidence of abuse of STAR (and many people did not even know who was involved in this anecdote or in others used to justify the end of the initiative). Regardless of the details and the wisdom of Peyton's particular work and family decisions, this isolated and unusual anecdote was not evidence of broad problems with STAR. A coworker who knew the situation well saw the homeschool story as a cover story for ending STAR after the merger:

> I think the real reason was management didn't like it. They can't keep tabs on their employees as carefully. So, it's kind of that trust issue . . . I don't really know if it was just management saying, "I don't like this because I'm not in control." And that honestly, I think that's what it comes down to at the end of the day.

Another damning anecdote was the case of a senior executive who set up a special meeting with employees and then had fewer people show up in the room than expected. We heard versions of this story from the perspective of the annoyed and insulted executives and from the perspective of the employees and frontline managers who thought the executives overreacted. One TOMO vice president said the low point in his support of STAR came when he set up meetings with small groups of IT professionals (who would not generally get to have discussions with an executive at his level) and some people asked for the conference call number, saying they preferred to work at home. He was incensed:

> This is one day in the whole year that I am asking for them to come in. I couldn't believe it. You are giving up the relationship [with the executive above you]? You are telling me you do not want that . . . Come on, guys!

The executive's annoyance is clear, and we saw his peers take these situations as personal affronts too. Jonathon explains that another vice president had visited an office where he did not usually work for "his little town hall" (i.e., a meeting with a large group of employees). The room was not filled. This was after the official end of STAR, and the vice president followed up with every manager to reiterate that all employees in his unit should be in the office at least three days per week. Moreover, the executive demanded that Jonathon and other managers provide written explanations about where each of their employees had been on the day of the meeting. Jonathon's five absent employees had been working on an outage (which takes priority over any meeting), on vacation, or ill. While he could give approved reasons for these employees' absences, Jonathon saw the expectation that everyone would be there in person as unreasonable. Employees in other cities were not flown in for the meeting, and that meant many people were already participating via web conference. As Jonathon says, the information shared in person was not any different from that in the slide deck shown via web conference. Yet he notes,

> Everyone had to give an accounting [of] where they were and why they weren't there. It was just bizarre.

In STAR, employees and frontline managers decide for themselves how to manage their heavy workloads and which meetings to prioritize. Choosing to skip a meeting that does not contribute directly to one's work product is acceptable, as is choosing to skip the commute and attend the meeting via conference call. In this case, we recognize that it was not wise or savvy to skip a special meeting with a senior executive. Patsy, a lead software engineer in a different part of the organization, heard one of these stories and argued that the employees were "juvenile" and wrong not to prioritize coming to see the executive in person. Still, in Patsy's view,

> That seems like a managerial discussion with that employee. Not a killer for all [of] STAR.[8]

In other words, these problems could be solved within the context of STAR, Patsy and others argued. A manager might advocate for certain meetings to be held in person or explain the value of a VP town-hall meeting. Jonathon did explain to his employees (after the fact) that not attending an executive's meeting "might be construed as disrespect." In other words, the emotional reaction from the executive was acknowledged, but he still found it "bizarre" to be asked to justify his employees' attendance.

At the large management meeting where the end of STAR was announced, a story about a vice president calling a meeting and getting poor attendance was used to publicly reassert old norms. One of the legacy ZZT vice presidents who seemed very influential among the integrated leadership team referred to stories about missed meetings directly. With a tone of incredulity, she said emphatically:

> It is not O.K. to be unavailable or, if a director flies in for a meeting, to say that today's a work at home day and so I am not coming in. It is not O.K. to do that.

These abuse stories reveal three important points. First, there were very few extreme cases that occurred but they were invoked repeatedly, circulating widely as real problems.[9] When we asked employees and managers about "abuse" that they had witnessed themselves, they almost never had specific problems they had encountered, but a substantial number referenced these few anecdotes. Second, employees and many frontline managers had come to see STAR as "the way we work here." In short, they had accepted the shift in control or decision rights from managers to employees with regard to when, where, and how work is accomplished. As Jonathon's response reveals, it was now bizarre for a manager to be asked to track his or her employees' presence (although managers did expect to monitor and evaluate employees' progress toward key goals). Recall that the town hall meeting that Jonathon was referring to occurred after the official end of STAR—but the STAR principles had stuck for both managers and employees. Third, these specific anecdotal situations could have been solved within the parameters of STAR. The baseline assumption of STAR was not that work *always* occurs remotely or that employees can do whatever they want, regardless of its impact on coordination and collaboration. Instead, a team that is fully implementing

STAR will regularly discuss how they want to work effectively together, with the manager weighing in as part of the team. Deciding to have certain meetings in person is perfectly acceptable, but that decision is supposed to be motivated by what the work tasks require and not exclusively by executives' preferences. The situations captured in the STAR abuse stories could have been handled differently with some coaching from peer managers, supportive executives, or HR professionals who fully understood STAR.[10]

In light of some of these stories one TOMO vice president initially advocated sustaining the initiative, but adding another round of manager training to it. According to this vice president, the problems that had arisen were not indicative of fatal flaws with STAR but of the limited skills of some of the frontline managers. So he offered "modified STAR" as a remedy and suggested giving managers more guidance on how they might articulate clearer expectations (like in-person attendance at meetings where executives would be present or in-person participation in certain design meetings), and evaluate work results more systematically. He argued that managers needed training to more confidently direct the flow of their team's work and evaluate their performance in the context of expanded employee autonomy. This vice president—who was the last real advocate for STAR within the executive team—saw that the rules of the game had changed with STAR but wondered if frontline managers had the right skills for the new game. He also hoped that this training would prompt another round of team discussions—similar to those already experienced in STAR training—about the dual goals of working effectively together and supporting people's personal lives.[11]

Instead, these stories were invoked as excuses for a decision already made by ZZT executives and others who were actively aligning themselves with ZZT's powerful leaders. The ultimate decision was to revert to a quite restrictive policy that came straight from ZZT and was consistent with their culture and preferences, even if it did not match the reality of how the global firm operated.

Anxieties about Collaboration

We also heard quite elaborated concerns about STAR negatively affecting collaboration and work quality from a few executives (but not from frontline managers). In our interviews and conversations soon after the merger and before a final decision about STAR was made, the influential vice president who had described STAR by saying that "it worked" also described what he saw as some unanticipated consequences of these changes. He worried that STAR discourages working together in closely knit groups. He argued:

> What made us effective was sitting in the room, not even in the cubicles [but together in the same space], with the free exchange of ideas . . . Now it is really "on demand." Unless you initiate a contact with somebody, it doesn't happen. There is none of the interactions that happen because you are sitting around. Those could be project related, or "I learned this" or "I am reading this."

This vice president had no specific complaints about the work getting done that he could point to, but he was concerned about whether employees felt connected to each other:

> It is like they are doing their part but they were not *part* of it.

Additionally, he feared that limited interactions would affect the quality of their work product because employees would not be as creative as they had been when they worked together more closely, in person. At the time of this interview, this vice president and the executive mentioned earlier were both advocating for a "next version of STAR" where teams would identify and prioritize some activities that they believed were better done in person. Those practices would be fully consistent with STAR as designed, and we saw that move as a strong implementation of the initiative. However, later on, this TOMO vice president joined with the legacy ZZT executives to set up even more restrictive rules. Soon after the official end of STAR, he told his managers to have their employees in the office five days per week.

These are legitimate concerns regarding collaboration and work quality; there is more research to be done on the trade-offs between increased control over when and where work is done and the value of easy exchanges with coworkers and managers. We would expect that the trade-offs between employee-driven flexibility and effective collaboration practices differ across different jobs, industries, and workforces. So we think the vice president who stressed collaboration raised important questions that should be evaluated carefully, across settings.

However, for the IT professionals and managers we studied, we did not find evidence that STAR caused collaboration problems or harmed the quality of work performed. We conducted a last survey specifically to investigate executives' stated concerns and possible unintended consequences of STAR. But we found that employees and managers who had been part of STAR were no more or less likely (than their counterparts from control group teams) to agree with statements like "I can reach others on my team easily when I have a question or issue," "I can reach my manager easily with questions," that "waiting on others slows down our work process," or that "my team has open and honest communication." And there are hints from that last survey (as well as the stories and quotes in previous chapters) that STAR promotes better team collaboration and performance. Employees in teams that had been part of STAR were significantly more likely to agree that members of their teams are able to bring up problems and issues freely (23% strongly agree, vs. 12% of those in control group). They also felt better about their work; significantly more employees from STAR groups agree or strongly agree that "my team produces high-quality work."[12]

Where do the concerns about collaboration come from then? At the time that the TOMO vice president shared these concerns, he had recently talked about STAR with friends who run start-up tech companies. The friends claimed that "jamming sessions" (especially the early stages of the project where the goals and design of the software are being hashed out) should happen in person, and this executive recalled those interactions fondly from his younger days. However, TOMO was a large firm that had already pulled people away from being "colocated" in close teams that could work together fluidly in person—years before STAR was launched. So even when managers required everyone to be in the office full time, as Peyton's new manager did, teams that are spread all over the country and world cannot get the full potential benefits of in-person collaboration.

Furthermore, the firm had already amped up the workload and divided technical problems into predefined segments and small jobs so that there was little time for professional development and little possibility for creative thinking to find new solutions. The vice president claimed that "We used to have brown bags, impromptu discussions, just talking about the work," and he worried that team spirit was suffering because coworkers were not "seeing each other, not going to lunch together." But our interview respondents said they have not had time for professional development in years. In fact, many had given up on lunch breaks, working over lunch at their desks instead. (Additionally, some STAR teams deliberately scheduled group lunches for those working in the same city and routinely blocked time in team calls to chat about personal life— protecting and cultivating their social relationships and teamwork.) While this vice president saw STAR and the remote work it facilitated as the problem, the speed up in work was occurring long before STAR and was evident in the control group too.

Finally, this executive's vision reflects a software development process that many IT professionals and managers appreciate—but that had not been present in TOMO for about a decade before STAR. He daydreamed about developers "buddy-coding" or working together side by side on a thorny problem, about standing around a white board strategizing about the structure of a section of software, and about jamming together in a large room where people can easily learn from each other, across functions. These practices are all consistent with a particular software development process (called "extreme programming" or "extreme agile"), but the firm had deliberately chosen a waterfall-like linear process where tasks are divided up and documentation is emphasized over in-person collaboration. In fact, the company was actively enforcing compliance with that process at the time of our study. Some of the IT professionals and managers we interviewed would prefer the other process, even if it pushed them to work more in the office. They admitted to "white-board nostalgia," but they recognized that the firm had gone a different direction. In short, the staffing strategy and the software development process that TOMO had adopted years ago prompted the problems that this vice president was now blaming on STAR.[13]

Executives seemed to be grasping at straws to explain the end of STAR. They needed something to say to the many employees and managers who were happy with it. Given the clear preferences of ZZT leadership and their greater power and influence within the merged company, the surprise is not that STAR ended but the fact that it took almost three years between the merger's official completion and the official declaration that the old ZZT policy (which required working in the office during core hours every day of the week unless a senior executive had signed off on another arrangement) was binding.

In between, there was a long period of ambiguity for IT professionals and managers. First, top management announced that STAR would be ending and something else would be coming. Then a new manager training was offered, which was called "modified STAR" by some. But the rollout was modest and fairly low-profile. During this period, there was also a shift in the power and influence held by different members of the executive team. The IT division was reorganized (repeatedly) after the merger, and many of the STAR champions left the firm. Those who did not leave quickly could see that the ZZT culture and policies were going to win out. Executives told us privately that "the signals were clear" that those who were not close to the ZZT crowd would not do well. For some senior executives from TOMO, we were told, the decision about whether to actively advocate for STAR or not "was all political."[14]

Exploiting Ambiguity—as Long as Possible

In the time between the official end of STAR and the turn to the restrictive ZZT policy, we saw wide variation in executives' guidance and even more variation in what happened on the ground. Some vice presidents followed up on the announcement of the official end of STAR by decreeing that employees should be in the office three days per week. Others announced that employees should be in the office five days per week, with limited exceptions approved by their manager. And some executives said that frontline managers should decide what made sense for their own teams. In all cases, the assumption of managerial control was reasserted. But the old rules of the game were not automatically accepted, and many middle managers and employees worked to preserve as much as they could of STAR ideas and practices.

Many middle managers chose to interpret the lack of a clear written policy as cover for continuing with STAR practices even after its official demise. For example, in an interview about a year after the official announcement that STAR was over but before the final ZZT policy was announced, Jonathon said that the executives

> have gone out of their way to say, "STAR is dead, STAR is dead, STAR is dead."

Jonathon's vice president told managers to have their employees work in the office three days per week or more. But because the top executives had not yet announced a new HR policy officially ("No news is good news"), he and his peer managers were laying low and allowing the same practices they did under STAR.

> We all decided as managers in our group [that] we're not bringing up this up. This is not even a topic of conversation in our staff meetings . . . We haven't gone to them and say, "Thou shalt be in the office three days out of five" and all. We will deal with it when we actually see something in writing from HR.

Celia is a frontline development manager under a vice president who said his "expectation is five days in the office, no matter what." But she ignored that:

> No published policy at this point. So what it means to me is just I'm kind of winging it still [laughs] until we have something in writing from our leadership team.

Celia chose to allow her team to work as they preferred—with some employees working almost exclusively at home—even though the director above her (who had not been part of TOMO before the merger) clearly expected people in the office. Celia eventually told the employees who had worked primarily at home that they would need to come in to the office more often. But because she had given their desks to contractors during STAR, she was not forcing them to show up every day, nor was she routinely checking that her employees with assigned desks were actually working in the office. In fact, one of Celia's subordinates guessed that she was turning down desks that became available, saying her team did not want to work "in the corner by the bathroom," because she knew he preferred to work at home. He appreciated that she was bending the rules for him, but he did not want her to get in trouble.

These frontline managers attempted to buffer their teams from the more restrictive rules, and many succeeded in keeping new practices in place through this period of ambiguity. But even though work at home and flexible schedules were still occurring, the decision rights had officially shifted back to managers (and specifically to executives). Under STAR, the decision of where to work was expected to be made by employees; managers were expected to focus on the work products rather than where or when subordinates were working. Many managers had accepted the logic that employees legitimately decide when, where, and how they work. As Hans said, his manager's guidance after STAR echoed the STAR training: "You get your job done. I don't care how you do it, or where you do it from, as long as you get your work done." Our survey of employees conducted almost a year after the official end of STAR found that those who had been randomized to STAR were still working at home significantly more than their control group counterparts, with post-STAR employees averaging almost half of their work hours at home or offsite.[15]

Some frontline managers expressed that the old rules of the game no longer seemed legitimate to them. When the more restrictive ZZT policy was officially announced in writing, the pressure to comply increased. But the expectation that employees and managers would follow these rules was still frustrating and disconcerting to many. As noted by organizational sociologist Tim Hallett, when a policy that had been informally ignored is actively enforced (a "recoupling" of policy and practice), there is likely to be distress.[16] Felicia, a manager who had been vocally supportive of STAR, told us in our last interview that her vice president had recently told them "STAR no longer exists," and "it's in the past and the past is the past." Since the beginning of STAR (several years ago, by this point), this team of production support staff had balanced their on-call work with the rest of their work as they chose:

> They've managed their own schedule. Most of them come into the office a couple of days a week. [It] just depends on what's going on. But they manage their own schedule.

Production support employees routinely need to work nights or weekends, but Felicia's employees often took time off during the day to make up for those sprints. After the final announcement of the ZZT policy, though, Felicia was told by her director, Kinsey, that she needed to make a formal request for their vice president to approve alternative arrangements for every person who would not be in the office from 9 to 5 p.m., five days per week. Felicia made a request that included almost everyone who reported to her, explaining that she cannot ask them to be on a call at 4 a.m. and then in the office during the regular workday. She laughed:

> If you want to give us a 9 to 5 job and make our jobs just 9 to 5 and then everything will have to be worked 9 to 5, then I mean that's a whole different story.

Before STAR, production support staff had worked these variable schedules and been on call almost 24/7, but now it was laughable to Felicia that management would expect that type of availability *and* expect her employees in the office five days per week.

At the time of this last interview, Felicia was waiting to hear what the vice president would say about this request. There was reason to worry, based on a recent story in which the executive had stopped by the office and found that some employees were not in the office. He turned to Kinsey and asked where they were, even though those employees were several levels below the director (i.e., not his direct reports). The vice president said, as recounted by Felicia,

> You should still know, every person in your organization, when they're in the office, when they're not in the office, and manage that.

This was nonsensical to both Kinsey and Felicia, who discussed that managers should be responsible for the performance and output of the team:

> It shouldn't matter when they're working or where they're working. If the work is not getting done, then you come to me and I'll be responsible for that as the manager.

Despite the STAR sensibility we still heard from Felicia, the ZZT rules were now in place, and so she was just hoping for official permission for her teams to work differently. These were not the only changes going on within the merged company at this point. Performance reviews had changed, the bonus system had changed, and project management staff had been cut so that frontline managers were even more overloaded than they had been previously. There were rumors that more managers would soon be told to move to the city where ZZT has its headquarters or lose their jobs. After detailing her frustrations with all of that, Felicia returned to the possibility that she would also need to tell her employees that they have to be available whenever a problem occurs, 24/7, while also working in the office during regular hours every weekday.

> And I told Kinsey, I'm not going to do that . . . So if you want to call that insubordination and fire me, then so be it.

The Bigger Picture: Why Is It Hard to Sustain New Initiatives?

Work redesigns (and other innovations, too) seem to be hard to sustain in the face of other changes. The end of STAR was driven by broader organizational changes—by the merger of TOMO with ZZT and the assumption that ZZT, as the acquiring company, would call the shots. Other firms have also pulled back from flexibility initiatives in recent years. Have those innovative policies and practices also been lost because of broader organizational changes?

To investigate that question, we read popular and business press stories about the decisions to revoke flexibility initiatives at seven large US firms between 2013 and 2017.[17] We began with some of the many stories about Yahoo CEO Marissa Meyer and her decision to stop telecommuting options at the company in early 2013. Yahoo's decision to pull back from their flexibility policy was salient to the employees and managers we interviewed at TOMO. For example, Hans explained that he did not hear a rationale for ending STAR. The message, instead, was:

> STAR is working, STAR is successful, and we are not going to do it anymore.

Hans (and others) surmised that the TOMO decision was influenced by other corporate revocations, even though he thought it is odd to be influenced by decisions in different industries and in dramatically different companies.

> It's basically it's just a couple of directors jumped on the bandwagon after what's her name, Molly [*sic*] at Yahoo who made a big point of saying, "It's not working for us."

We saw commonalities across the decisions at Hewlett-Packard (HP), Bank of America, Best Buy, Honeywell, Aetna, and IBM. Some of the lost policies were fairly standard work-at-home arrangements that we would classify as flexibility as accommodation. Other companies had adopted what we would call dual-agenda work redesign approaches with team meetings to consider how work is accomplished and coordinated, and a shift to increased employee control over when, where, and how work is done. In fact, we had studied the Best Buy initiative (ROWE, which is a precursor to STAR) and found many positive effects for employees and the firm.[18] The executives making decisions at the time of our Best Buy study were thrilled with those findings and proud of ROWE. But after a new CEO joined the firm, ROWE was soon ended.

All of these revocations occurred in firms facing significant organizational changes or significant business challenges because technologies or smaller tech companies were "disrupting" (to use the corporate lingo) old business strategies. With Best Buy and Bank of America, for example, e-commerce and e-banking mean customers are less likely to come into stores or banks to purchase the firms' products and services. People can easily search for the cheapest or easiest option online. While the common context is new technologies and an increasingly competitive landscape, in the majority of these cases there is *also* new leadership at the very top of the organization. Often that leadership change follows a major organizational restructuring or merger.

Executives involved in these decisions offer a common critique: that flexible work practices supposedly reduce collaboration and so make it harder to innovate. In these tough business situations, the claim is that all hands are needed on deck, and that means in the office. There is hope that more in-person interactions will foster more innovation and get the firm past the present business crisis. The "all hands on deck" phrase was used in the announcements ending Best Buy's and HP's programs, for example. And the new chief marketing officer of IBM, Michelle Paluso, announced that:

> It's really time for us to start bringing our teams together, more shoulder-to-shoulder. There is only one recipe I know for success, particularly when we are in as much of a battle with Microsoft and the West Coast companies as we are . . .
>
> Bringing great people with the right skills, give them the right tools, give them a mission, make sure they can analyze their results, put them in really creative inspiring locations and set them free. That's the recipe I have always relied on and counted on.

Collaboration in person is viewed as powerful and perhaps even magical, as Paluso continues:

> There is something about a team being more powerful, more impactful, more creative, and frankly hopefully having more fun when they are shoulder to shoulder. Bringing people together creates its own X factor.

These messages were suggested when the TOMO decision was announced as well, by the ZZT vice president who said that "collaboration is the new blue." But, as we have seen, TOMO's IT professionals and frontline managers were far from shoulder-to-shoulder and instead were deliberately spread out over the globe. The same is true in many of these other large organizations.

What is not stated in these official accounts is that executives are downsizing and laying off employees at the same time they are pulling back from new ways of working. In all six decisions that came after Yahoo's initial announcement, firms laid off sizable numbers of employees around the same time that the flexibility policy was revoked. It is plausible—though we do not know this for sure—that those who are planning layoffs know that the revocation of flexibility will be unpopular. Ending a popular initiative may reduce the number of people who are laid off (with associated severance packages and bad press) if some employees "voluntarily" leave out of frustration with the new inflexibility. Insiders hint at that logic in the case of IBM, where the company had allowed extensive telecommuting and remote work for the previous fifteen years. Many employees had taken IBM jobs even though they lived far from a large IBM office, or had moved while working for the company. After the IBM decision that all marketing staff should be colocated in a few strategic offices, employees were given thirty days to decide whether they were moving to one of those locations or leaving the firm. The IBM decision was described by employees speaking anonymously with a reporter as "a downsizing effort. One referred to the colocation move as 'the massacre.'"[19]

Looking beyond work redesign initiatives like STAR, it is clear that management innovations of various types are fragile and apt to be lost when there is significant organizational change and new leadership. It is easy to assume that if a firm drops a new policy or initiative, it must mean the innovation did not work. But that is not necessarily the case. We know that STAR worked (from the perspective of managers and employees, with benefits to employees, families, and the firm, including bottom-line implications for turnover), even though it was not sustained. Other studies document that practices and policies that have been proven successes do not necessarily last either. Economist Nicholas Bloom and colleagues recently evaluated whether manufacturing plants in India that had implemented a different set of management innovations sustained those practices or not. (The innovations they studied addressed manufacturing processes such as quality monitoring on the production line, building in more time for cleaning and maintaining equipment, and other practices unrelated to our type of work redesign.) The research team had run a randomized field experiment where those new management practices were conclusively proven to increase productivity and performance. Yet when the research team returned about nine years later, around half of these practices had been dropped. Moreover, practices were more likely to be dropped when the top manager at the plant had changed, when the senior executives at the firm were busier, and when the practice was less common within that industry.[20] STAR faced all three of those threats: new leadership, distracted senior executives (who were focused on the enormous work of integrating the company and also concerned with protecting their own turf in the shifting executive team), and a dual-agenda work redesign that was unusual in the industry.

Yet new ways of working and managing, like STAR, may also be durable. Because this approach prompts a collective critique of traditional ways of work and changes the rules of the game deliberately, the official end of STAR does not mean the end of STAR thinking. There are lasting changes in what seems sensible, and in what is expected of managers and of employees as they work together. Frontline employees and managers may comply when pushed to do so—since not everyone is like Felicia and ready to be fired for insubordination—but they also see the reinstated rules as irrational, and they question these decisions privately. The employees and managers who have worked in new ways are likely to look for other opportunities to do that again. And they will be joined by others, including younger workers, who are ready to push for new and better ways of working.

Chapter 8

⌘

CREATING SANE AND SUSTAINABLE JOBS

Even good jobs are becoming more intense and more insecure—and changes in technology and global markets mean that is likely to be true going forward. In our study of TOMO's IT professionals and managers, we have shown that overload harms employees' health and well-being as well as affecting their family lives. Overload also harms organizational performance through burnout, turnover, and reduced quality, creativity, and collaboration.

Overload arises because firms ask more and more of fewer and fewer employees. Research often emphasizes that employees have internalized the firm's goals or broader cultural ideals about devotion to work, and so people willingly push themselves hard. The professionals and managers we studied do have a strong professional identity and want to take pride in their work. But the overload and related intensive work practices are driven by the real sense that cutting hours or limiting availability or saying "this is too much" will put your job at even greater risk.

Overload, long hours, and near-constant availability have implications for gender inequality as well. In our sample of IT professionals and managers, we saw few gender differences in the intensity of work or in the benefits of new ways of working. But the women who are working in this firm and in the type of IT jobs we studied are a select group: those who have stuck it out working long hours in a traditionally male-dominated field. The gender implications of taming overload and creating flexibility as a new norm are more evident when we step back to consider the workforce more broadly. Women have been and still are expected to do more family caregiving. Middle-class mothers are charged, in our culture, with giving all their time, energy, and focus to their children as well as supporting parents, in-laws, or other adult relatives who need them.

And so, faced with inflexible and intensive demands at work and high expectations in the family domain as well, some mothers end up scaling back or leaving their jobs for a time (particularly when their spouse earns an upper- or upper-middle-class income). Those decisions have consequences for women's earnings and future job prospects and, in the aggregate, reinforce gender inequality in pay and advancement. If professional and managerial jobs were slightly less intensive and more flexible, we could keep more women in the fields and firms where they have gained experience and position more women to advance up the ranks. These changes would also make it more feasible for men to take on the family care obligations that many want to fulfill, while also living up to cultural expectations for men regarding full-time paid work.[1]

Clearly mothers, fathers, and those caring for ailing relatives would benefit if they could get out from under intensive work patterns that produce feelings of overload. But this is a much broader issue. We have shared story after story of employees—including single individuals, married and childfree people, and older workers—who are eager to do excellent work *and* to take better care of themselves as well as pursue personal priorities, whether that is an adult hockey league, volunteer commitments, a new training opportunity, or more time connecting with friends and family. Work has crowded out so much that they might have done. Despite the compromises these employees have already made by pulling back from family, community, and personal goals to concentrate on their jobs, there is *still* a sense of overload, that there is not enough time to do all that is asked and expected at work. Cutting back on hours or saying no to work requests feels risky, given all the downsizing, offshoring, and automation of processes that these professionals and managers have already survived at TOMO or experienced in previous jobs. While we have not discussed younger workers specifically, other analyses of millennial workers describe them as frantically trying to find a way to some economic security by hustling harder and working longer, which contributes to their sense of burnout at young ages.[2] Many different workers—of all genders, ages, life stages, and many different occupations—would agree with Hayward, the dad who told us that "something has to change."

But not all changes are helpful. We have argued that there are real downsides to some popularly promoted changes, including common modes of workplace flexibility. When flexible work patterns are understood as accommodations and are individually negotiated, those who work different schedules, work at home extensively, or trim their hours are implicitly violating the expectations of what ideal, fully committed workers will do. These employees rightly worry about flexibility stigma and possible career consequences for pursuing flexibility under these conditions.

There is also a real risk that half-measures, such as a single policy change to allow everyone to work at home, will actually exacerbate overload and be experienced as an additional push toward work intensification. Such employer-driven flexibility in the form of expectations to be always available can be daunting. In this case, the freedom to work whenever and wherever you want can create more pressure to be available everywhere, all the time, if the existing organizational culture and reward system are not simultaneously called into question.[3] With a dual-agenda work redesign approach like the STAR initiative we studied, the rules of the game change—such that different ways of working become the new normal, accepted as the default way of working, and not stigmatized. Protecting personal time and health becomes an explicitly supported goal, along with actual work performance and productivity.

We have demonstrated that this work redesign approach can benefit companies. The case of STAR at TOMO shows this conclusively, and we also highlight other research—from a variety of contexts and workforces—that provide support for that idea. TOMO let us in to address three key issues: burnout, turnover, and the related sense that coordinating work across the globe meant that people felt stretched too thin. Our findings from the STAR field experiment and related interviews demonstrate reduced burnout as well as increased job satisfaction, and reduced odds that employees and managers choose to leave the company.

We also find positive effects on the other side of the dual agenda: the STAR innovation benefits employees in terms of health and well-being and their family and personal lives. In addition to some important shifts in stress and psychological distress, these IT professionals and managers shared stories of being able to exercise, eating better, having more control over their work time, and improved sleep quality and quantity.[4] We see that these changes at work cross over to benefit the children of these employees as well. Data from pairs of TOMO employees and their adolescent children show STAR benefits with regard to time spent together, adolescents' sleep, and adolescents' ability to handle everyday stress. Employees in STAR report feeling better about how work and the rest of life fit together, and we hear many stories about reduced guilt, well beyond parents and caregivers. People know they can put the pieces of their lives together in ways that work better for them.

Nonetheless, we saw firsthand that change is hard. Even though STAR worked in the sense that it benefited the firm and employees, it did not survive the leadership changes that came after the firm merged with another organization. New executives were now weighing in on company policies with the default assumption that the acquiring company would call the shots. These executives from that firm were perfectly comfortable with status quo assumptions about when, where, and how work is done and who should have control—that is, the managers—over those decisions. This is disappointing, but perhaps not surprising.

What is the path forward? To make work sane and sustainable for more people, we conclude that both private sector initiatives and public policy changes are needed.

Changes that Employers Can Make

Businesses, and other organizations such as nonprofits and government agencies, need to recognize the costs of the *current* ways of operating. New initiatives to redesign work are more attractive when executives, managers, and employees consider the unintended and usually unrecognized costs of the status quo's push for long hours and constant availability. These costs include reduced engagement, burnout, and turnover tied to long-term exhaustion and frustration with never getting time really away from work. In addition, overload makes it much harder to do cutting-edge work and develop innovations that create real value for the firm moving forward. Firms should also consider the healthcare costs that arise from such stress-related conditions. Recall the professionals and managers we interviewed who had mystery hives that specialists were trying to diagnose, whose sleep was so disrupted that they talked to themselves, whose chiropractors recognized their neck and back issues as classic symptoms of IT work, and who suffered heart attacks and strokes in middle age. Employers lose money in reduced productivity, absences, and higher healthcare costs when current ways of working chip away at workers' health in both dramatic and mundane ways.[5]

Assuming that decision-makers inside companies and other organizations see the potential value of making changes, what changes might they make? Our study serves as a strong recommendation for STAR—and all the materials we used in TOMO are freely available on the Work, Family, and Health Network website for interested managers and employees to review and implement in their own workplaces.[6] It would be worthwhile to test these proven tools in a wide variety of workplaces (and we would be excited to hear about the results).

There are also other initiatives that we believe to be promising. Like STAR, these initiatives involve a collective process where employees and managers attempt to create a new normal—to make some significant changes in how they do their work and how they interact after looking critically at the status quo. Through participatory dialogue, employees and managers diagnose the issue as an organizational problem—not just a private trouble or hassle.

In fact, dual-agenda work redesigns are not new. We first learned about the excitement of team efforts to reimagine work processes from the collaborative work of feminist organizational scholars in Boston including Lotte Bailyn, Joyce Fletcher, Deborah Kolb, Rhona Rapoport, Debra Meyerson, Robin Ely, and their colleagues. Beginning in the 1990s, these "action researchers" worked with companies and nonprofit organizations on dual-agenda change initiatives. Their explicit focus has been on gender equity and work effectiveness as the dual goals, with the recognition that work–family or broader work–life concerns are often part of the story here. Their approach is in some ways similar to STAR, but they used a more open and flexible process with more varied changes. Like STAR, these changes ask employees and managers to "name the norm" or identify underlying assumptions behind their everyday work practices and then help people to consider how the current ways of working and evaluating each other create unintended consequences that affect both individuals and the organization's performance.[7] These scholars argue, as we would, that it is the process of doing this institutional work that is key to the change, not the specific behaviors that are altered.

Two more recent examples of work redesign initiatives are the Predictability, Teaming, and Open Communication (PTO) project that Harvard Business School professor Leslie Perlow launched at the consulting firm BCG and later implemented in other firms, and the Results Only Work Environment (ROWE) developed by Cali Ressler and Jody Thompson.[8] PTO provides a space and a process for teams of consultants to plan and check in on their work together. In those conversations, employees and managers openly discuss emerging and ideal team norms, shared and individual priorities, and also set a "time-off goal." For example, a consulting team might aim to have each person leave the office by 6 p.m. one night of the week. Some could have dinner with a spouse, others would choose a night when they have social plans, but all would stay offline the rest of the night. The team then works to make the time off happen in the context of highly interdependent work, routine late nights, and industry norms of instant responsiveness. We also studied ROWE, implemented first at Best Buy Co., Inc., as one of the pilot studies that directly informed STAR. Many pieces of STAR are directly borrowed from the ROWE initiative, so we will not recap them here.

Both of these initiatives, PTO and ROWE, motivate change by identifying the inefficiencies and ineffectiveness of particular work practices for the organization and for a given team. Both initiatives pursue a team-based approach to discuss how work is working for individuals and to implement changes in everyday practices. While employees quickly see the benefits for them personally, these approaches both go well beyond offering flexibility as an accommodation for a specific individual. There are some intriguing differences in strategy, however. PTO prompts teams to identify one change they will implement, with the idea that starting with a common focal point can then open teams up to pursuing a variety of changes. ROWE (and STAR) point to broader changes, with more customization and variation in new work practices from the beginning.

In Europe and particularly the Netherlands, there has been enthusiasm about what is called New Ways of Working. In a knowledge economy, the argument goes, workers can and should be "empowered to work more efficiently and effectively."[9] The term New Ways of Working refers to changes in physical space, including moving away from private offices or separate cubes to shared and open workplaces, and changes in technology that facilitate working at home or other remote locations. In some descriptions of New Ways of Working, there is a recognition that management style and organizational culture need to change too. For example, some initiatives point out that managers now need to trust employees to do their work outside the office or propose that ideally employees will determine how they can do their best work (shifting control, in our terms). On the other hand, sometimes it seems that the social dimensions of these New Ways of Working get little attention, and there is an assumption that changing office spaces and adding technologies will be enough to transform work.

Consulting groups in the United States also offer guidance on team-based approaches to flexibility that fall somewhere between flexibility as accommodation and more participatory dual-agenda work redesigns. For example, the consulting group WFD pioneered team-based initiatives that encourage flexibility as well as effective team processes. WFD consultants or in-house facilitators interview employees and managers about their current practices, their perceived expectations, and their sense of the company and team culture. One goal is to identify unspoken assumptions, expectations, or stigmas that may have discouraged the use of existing flexibility policies. Then change agents develop guiding principles for senior management consideration. For example, guidelines might hit on topics like: If you plan to work at home on a given day, how is that communicated? What types of meetings will we aim to do in person, because we believe that is more effective, and what types of meetings or interactions can happen with remote participants? After senior managers have signed off on the principles, the full staff then reviews them (and gets a refresher on related company policies). This means everyone is oriented to the new expectations and norms, even if they do not anticipate changing their own schedule or work location. Employees and managers try out the new principles for a few months and then reconvene to make adjustments or to get training (such as how to use web-based meeting platforms more effectively) that will support flexible work practices.[10]

Other recent innovations include a "systems change" approach informed by behavioral science research. A research group called ideas42 worked with the Better Life Lab at New America and the Robert Wood Johnson Foundation to develop and test interventions that might improve work–life balance, health, and work effectiveness. They aim to encourage what they see as "better choices" by individual employees and managers and cumulatively change the culture that way.[11] For example, they suggest rethinking collaboration practices (including being deliberate about how meetings are set up and blocking out time for concentrated work), recognizing previous expectations or norms around face time and long hours (and encouraging time away via vacations and everyday disconnections), and building in more slack time to account for the realities of work delays. Many of these changes are familiar from STAR—which is not a surprise, since our research and related studies are cited as background for their Better Work Toolkit.

What is new here is the explicit discussion of the ways that cognitive shortcuts and biases make it harder for individuals to do what they know would be sensible and efficient. Small nudges can be valuable for changing behaviors. For example, a firm with a hard-driving culture might offer a bonus to employees for each full vacation day that they are logged out of the system (and not checking or responding to emails, texts, or IM). The bonus might be additional vacation time, a small cash bonus, or a donation to a charity the employee cares about. An employee who is taking a vacation day but logging into email would be nudged with a question whether they really want to get online—and lose the bonus—or not. Other suggestions include autoreplies for emails sent outside of regular business hours that affirm the need to rest and re-energize, and explain that an immediate reply is not expected. We can see how this strategy would prompt teams to discuss what practices they want to pursue in order to work at their best but still have time for other commitments, leading to discussions similar to those in the STAR work redesign.

Some innovative companies are also making related changes on their own—even if they do not label the changes as dual-agenda work redesign. Menlo Innovations, a software development and design firm, is known for their innovative work culture. Cofounder and CEO Rich Sheridan decided to create a different company culture after having "lived the death march life of corporate America" where long hours were expected, and work demands prompted "irrational, unreasonable" family sacrifices.[12] Menlo Innovations' approach draws on the key elements of work redesign by setting up a culture that works for everyone (rather than trying to help or accommodate parents specifically), interrogating what the informal expectations are in addition to changing formal policies, and framing these ways of working as good for both the firm and for individuals. However, the specific strategies that Menlo Innovations follows are quite different from those of STAR as implemented at TOMO. For example, Menlo Innovations management sets up teams of two who work together closely, in person and at the same tables, on a given task for a week at a time. This strategy is used because it minimizes the need for meetings and avoids multitasking, allowing for focused work and more realistic estimations of project time lines. There is a deliberate effort to work smarter in order to work moderate hours. The expectation—for everyone—is that the end of the eight-hour workday means the end of working for the day; emails and work calls are discouraged in the evenings, mornings, or weekends. The reality of family life and caregiving is also acknowledged by welcoming babies and toddlers in the office—for as long as they and their parents are happy with that arrangement—and by hosting a Menlo summer camp for older kids. These are intriguing changes because employees have little apparent choice in how they put their work and personal lives together on a daily basis (and control is a critical part of STAR's benefits), but the firm has deliberately reorganized work and created unusually clear boundaries in order to foster focused work, explicitly support life outside of work, and address overload.

Organizations can also redesign work to include more variety in the hours required, creating part-time options and not-so-big jobs in professional and managerial positions.[13] The STAR initiative aimed to make full-time positions more manageable and less stressful, but another possibility would be creating attractive jobs with fewer hours (and less pay and pro-rated benefits). Part-time professional work would likely appeal to a variety of employees, including some older workers, some parents, some people with health crises or limitations, and employees who are prioritizing going back to school or a community commitment. Their appeal would be greater if employees knew that they could return to full-time positions after a period, if they chose, and if workloads were trimmed and tracked so that part-timers do not end up working just as many hours for part-time pay. Teams or work groups would need to have deliberate conversations about coordinating work and communicating effectively with some people on part-time schedules, as we saw with STAR's increased remote work and variable work times. Otherwise, we might see occasional accommodations that are negotiated individually but viewed as risky, particularly when layoffs are common, or understood as a permanent dead end for a career. Law firms, medical practices, and some consulting companies have experimented with part-time options for professionals, and several European countries require employers to allow shorter hours whenever feasible. There are good models that can be integrated with dual-agenda work redesign strategies.[14]

While we have focused on professional and managerial jobs, unpredictable and variable schedules, always-on availability, and new staffing strategies are also problematic for workers in other fields. Hourly workers in the service sector—particularly in retail, hospitality, and food services—are often eager for *more hours* and for *more predictable hours*. Many of these workers face real precarity without the economic resources (such as savings and spouses earning good wages) that can buffer them from crises as well as intense stress. Inadequate hours, unpredictable schedules, and a lack of control at work impact these workers' health and well-being, their ability to care for their families, and their capacity to perform well on the job. These jobs have always been bad, in terms of relative wages and limited control, but they are now bad in new ways too. In retail and restaurants, for example, many workers are expected to be always available for work and to come in and work at the last minute. These workers are also forced to accept fluctuating hours, canceled shifts, fewer hours than desired, and unpredictable income flows, since these hourly workers do not know how many hours they will get from week to week.[15]

Overload is not the core issue—and many of these workers would like to work *more* hours so they can bring home more pay. Yet there are some similarities between the professionals and mangers we have studied and workers making much less money in retail stores, hotels, customer service centers, and elsewhere. In all of these settings, workers' sense of control over their schedules is limited and their open availability for work is expected. Across industries, technology has facilitated these problems. Among the hourly service workers, "just-in-time" staffing software tracks the customer flow and rejiggers schedules accordingly. Technologies also track exactly what each worker produces or sells, creating pressure to do more even when staffing is lean or equipment is unreliable.[16] Among the professionals and managers, technology facilitates global labor chains and coordination across time and space. Automation and AI assistance may soon put jobs at risk across industries, with fewer cashiers needed in retail stores and fewer software testers needed too.

Organizational changes can benefit employers and employees in many types of industries and for a wide variety of jobs. Our experiment with STAR at TOMO demonstrates this for professional and managerial white-collar employees. But there are exciting innovations in other settings too, and these innovations also begin with recognizing the costs of current practices. Staffing retail stores with a primary focus on matching store traffic closely to worker hours actually creates other problems, such as high turnover, absenteeism, and tardiness as well as short-cuts that cause problems with stocking, tracking of goods, and customer service. Retail firms can avoid this vicious cycle and set up a *virtuous* cycle with more stable schedules, cross-trained and flexible staff, and smooth operations at both the peaks of customer demand and at other times. A recent experiment with more stable scheduling in the GAP stores showed clear business benefits, with increases in sales and productivity tied to the retention of more experienced associates. Another experiment in call centers in China found that working at home brought benefits in terms of higher satisfaction, lower turnover, and increased productivity, particularly when frontline employees had a say in where they worked.[17]

Changes That Individual Managers and Employees Can Make

We have argued that the causes of overload are organizational, including specific management practices and staffing strategies, and that real solutions involve organizational changes including shifts in everyday practices and reconsideration of the assumptions that guide evaluations of individual and team performance.

Work redesign initiatives such as STAR and other programs provide possible paths forward; however, sometimes those paths are blocked by executives and managers who are not ready to try new ways of working. In that situation, frontline managers and individual employees can challenge the entrenched culture in small ways. We think of these as "in the meantime" changes that will hopefully lay the groundwork for broader reforms down the road. We provide some ideas for pursuing those changes here and in appendix 3, Ideas for Action. If you are an employee or a manager who would like to do things differently but do not have the authority to launch a formal work redesign initiative on your own, please read appendix 3.

Frontline managers and other employees can start conversations that raise simple dual-agenda questions. The goal here is to destabilize the status quo and help yourself and others imagine new possibilities; recall that this is what scholars call institutional work and "naming the assumptions." You might ask: What are we losing by working under the status quo and trying to soldier on? In other words, what isn't working currently that we have not yet fully discussed? How could we work more effectively while also working in a less intensive and more sustainable way? How can we facilitate more flexibility, in the form of more varied schedules, more work offsite, and more protected blocks of time for getting the real work done? What current tasks or meetings could we set aside so that we can actually do our best work on our top priorities? How can we use connectivity tools and technologies to communicate smoothly when needed, but not expect instant answers and constant availability? How can we encourage time away from work—taking real vacations, taking weekends fully off, and finding uninterrupted recovery time most evenings? What do we gain, as a team and as an organization, by supporting each other's family and personal obligations, goals, and interests?

These kinds of questions can feel risky, particularly if those who are evaluating the work performance (of an individual or a work group) still assume that longer hours always translate into higher productivity, that responding immediately to any work issue or question reveals a person's commitment to the job, and that being in the office later or longer legitimately positions a person for the next promotion. Even small changes may feel unwise if the organization is preparing to reduce staff or reorganize. Standing out in a culture that accepts overload as inevitable feels like a gamble, particularly when there is a threat of job loss. There are many times that professionals and managers will want to stay quiet, not rocking the boat for fear of falling out of it. Workers in lower-status jobs, who are paid much less and not viewed as the talent the company wants to retain, are even more likely to stay quiet, even when the changes they might suggest would benefit the firm and them personally.

But it is worthwhile to seize on times when conversations about new ways of working can happen. Anyone can be a "tempered radical," to use Debra Meyerson's term for those who "work quietly to challenge prevailing wisdom and gently provoke their organizational cultures to adapt."[18] Managers can begin these conversations within their work groups and float the idea of working differently with their own peers. Employees can change their own behavior quietly by running project meetings differently, by turning off email and messages for heads-down time some afternoons, by stating that no reply is expected when sending emails over the weekend, and by explicitly supporting coworkers' vacations, leaves, and other time fully off of work. Employees might point out that the time line a manager has proposed feels unrealistic given the staff assigned to the project. That conversation may seem like a stretch and a risk, but it can be done politely and professionally. One overloaded employee told us that she brings her long list of current projects to her manager and nicely asks for help prioritizing. It quickly becomes clear that it can't all get done, so the manager needs to find additional staff to help her, or adjust his expectations. The fact that it does not feel appropriate, in some organizations, to even point out that demands are unrealistically high is part of the problem.

These small changes amplify when discussed with coworkers or a supportive manager and when framed as a dual, win–win agenda. This can be the path to a critical mass viewing work redesign as a worthwhile move for the organization, as well as for its employees. At a minimum, employees and frontline managers can change how they interact with others to avoid reinforcing dysfunctional practices. Jody Thompson and Cali Ressler, who developed ROWE and were a critical part of STAR, emphasize that anyone can eradicate what they call "sludge," the everyday language and routines that reinforce old norms regarding face time and long hours. That means not giving awards (or even informal recognition in team meetings) for working on weekends, being in the office past midnight, or interrupting vacation to participate in conference calls. Instead, employees and particularly managers can focus explicitly on work objectives and what is needed to do that work well. These conversations can also help clarify the right performance metrics, realistic time lines, and what excellent work looks like in particular teams. Thompson and Ressler talk about this as "managing the work, not the workers," and this framing can increase employees' motivation too. These changes may help improve performance evaluation processes and chip away at the assumption that long hours and constant availability are valid indicators of productivity, quality, or commitment. This institutional work catalyzes further changes in the rules of the game through conversations and quiet experimentation.

Employees and frontline managers can also model a more supportive culture by sharing their own personal lives and family priorities and admitting—rather than hiding—when they have rearranged their work to take care of the rest of life. Support for others' personal and family lives can be offered to coworkers and subordinates at all ages and life stages. Teams can deliberately and proactively recognize everyone's care work, family and community engagement, and personal care needs (like sufficient sleep). Doing so reinforces the importance of life outside of work and means that intensive and intrusive work is recognized as problematic for all. Employees and managers should also recognize that people's preferences for integrating work and the rest of life or keeping their roles and times distinct vary. The idea is not to present one new model of complete work–life integration and high levels of sharing, but to see how coworkers and managers can customize their work practices in ways that work well *for them* while still keeping group goals and needs in mind.[19]

Managers, in particular, can help move their organizations toward better ways of working even when there is no official policy or new program. First, managers who have the discretion to approve flexible work arrangements (under a flexibility-as-accommodation policy) can change their default assumption to assuming that different schedules and work locations will work well in most situations. Company policies often require that employees who seek an accommodation make a business case for working differently; this means they need to justify how they can do the work and also show how the new arrangement will benefit the firm. The underlying assumption here is that the current (inflexible, intensive) work patterns are optimal and the only reason to allow changes is to reap even more productivity from their employees. But that assumption is often wrong. Managers can assume that requests for flexible work options are worthwhile and approve them unless there is a particular situation that makes experimentation tricky. Even jobs that seem to require high availability or contact with clients can be accomplished in different ways with innovative coordination routines that exploit new connectivity technologies, but also set some boundaries so that work is not endless. Changes in when and where work occurs often also require modest changes in *how* the work is accomplished. But that does not mean the old, rigid ways are better or are the only feasible arrangement.

Managers can also check themselves, assessing whether flexibility stigma is creeping into their evaluations. There should be no career trade-off where employees who are allowed to work flexibility are as-sumed to necessarily move more slowly toward a promotion or get a smaller raise. Work results can be evaluated (with appropriate pro-rating if the employee has reduced hours and workload) rather than evaluating where the employee works, what the employee's specific schedule is, or how often the employee pulled late hours. If a performance problem is evident with an employee who is working flexibly, that problem should be treated as an issue to resolve with that specific employee. Performance problems are not necessarily evidence that more traditional work patterns will improve the situation. Some employees who are not rated as high performers (and so often not eligible for flexible work arrangements under accommodation policies) could very well perform *better* if they rearranged their work to better align with their personal needs and style. Managers can remind themselves to attend first and foremost to the quality and timeliness of the work, not evaluating their direct reports based on their compliance with an intensified ideal worker norm where productivity and commitment are equated with long hours and constant availability.

Changing the Public Policy Context

A more sustainable future of work also requires updating the outdated public policies that were originally fashioned for the work and the workforce of the middle of the last century. Work redesigns implemented at an organizational or team level, like the one at TOMO, are important innovations that dislodge old expectations and provide a "proof of concept." But they are not sufficient for producing new ways of working in the country at large. Even successful organizational strategies for change are always at risk, as we saw with the revocation of STAR after the merger. High-road employment policies are also more likely to be pursued by organizations with relatively privileged professional, managerial, and technical employees or workforces represented by a union, and the strains felt by hourly workers in service jobs and less advantaged workers are too often ignored. Public policy initiatives aimed at reducing overload and addressing unpredictable hours can institutionalize new ways of working as both the way things are and the way things should be for everyone.

Public policies need to provide sufficient safety nets for today's, and tomorrow's, realities. That means providing workers with greater control over their work schedules while simultaneously recognizing their important priorities and commitments outside of work. Labor laws in the United States were designed in and for the industrial era when blue-collar work prevailed; when white-color organizational work was expanding and often meant a stable career moving up in one firm; when paid work only happened at workplaces (except for farmers and quite limited home production); and when unions represented more workers and negotiated wages, hours, and safety rules with more employers. Those policies also assumed that most workers were engaging in a "separate spheres" strategy where the male breadwinner earned a wage sufficient to support a homemaker wife to care for their home, children, and infirm relatives, as well as for the male workers themselves. As the economist Heather Boushey puts it, the primary law regulating work time in the United States, the Fair Labor Standards Act, was drafted "before computers were invented and when the most important scheduling problem was over work for hourly employees." Boushey also reminds us that for decades, US businesses relied on "the American Wife" as a "Silent Partner" whose contributions undergirded the work of paid employees.[20] Clearly, our nation needs to update its safety nets and labor regulations to reflect changes in the workforce and in the types of work done, the instability of employment relationships, and the variety of workers' personal situations today.

This fundamental mismatch between twentieth-century policies and practices and twenty-first-century realities has spawned expectations that employees will somehow work at work (by being in the office or worksite certain rigid hours) and also work anywhere, anytime (bringing work home to try to accomplish impossible demands and deadlines). This flexibility for business needs means that employers push for longer hours for salaried workers and expect many hourly workers to be available to come in as needed, with no predicable hours (or income), no predictable schedules, and no set number of hours as a minimum.

One critical policy change would be to revise overtime laws so that professionals and other workers who are now classified as exempt from the current Fair Labor Standards law are also paid overtime wages. That change would mean the costs of long hours would be shared more equally between employers and their workers. Employers would then have financial incentives to reconsider the strategy of running lean, pushing their smaller workforces to work long and hard. The Obama administration proposed new overtime rules to raise the income threshold (from around $25,000 annually) so that more employees would be eligible for overtime pay. Court cases and changes directed by the Trump administration meant these rules did not go into effect as initially planned but—as we are revising the book—the Department of Labor is proposing to raise the threshold to around $35,000 annually. Regardless of whether or when that happens, the public conversation about the need to update the rules for overtime pay has begun, and it can go further.[21]

An expansion of overtime coverage may sound crazy to American ears but most workers, including professionals, in other rich countries have a standard workweek specified and receive overtime pay when they exceed that standard. For instance, France has an official workweek of 35 hours. While French professional workers may not always track their additional hours or receive the additional pay, the legal standard sets a more moderate threshold as a cultural norm that can be enforced by law in egregious cases. Additionally, France recently passed a "right to disconnect" law that says employees can't be forced to respond to evening or weekend emails. A somewhat similar bill was proposed in the New York City council. Employees may sometimes check emails and respond to them, but they cannot formally be penalized for protecting their time off of work. So even though these regulations are hard to enforce—and sometimes employees will want to ignore them—these green shoots of innovative legal standards challenge employers' and employees' expectations regarding workers' unlimited availability for work.[22]

Beyond incentivizing moderate hours by requiring overtime pay, labor law could provide protections to employees who refuse to work long hours. Currently, requiring mandatory overtime is allowed in the United

States for hourly workers and salaried employees can be pressured to put in very long hours, come in on weekends, take early morning or late night meetings, and be responsive to calls, texts, and emails at all hours. But legislation could set a total number of work hours after which a worker cannot be compelled to work. New laws could also identify a maximum number of days or shifts per month when overtime can be required, with the right to refuse overtime at other times. Sweden's Working Hours Act sets the workweek at 40 hours per week and covers nearly all employees, including managers who are not senior executives. Overtime is capped at 200 hours per year, with a maximum of 50 hours per month. Sweden is highly unionized with quite different social policies and priorities than the United States, of course, but this is one example of a workable standard that would alter the current situation in which many American workers feel they have to work as long as they are asked or risk putting their jobs in jeopardy.[23]

Broader access to flexible schedules and remote work options can ease the stress of working longer hours or being available after work and on weekends, as we saw with the IT professionals and managers moving into STAR at TOMO. These too can be implemented through legislation. For example, several countries (including the United Kingdom, Australia, and Germany) have laws that provide a right to request flexible work arrangements. Note that these are "soft" regulations; they do not mandate that employers allow their workers flexible arrangements. Instead, the law establishes that employees can *request* a schedule or work location that works well for them, and that employers must seriously consider the request and approve it unless there are concrete business needs that make it infeasible. In practice, employers still have considerable leeway to approve or deny flexible work requests, but this legislation constitutes a new, publicly proclaimed expectation that organizations should and will consider flexible work options fully.[24] This represents a shift from the current US practice—requiring employers to say why the new arrangement could *not* work rather than asking the employee to prove, in advance, that it can. In many countries, employees who believe their request was denied for illegitimate reasons can appeal to a government agency or employment tribunal.

Part-time schedules are also covered by these right-to-request laws, and the European Union has part-time parity laws that require similar hourly pay rates for those working part-time and pro-rated access to other benefits. Of course, some employees still hesitate to seek part-time work because it is less clear that they have a right to return to a full-time position when they are ready. This can discourage men's use of that option, in particular.[25] Even so, there is a clear and public statement that part-time work is a reasonable and available choice, and many do take it.

Paid time away from work also makes intensive work and overload a bit easier to bear. Paid vacations are provided by law or by collective bargaining agreements (negotiated by unions) for most workers in most industrialized countries. In the United States, paid vacations are offered as an employer-based benefit provided to most but not all employees.[26] Paid vacations are more commonly available to professional and managerial workers—but those workers often experience some pressure not to take their full vacations or to check in while officially on vacation.

Paid sick leaves and paid parental leaves are also provided in most other rich countries; indeed, the United States is the only industrialized country in the world that does not provide paid maternity leave for new mothers, though now a few US states do have paid family leave laws. Paid leaves are generally administered as social insurance programs, which means that all employers contribute to a leave fund (and sometimes employees pay in too, via payroll taxes). Workers receive partial pay from those funds. Research on leave-taking in other countries and in California, where paid family leave insurance has been in effect for well over a decade, demonstrates that short and moderate leaves (of less than one year) encourage continued employment by mothers and support families' financial, emotional, and physical well-being.[27]

Paid family and medical leaves signal that we, as a society, recognize the value of time outs—the ability to step away from work for short but critical periods of time when children are born or adopted, when family members need care, or when workers themselves are seriously ill. With legislation around paid leave, employees know they can legitimately take some time off during these critical periods of their lives—without endangering or giving up their job in the long term. Employers also get the message that they need to work around these leaves rather than refuse them or informally discourage them. Currently, paid leaves are available disproportionately to workers who earn more and are in professional or managerial jobs. But we need laws that bring paid leaves to all workers and that provide legal protections if and when the employee needs a back-up in negotiating with a recalcitrant boss.[28]

In addition to policy changes focused on long hours and limited leave times, new labor legislation should target unpredictable hours. Unpredictable hours are problematic for professionals and managers who do not know when they will be called on to fix a problem, reply to a client, or simply reassure a boss who has a question. But unpredictable (and long) hours are also problematic for warehouse workers and delivery drivers who are overloaded, exhausted, and doing physically taxing work. In these cases, the company has promised customers a quick delivery and so management pushes harder and harder, with real consequences for employee well-being. For example, "pickers" and other warehouse workers report that frantic speed combined with the physical requirements of the work causes health problems, including miscarriages, and some are trying to collectively push back on these demands.[29] In these and many other settings where shifts can be extended with little notice, workers often feel they have no choice but to leave their jobs. High turnover is routinely accepted even though the associated costs to the firm might be reduced with a different staffing and scheduling strategy.[30] Reforming overtime laws, forbidding or limiting mandatory overtime, and actively enforcing more generous leave laws would help workers in these situations.

Other workers have unpredictable schedules combined with too few, rather than excessively long, work hours. There are public policy changes that could address this situation too. In fact, several cities (including New York City, San Francisco, and Seattle, with new policies being debated each month) and one US state (Oregon) have adopted "fair workweek laws" that set some standards for work schedules. These regulations have so far targeted retail, food service, and hospitality industries and larger employers in particular. Under these laws employers must provide more advance notice of work schedules (with a requirement that schedules be posted two weeks in advance) and pay more when there is an unexpected schedule change or when the worker is asked to be on call to come in as needed. Employees are able to decline additional shifts or additional hours at the end of a shift (addressing mandatory overtime problems). Additionally, "clopening" shifts, where a worker closes up a store one night and opens it the next morning, are discouraged. In some regulations, there is also a right to request a different schedule with the idea that workers need some say in how their work hours fit with school, family, or with another job. The overarching message is that employers cannot just set schedules as they choose but must work toward predictable and reasonable schedules for these hourly workers.[31]

Fair workweek laws are particularly important in the United States where employers can hire workers without promising a certain number of hours per week. For hourly workers, this means that their income may fluctuate substantially and they may be officially on a given employer's payroll without actually earning much or anything. As one news story about schedules and recent laws raising the minimum wage asked, "What good is a wage boost if workers don't know how many hours they're working every week?"[32] In other countries this is called a zero-hours contract, and there are policy discussions and public concern about the economic insecurity that these contracts create for workers and their families. In the United States, this situation is common. In fact, we don't even have the language—the label of "zero-hours contract"—to highlight when hourly workers have no promised hours and little say regarding how many hours or when they work. That is our default. But Seattle's new regulation, called the Seattle Secure Scheduling Ordinance, covers these scheduling practices, including requiring employers to provide a good-faith estimate of the median hours a new employee can expect to work and to offer existing employees additional hours before new employees are hired. Since this ordinance is quite new, this is a work in progress. We will need to learn more about how to implement secure scheduling in a way that feels feasible for employers as well as helpful to employees. This is another example of how policies can attempt to address the *number* of hours offered, pushing toward more stable incomes and more predictability for hourly workers in the service sector.

Designing a Better Future

The crux of the story we tell in this book is that employers currently have almost total say regarding work time and workload. Faced with a global and sometimes volatile economy and the threat of technology "disruptions" to their businesses, employers have tried to demand more from their workforces while also cutting staff (in the United States and other expensive labor markets), shifting work offshore, and using technology to streamline work processes, knit together global teams, and replace workers. This means that a growing number of salaried workers face long hours and overload, with their jobs crowding out everything else in their lives. In addition, growing numbers of hourly workers must cope with inadequate hours and chronic unpredictability, making it hard to plan their lives and manage financially.

In the United States especially, employers call the shots on work time and schedules in a unilateral way. [33] Even when some organizations offer creative and flexible options—as we saw with TOMO's willingness to bring STAR in to its IT division as part of this study—that is understood as the employer's decision. Flexibility initiatives and the dual-agenda work redesigns we have evaluated are therefore unequally distributed, more likely to be available to the high-status professionals, managers, and skilled technical workers that management seeks to recruit and retain. But as we have seen, those more flexible and supportive ways of working are far from guaranteed, even for privileged and sought-after workers.

We have outlined possible policy changes addressing long and unpredictable schedules leading to both overload and inadequate work. But governments are also employers, and as such they could pave the way for new ways of working even in the absence of legislation. Specifically, city, county, state, and federal units could redesign the clockworks of work and improve safety nets for their civil service workforces. In this way, the public sector could become a model for innovative practices for employers in private and nonprofit sectors.

Another path forward is to formally and collectively negotiate scheduling and related staffing practices, with employees' voices represented by unions or through works councils. Only 11 percent of US workers are union members, but that does not mean the remainder are opposed to unions or uninterested in having a say in how their organizations are run. In a 2017 survey, nearly 50 percent of nonunion workers say that they would vote for a union in their current workplace. And over one-third said that they have less input than they want on how they do their jobs, their schedules, and the time available to do their work.[34] Works councils (which are common in Germany and found in other countries too) allow elected employee representatives to work with management to make decisions at local workplaces, and also seat worker representatives on corporate boards. With works councils, company policies regarding schedules, workload, and more would be vetted and even cocreated jointly by management and by employees on the ground. A negotiated system would also make it harder for a CEO or small executive team to yank a given policy or program, as we saw happen with several initiatives (including STAR) in US companies with unilateral control by employers.[35]

The United States also needs an updated and redesigned safety net that can address the growing precarity of work. Part of our argument has been that employees are wary of pushing for sane, sustainable schedules and reasonable workloads in the context of high job insecurity. When everyone is running scared, it is risky to slow to a walk. That is true even if a more moderate pace would produce higher quality work products, foster creativity and innovation, reduce turnover, and therefore benefit the organization.

Policy changes are required to better address the risks of shifting employment relationships today and tomorrow. Important benefits such as health insurance and retirement need to be portable in order to reflect the reality that workers change employers more often. Even more fundamentally, our social safety net needs to adapt to the fact that *workers*—those who do the labor that produces profits—are less often *employees* of the organization earning that profit. (As we discuss in appendix 2, our study was only able to include the US employees of TOMO even though their work, and the firm's business strategy, was intimately intertwined with contractors in the United States and India.) With growing numbers of independent contractors, freelancers, gig workers, and others who are officially self-employed, we need new options for portable benefits that are not tied to an employer. These benefits also need to be affordable for these workers who are already absorbing much of the risk in this emerging system. Unemployment insurance also needs to be updated to address the needs that contracted and contingent workers face. Even for regular employees, unemployment insurance needs an update. Like scheduling laws, the current laws regarding benefits and unemployment insurance are built around the experiences of manufacturing workers in the middle of the twentieth century. There is an assumption that displacement is rare and alternative work is plentiful, so a relatively low wage replacement rate and relatively short-term benefits are appropriate. But new technologies, which facilitate global labor chains and also automation, plus rabid markets may make displacement much more common and reveal the inadequacies of our policies for unemployed or underemployed adults.[36]

Some of the policy innovations we propose may seem foreign—literally—but evidence from European countries demonstrates that a more supportive and secure system is possible. We also see creative policy moves in a variety of US cities and states today. Moreover, work itself feels increasingly foreign for older Americans used to orderly career paths and conventional 9-to-5 work time expectations. Millennials, by contrast, are well aware of the changing landscapes and timescapes of our global digital economy. This generation expresses different ideals about how women and men will put their work and family lives together, but they are confronting work organizations that do not allow them to pursue those ideals.[37] Millennials now represent the largest group in the US workforce (and a growing force politically, too). These workers may be ready to push, together with older generations, to both redesign work and update employment laws in ways that assume a tech-facilitated global economy and that prioritize workers' real commitments to care for themselves, their families, and their communities.

The future of work is here. We see the problems of unregulated work time and unpredictable schedules at both the high end of the occupational and economic spectrum and at the bottom end. Employers feel pressured by the market to push for doing more with less and to find new ways to lower costs, including labor costs. Technologies facilitate global labor chains that mean professional knowledge work can now be performed by those who are paid much less because they are working in less developed economies or working as subcontractors, officially employed by another firm. IT professionals and attorneys, accountants, some medical specialists, and others are facing the realities of offshoring and downsizing that previously hit manufacturing, and artificial intelligence and automation will soon exacerbate that insecurity. Technologies also seduce us to be always on and always available to work. The lure is not so much our love for our work per se, but the ease of blurring boundaries by checking our phones and messages plus the pressure to do all we can to keep up, in hopes of keeping our jobs. Of course, individuals can be smarter about how much we let work take over our lives and how many hours we put in before deciding we must protect our sleep and our health. But individuals do not have the leverage to make those changes happen on their own. The good news is that together, we do. It is time to make that happen.

ACKNOWLEDGMENTS

⌘

From Erin and Phyllis:

We are grateful to the National Institutes of Health and the Centers for Disease Control for developing the vision for and supporting the work of the Work, Family, and Health Network through the Eunice Kennedy Shriver National Institute of Child Health and Human Development (Grant # U01HD051217, U01HD051218, U01HD051256, U01HD051276), National Institute on Aging (Grant # U01AG027669), Office of Behavioral and Social Sciences Research, and National Institute for Occupational Safety and Health (Grant # U010H008788, U01HD059773). Grants from the William T. Grant Foundation and the Administration for Children and Families provided additional funding to the network. We appreciate the support of the Alfred P. Sloan Foundation, where Kathleen Christensen found a way to help us launch the work that became this project.

We are very grateful to the over 1,000 IT employees and managers who shared their perspectives with us in surveys and in-depth interviews (and sometimes wore sleep trackers and spit into tubes for cortisol analyses, too). We enjoyed learning about your lives and we appreciate your generosity. We could not have done this study without the internal champions and advisers to the study, who cannot be named here but who were unfailingly eager, thoughtful, and willing to work with us so that we could pursue our scholarly goals within their firm. Thank you to the advisory committee and especially to the great team we relied on for access, early orientation, and guidance as the project unfolded.

We have been privileged to work with many terrific collaborators in the Work, Family, and Health Network and to have an inspiring research team at the University of Minnesota. Those wonderful people are all named in appendix 2, and we are sincerely thankful to have worked with each of you. A few people were steady forces pushing this project forward over many years and in many ways, so another round of thanks are required for Rachel Magennis, Jane Peterson, and Kim Fox. Our Minnesota research team benefited from the creative, can-do attitude of those leading the Minnesota Population Center (now the Institute for Social Research and Data Innovation), especially Steve Ruggles, Cathy Fitch, and Kris Michaelson. We also knew that the Department of Sociology, and specifically chairs Liz Boyle and Chris Uggen and accountant Hilda Mork, had our backs.

As we turned in earnest to writing the book, we benefited much from Yagmur Karakaya's research assistance. Yagmur worked on coding and analysis in response to specific queries but also brought us new literatures, listened to and challenged emerging lines of argumentation, and enthusiastically supported the book as it came together. Thank you very much, Yagmur, for the hard work and for freely sharing your smart ideas and energy.

We are so pleased to have had the chance to work with Meagan Levinson at Princeton University Press. Meagan has appreciated the book from our first discussion of the project, but she has also pushed us to write better and be bolder. And every conversation and interaction along the way has been supportive of those goals and of us. Thank you again, Meagan.

From Erin:
My thanks go first and foremost to the incredible Phyllis Moen, a true friend and a true mentor. It has been incredible fun to spend over a decade collaborating closely, and I am so glad we did this together. This project has relied on so many other people who offered their labor, intellectual insights, and companionship along the way. Our appendix 2 describes the essential contributions of those involved in the data collection and early analysis for the book, and I thank each of you again. The Network collaborators educated me in interdisciplinary team science but also provided wonderful guidance on how to enjoy life and our jobs. Thanks especially to Lisa Berkman, Orfeu Buxton, Cassandra Okechukwu, David Almeida, Susan McHale, Ellen Kossek, Leslie Hammer, Georgia Karuntzos, Jeremy Bray, Mary Durham, Ginger Hanson, Lis

Nielsen, Roz King, and Lynne Casper. During the data collection stage, which occurred during the craziest years of parenting, my good friends kept me going. Thank you in particular to Kathy, Kate, Kitty, Karen, Lianne, Pam, Sara, Shelle, Sofi, Gail, Nancy, Krista, and Shannon for the encouragement, reassurance, and support.

During the writing stage, I received encouragement and helpful comments from near and far. Thank you to Deborah Ancona, Evan Apfelbaum, Lisa Berkman, Kara Blackburn, John Carroll, Emilio Castilla, Shelley Correll, Rae Cooper, Jared Curhan, Heejung Chung, Jack Dennerlein, Greg Distelhorst, Frank Dobbin, Barbara Dyer, Martin G. Evans, Roberto Fernandez, Kim Fox, Lena Hipp, Kathy Hull, Sandra Kalev, Kate Kellogg, Sarah Kaplan, Sasha Killewald, Tom Kochan, Laura Kubzansky, Meg Lovejoy, Yvonne Lott, Martha Mangelsdorf, Ann Meier, Melissa Milkie, Paul Osterman, Leslie Perlow, Michael Piore, Ray Reagans, Leah Ruppanner, Brigid Schulte, Pam Stone, Scott Schieman, Cat Turco, Steve Vallas, JoAnne Yates, Kathrin Zippel, and Ezra Zuckerman. I am particularly grateful to Lotte Bailyn and Susan Silbey for talking with me repeatedly about the book and for inspiration.

Amy Buxbaum and Vanessa Conzon conducted additional analysis during the writing stage and shared helpful comments, while Ieva Paulauskaite and Jacob McAuliffe supported this work with bibliographic, graphic, and administrative assistance. I also enjoyed collaborating with Marjaana Sianoja on a new daily diary paper, which affected my thinking about the book. I appreciated editorial suggestions and smart questions from PhD and MBA students at MIT Sloan. Those students included Ellie Azolaty, Amy Buxbaum, Brittany Bond, Alex Kowalski, Christine Riordan, Xavier Vargas, George Ward, Duanyi Yang, and the students enrolled in 15.S03 Spring 2019. Special thanks to my sister, Caryn McGarrity, an HR professional who read the first chapters to advise us on clarity and style, and to my friend Doug Smalley, an IT professional who read our descriptions of different roles and processes to check that they were both accurate and general enough that they would not identify the firm.

We also benefited from audience comments at two ASA talks in 2017, a Work Family Researchers' Network talk in 2016, and from early book talks at the Institute for Work and Employment Research seminar at MIT, the Economic Sociology seminar at Harvard, the Harvard Business School, the Gender & Tech conference at the Harvard Kennedy School, the Weatherhead Initiative on Gender Inequality at Harvard University, Emory University Goizueta Business School, Stanford Graduate School of Business, University of Sydney Business School, University of Toronto Rotman, and Yale School of Management. My thanks as well to Dean David Schmittlein and Deputy Dean Ezra Zuckerman at the MIT Sloan School of Management for summer support and for their interest in my work.

My writing group has been with me almost daily over the last two years, cheering on each "5" icon representing 500 new words drafted or 5 pages edited and reassuring me on days that neither happened. Thank you to Agnes Bäker, Eszter Hargittai, Elizabeth (Lisa) Margulis, and Nancy Thompson, with a special thanks to Eszter for setting up our systems and keeping us going. My extended family (including Caryn, Patrick, Jerry, Linda, Sharon, Lois, Bruce, Peter, and Laura) has been cheering me on this academic journey much longer! Thank you for the enthusiastic support of this project and of me.

I started the fieldwork in TOMO when my children were in diapers and elementary school; they are now a tween and a teen. Thank you, Noah and Graham, for understanding when I repeatedly got on a plane to do more interviews, go write with Phyllis, or give a talk. Thank you especially for jumping with joy and for the spontaneous hugs when I told you the book was submitted. None of this would have been possible without the emotional support and the instrumental support that my wonderful partner, David, has provided, day by day and year after year. Thank you, Noah, Graham, and David for reminding me of the joys of family life even when work was genuinely engrossing and for your steady love. I am lucky indeed.

From Phyllis:
After twenty-five years, I moved from Cornell to the University of Minnesota for many reasons, including grandchildren James and William, but the opportunity to collaborate with Erin Kelly was a key attraction.

Little did I know how closely we would work together and how much her family—David, Graham, and Noah—would come to feel like my own. They, the Work, Family, and Health Network, and this project have helped sustain me through years of loss, including the death of my daughter Melanie and the caregiving and then death of my husband, Dick Shore. My dear friend Urie Bronfenbrenner always said we are the people in our lives. Network members Lisa Berkman, Orfeu Buxton, Cassandra Okechukwu, David Almeida, Susan McHale, Ellen Kossek, Leslie Hammer, Georgia Karuntzos, Jeremy Bray, Mary Durham, Ginger Hanson, Lis Nielsen, Roz King, and Lynne Casper have touched my life more than they can ever know.

Sustaining as well was my year at Stanford University's Center for Advanced Study, which brought new sources of support and encouragement for this book and for life—Margaret Anderson, Maureen Perry Jenkins, Mick Smyer, and especially Carol Heimer. This magical year was made possible in part by the College of Liberal Arts at the University of Minnesota with its amazing dean, John Coleman. Erin and I shared productive writing time both at the center in 2016 and at Harvard as a result of my Radcliffe Fellowship the summer of 2018.

I am grateful for the graduate students I worked with most closely—Kelly Chermack, Samantha Ammons, Elaine Hernandez, Quinlei Huang, Shi-Rong Lee, Anne Kaduk, Eric Tranby, David Hurtado, Miquel Marino, Soomi Lee, Nicole De Pasquale, Rachelle Hill, Reiping Huang, Erik Kojola, Yagmur Karakaya, Jack Lam, and Wen Fan—who became true collaborators and coauthors on this project. I am always grateful for Jane Peterson, who has helped me find more references than either of us can ever remember. Rachel Magennis kept me, as well as our project, on track. Michael Oakes's methodological skills provided new insights and tools. Steve Ruggles, who heads the Institute for Social Research and Data Innovation at the University of Minnesota, remains a pillar of support.

Erin and I began this research and writing project with the goals of making it meaningful, productive, and fun. We succeeded on all three, celebrating our own and team members' birthdays, achievements, marriages, babies, moves, and other life-course transitions. Throughout, we have helped one another contain the overload in our own lives.

APPENDIX 1

⌘

OVERVIEW OF SOFTWARE DEVELOPMENT PROCESS AND JOBS

Title	Role	Key Tasks and Interactions
Planning Stage		
Business Unit	Client	Identify problems that seem to require IT solutions; negotiate budget and time line; report on problems once launched
Program Manager	IT—business liaison	Work closely with business unit to understand problems for business; confer with systems engineers on possible IT solutions
Systems Engineer	IT—technical expert	Work closely with program manager, business unit to understand needs; identify possible IT solutions (small changes, off-the-shelf options, or new software); develop requirements (technical description of what IT solution will do)
Development Stage		
Analyst	IT—technical expert	Flesh out requirements (technical description of what IT solution will do) and update as project evolves; work with systems engineer, developer, project manager
Project Manager	IT—process	Develop staffing plan for given project, adjust if budget or requirements change; monitor progress (status updates) and track metrics for project; work with developers, testers (onshore and offshore)

Continued on next page

Title	Role	Key Tasks and Interactions
Developer (Software Development Engineer)	IT—core technical role	Write and revise code; work with analyst, project manager, testers
Tester (Quality Assurance, QA)	IT—technical expert	Write test cases to evaluate code for bugs, usability for intended end users; work closely with developers, project manager; coordinate with many testers offshore
After Launch (Ongoing)		
Production Support	IT—business, technical	Respond to problems (tickets) that users experience; resolve problems by making technical fixes or consulting with developers, if needed; rotate on-call duty so support is available 24/7; coordinate with production support groups offshore, developers onshore
Database Administrator	IT—technical expert	Capture data from systems that are already operational to track use, outages, etc.; determine how to securely store, access data that is required by regulations; responsible for development and maintenance of these systems; minimal coordination with other groups

APPENDIX 2

⌘

METHODOLOGY AND REFLECTIONS ON CORPORATE FIELDWORK

The Work, Family, and Health Network

We conducted this research as part of a bigger team, the Work, Family, and Health Network, which officially lasted from 2006 to 2016. Some collaborations have continued through today, as has a lasting sense of connection to these researchers. First, we will provide the official introduction: the Work, Family, and Health Network was an interdisciplinary research team that was funded by a cooperative agreement through the National Institutes of Health (NIH) and the Centers for Disease Control and Prevention (CDC): Eunice Kennedy Shriver National Institute of Child Health and Human Development (NICHD; Grant # U01HD051217, U01HD051218, U01HD051256, U01HD051276), National Institute on Aging (NIA; Grant # U01AG027669), Office of Behavioral and Social Sciences Research, and National Institute for Occupational Safety and Health (NIOSH; Grant # U010H008788, U01HD059773). Grants from the William T. Grant Foundation, Alfred P. Sloan Foundation, and the Administration for Children and Families provided additional funding. The contents of this publication are solely the responsibility of the authors and do not necessarily represent the official views of these institutes and offices.

Now the unofficial story, as we understand it: the Work, Family, and Health Network was conceived and developed by Lynne Casper (when she was a program officer at NICHD), Rosalind B. King (a program officer at NICHD), Lis Nielsen (a program officer at NIA), Greg Wagner (a program officer at NIOSH), and others (notably Regina Bures and Rebecca Clark) at the NIH and NIOSH. The goal of the network was to integrate, advance, and amplify research on the work–family interface and on the relationship between the organization of work and health and well-being. The program officers who envisioned this collaboration wanted to pull together researchers with expertise in workplace policies and programs, parents and children's development, diverse workforces including the concerns of aging workers, and more. They had seen exciting studies with implications for public health, but the research was scattered and scholars seemed not to know each other or to talk past each other. As with most academic research, there was more attention to getting published than to getting the word out more broadly to the people who might use the findings. They wanted to promote both rigor and real-world relevance.

With those goals in mind, the NIH and NIOSH program officers set up the network as a cooperative agreement, an unusual type of grant with shared leadership. This was supposed to be truly cooperative —with key decisions made jointly by the principal investigators and staff scientists— and transdisciplinary, meaning the researchers involved learned enough about other disciplines to form something new rather than just represent the fields they were trained in. The selected research teams had substantial time to learn from each other and identify exactly what we knew about the interplay of work, family, and health and what we still needed to learn. The NIH and NIOSH officers also built in time to conduct pilot studies that would help us work together to conduct a randomized controlled trial (or field experiment) in order to rigorously evaluate the effects of a particular workplace change. And they insisted on devoting the time and energy to make this research matter to a variety of audiences including interested employers, workers, advocacy groups, and policymakers.

Phyllis and Erin applied eagerly to join the network because we were both drawn to research that has real implications for practice and for people's lives. We were tired of documenting the challenges of contemporary work and the stresses in contemporary families. We wanted to be a part of making change. But we did not fully understand then how this work would change us. Erin often says it was like a decade-long postdoctoral fellowship, because we learned an enormous amount and it has taken our research and careers in new directions.

Our network colleagues are an amazing bunch who brought deep expertise in developmental psychology, economics, occupational health, policy evaluation, psychology, organizational behavior, sleep science, social epidemiology, and sociology. In addition to the program officers who participated as staff scientists and the two of us, the core of the network included, at various times, David Almeida (Penn State), Lisa Berkman (Harvard), Jeremy Bray (RTI and then University of North Carolina Greensboro), Orfeu Buxton (Harvard and then Penn State), Kelly Chandler (Penn State and then Oregon State), Ann C. Crouter (Penn State), Jim Dearing (Kaiser Permanente Center for Health Research), Mary Durham (Kaiser Permanente Center for Health Research), Leslie Hammer (Portland State and Oregon Health Sciences University), Ginger Hanson (Kaiser Permanente Center for Health Research), Georgia Karuntzos (RTI), Ellen Kossek (Michigan State and then Purdue), Susan McHale (Penn State), and Cassandra Okechukwu (Harvard). There were six teams or centers, with each headed by one or two principal investigators, but the list of key research staff would be even longer. We also benefited from the wise counsel of our early faculty collaborators at Minnesota, Patricia McGovern, J. Michael Oakes, and Andrew Van de Ven.

Our research team at the University of Minnesota was phenomenal; each person brought something different but very helpful to this endeavor. Graduate research assistants during the pilot study included Sam Ammons, Kelly Chermack, Rada Dagher, Eric Dahlin, Elaine Hernandez, Rachelle Hill, Qinlei Huang, Reiping Huang, Donna Spencer, and Eric Tranby. Graduate research assistants during the TOMO period included Wen Fan, Jacqui Frost, Kia Hiese, Erin Hoekstra, Anne Kaduk, Yagmur Karakaya, Erik Kojola, Sarah Lageson, Jack Lam, Shi-Rong Lee, Raphi Rechisky, and Madison Van Oort. Research associates and postdoctoral researchers included Kim Fox, Katie Genadek, Julia Miller-Cantzler, Holly Whitesides, Laurie Pasricha, and Jon Vaughn. We learned from each of you and appreciate all you did for the project.

Undergraduate research assistants primarily worked on transcription, de-identification, and data management. Our tireless undergraduate team included Safiyyah Abdul-Alim, Sarah Aufdermauer, Rebecca Barney, Natasha Bistodeau, Collena Coleman, Charles Crawford, Gina Dominichetti, Matt Forstie, James Frickstad, Anasmita Ghosh, Samantha Ihrke, Erin E. Kelly, Kelsey Knish, Gino Marchetti, Kirkland Marine, Laura Miller, Bao Moua, Taylor Nelson, Ryan Pottebaum, Michelle Pose, Marika Reese, Ashley Rolffs, Emily Schulz, Allison Stambaugh, Paige Stroshine, Mike Vasseur, Caralin Walsh, Will Wojcik, Meghan Zacher, and Shirley Zhao. Thank you for the careful attention and your good cheer working on often tedious, but important, tasks.

For the first three years of the network, the principal investigators and some of our graduate students met regularly to teach each other about topics like how to measure sleep well, what we actually meant by work–family conflict, how to ask adolescents about their lives, strategies for building research partnerships with employers, and more. We brought in speakers beyond the group and spent time working together on the four pilot studies that we were conducting. The Harvard team studied four nursing homes to learn about that workforce and to develop new strategies for measuring cardiometabolic risk, sleep, and resident outcomes (which is an important performance measure for these organizations, as well as an important public health concern). The Penn State team went into hotels to study their frontline managers and staff and to fine-tune the daily diary methodology with both employee-parents and their children. The Portland State/Michigan State team partnered with a group of grocery stores, under the direction of Leslie Hammer and Ellen Kossek. They validated new scales for family-supportive supervisor behaviors and also developed a short training for frontline managers that incorporated tracking interactions with employees to try to build new habits of expressing support more actively. We conducted our pilot study at Best Buy Co., Inc., where we studied the implementation of the ROWE initiative in the corporate headquarters and practiced integrating qualitative fieldwork and interviews into a study of an organizational change.

All of these pilot studies directly informed the field experiment at TOMO and a parallel study in thirty long-term care sites or nursing homes. The two pilot initiatives (manager training on supporting family and personal life and ROWE) were woven together to create STAR. First, though, we went into TOMO and into the nursing homes to learn about their concerns and how we might customize the pilots for these work-forces. That customization work involved Leslie Hammer, Ellen Kossek, their students, our students, and the organizational development con-sultants Jody Thompson and Cali Ressler, who had pioneered ROWE and would facilitate the delivery of STAR. We turned to Kent Anger and Ryan Olson, both scientists at the Oregon Health Sciences University, to develop the tools to track and encourage supervisors' supportive behaviors.

The network's website (www.workfamilyhealthnetwork.org) provides all the STAR training materials, including the version used at TOMO and a version customized for the healthcare study. It also has links to over one hundred research publications from the network and guidance on how researchers can get access to the survey and health data to take these lines of research even further.

This book represents our learning together—even though the analy-sis of the context at TOMO and our readings of the qualitative data are our own. Doing that kind of interpretive analysis as a committee of ten or more is not feasible or desirable. But we could not have done this proj-ect, nor would we have wanted to do it, without our wonderful network colleagues.

Doing Research in and with a Corporation

Our work required access to a large organization *and* permission to make changes to their policies and practices by introducing STAR as a pilot to some work units. This is a big ask, and our ask got even bigger because the network concluded that for the best science, we would only study organizations that agreed to randomize some work groups to treatment or intervention conditions (STAR) while having other units continue on as a control group, operating under previous company policies. Additional-ly, to obtain the best possible data (in terms of response rates, cover-age, and quality), we wanted to do in-person surveys on company time and we wanted to do four waves of those surveys plus semistructured interviews along the way. We required dedicated small conference rooms as private spaces to conduct data collection for months on end. All employees and managers participating in the study did so on work time, with a project code that meant their billable hours for a given week included time spent on the study. Ironically, these salaried employees probably worked later since they took time away to answer our questions about overload and intensive work. The rollout of STAR training sessions and subsequent activities also occurred on company time, with a project code provided for that as well. Invariably, any project of this size is something of a disruption, requiring considerable coordination time from key staff. We also asked for access, desk space, and informal support for the study site managers and STAR coordinators (researchers hired by us and reporting to us) who collected much of the qualitative data we have analyzed here. Having those embedded researchers on-site daily was key for building relationships as well as gathering rich data.

Getting In and Getting to Know Each Other

We were fortunate indeed that TOMO invited us in and met all of these requirements. They accepted this "research partnership," which is a term we used repeatedly to distinguish our work from paid consultants who would do management's bidding and primarily answer management's questions. Additionally, the executive sponsors and HR managers who served as critical gatekeepers actively tried to protect the study and initiative through the upheaval of the merger. We remember vividly the day the merger was announced—in the press at the same time the TOMO employees got the news from their CEO—and we feared that we would be shown the door. Instead, these insiders worked behind the scenes to keep the project going through the originally planned end date.

Why did leadership agree to participate and human resource managers seek to sustain this study? Both business reasons and personal commitments seemed to motivate their involvement. A director who had heard of ROWE at Best Buy (and our earlier research evaluating ROWE) brought that initiative to the attention of his vice president, who shared the information with his trusted HR manager and the top HR executive for the IT division. These two women became early and primary informants, guiding us through getting in to the organization, planning a design that met our needs and their objectives, carefully introducing the study to get support from key executives, and negotiating differences between our time line and reporting style and corporate norms.

From our first meeting with those HR professionals, we sensed their excitement about the possibilities inherent in a dual-agenda redesign study. One would later say, as she was leaving the firm after the merger, that this project was the most meaningful work she had done in her time at TOMO. HR professionals are often looking for ways to both support employees and be what they call "strategic partners" whose programs or initiatives contribute to business goals and the bottom line. Early on, these HR professionals saw STAR as a potential solution to multiple problems they had identified. They recognized that always-on expectations and stretched hours accompanying the firm's "follow-the-sun" (offshore) model were risky and sometimes counterproductive. They saw that many managers were not updating their expectations regarding time in the office, despite requiring work at all hours including late-night and weekend work from home. Yet they did not know how to encourage those "old-school managers" (to use employees' language) to manage differently. Moreover, the firm itself was engaged in other practices, such as increased documentation, that increased work demands and hours. These HR professionals had previously been called in to solve morale problems after a vice president had declared that all employees had to work on-site five days per week. They struggled with how they could improve employees' attitudes without contradicting the executive's presumed authority. They were charged with reducing "regrettable losses," or the turnover among employees with highly valued skills and those rated as high performers. They knew, from their involvement in recruiting, that the company was seen as stodgy rather than innovative, and they wondered how they would recruit the best talent among the younger generation. As the research project progressed, these gatekeepers came to see that STAR was benefiting employees and managers, and believed those improvements in morale and engagement would pay off for the firm.

With the help of these HR informants, we worked to build a broader network of potential champions. The term "champion" is often used in corporate settings to refer to people who advocate for a given policy, program, or strategy. We knew the changes that might happen with STAR were what appealed to them. But we also needed to get them on board for the *study design*, which involved following both the STAR groups and control groups who would not get the STAR initiative over repeated waves of data collection. We reported the positive findings from the pilot studies (including our evaluation of ROWE at Best Buy and Leslie Hammer and Ellen Kossek's supervisor training research) while also stressing that we were researchers who would evaluate STAR rigorously and report whatever we found. We had to sell the idea that the STAR change initiative could help the company while also underscoring our identity as independent scholars, and this meant acknowledging the reality that STAR might hurt the firm, employees, or their interests specifically. Over and over, we reminded people in TOMO that we were interested in a broad set of questions about work, family, and health and that we would publish whatever we found (although we would not name the firm or individuals in it). We soon met several vice presidents and the more supportive executives then discussed the project with their peers, laying the groundwork for our subsequent conversations. Our discussions with the legal department (which were essential for finalizing the nondisclosure agreement) came after several influential vice presidents were on board and after human resources had introduced the plans. This meant those charged with protecting the firm saw that insiders wanted this to happen.

The IT executives often framed STAR as a plausible way to update their culture to reflect the reality of the global labor chain or, as they called it, the "follow-the-sun model of software development." They hoped to avoid burnout and turnover and also to promote improvements in productivity or performance—even though the executive team disagreed among themselves how that was best measured. In one meeting, which included the lead economist in the Work, Family, and Health Network, Jeremy Bray, we probed which measures of productivity and performance the directors and vice presidents in the room wanted us to concentrate on. We wanted to be sure to measure what mattered to them. They went around the room critiquing every proposed internal measure, with one vice president telling us why we should not trust a particular metric and the next telling us why the metric proposed by the previous vice president was worthless. It was instructive to hear that the performance measures they used to evaluate their staff—and often the measures their superiors used to evaluate them—were seen as unreliable, poorly reported, easily gamed, uninformative regarding the quality of the work, and insufficient for capturing individual contributions to large projects.

We did our best to test STAR on multiple measures, since they did not agree on the most important business outcomes. But our analysis of performance and productivity was complicated by the fact that most of those measures track applications or programs, and few applications or programs were completed entirely by STAR teams or by teams working under the company's usual practices. We had to estimate the effects of applications developed by 60 percent STAR teams and 40 percent control group teams, for example, making that analysis very noisy. Jumping ahead several years, in the large management meeting where the end of the STAR pilot was announced, a senior executive presented the positive findings from the perspective of employees' experiences, job satisfaction, and low turnover and then reported the null results on productivity and performance. We were disheartened to see him frame those findings as evidence that STAR didn't work when we understood the issue as complicated and messy data that nonetheless showed no evidence of new problems for the firm. In other words, the insiders knew all the problems with their internal measures, and yet this senior executive had pinned his assessment of STAR solely on moving those metrics.

Returning back to the early stages of the study: we also set up an internal advisory group that included the vice president who first brought up the idea of a work redesign initiative, a number of frontline managers and IT professionals representing different job functions, plus employees who worked with internal data such as HR records and productivity and performance metrics. We met with this group repeatedly in the first two years of the study, asking for their input on the data collection plans and on communications about the study and about STAR (which came separately and with distinctive voices, since STAR was introduced as a company pilot). We conferred with these individuals as questions came up or to learn more about various roles, different people, or possible data sources.

The company also let us in because we offered quite a bit, along with asking quite a bit of them. The network could provide extensive consulting and training, at no direct cost to the firm, because the funding from the National Institutes of Health and the National Institute for Occupational Health and Safety covered the development and delivery of the STAR workplace intervention we were studying. Given the firm's financial situation (especially before the merger), the partnership made it much more feasible for the IT division to take action to address the problems of overload, burnout, and turnover and to move toward being known as an innovative and unusually flexible organization. Aside from the financial contribution of providing training and evaluation at no direct cost to them, we offered status and affirmation of specific executives' identity as smart and rational decision-makers. In terms of status, executives often brought up the NIH and CDC funding, and it did not hurt to have Harvard as one of the participating institutions. In terms of identity, the senior executives believed themselves to be both innovative and data-driven. STAR was clearly innovative, and we explained in our early meetings how this dual-agenda work redesign approach went well beyond common flexibility policies. They hoped that adopting STAR would differentiate them from other IT companies in the area, helping with recruitment and with the firm's brand. And by supporting a randomized controlled trial (by letting us in and letting us do the research right), these executives were signaling to themselves and to others that they cared about data and about rigorous scientific evidence.

Who Was In and Who Was Out

Once we gained access to TOMO, we needed to clarify who would be eligible for the study and, among those, who would be eligible to participate in STAR (should their work group be randomized to that condition). Our research design and our budget drove some of this. We needed to concentrate data collection in the largest work sites, because we were collecting survey and health data in person and on-site. The RTI team (led by Jeremy Bray, Georgia Karuntzos, and Frank Mierzwa) within the network hired and supervised field interviewers, many of whom lived in these communities, but we had to consider travel costs for facilitators and some research staff. TOMO's IT employees worked in at least ten cities in the United States, but we decided to include employees and managers in the two metro areas with the largest number of IT employees; this decision meant that over three-quarters of the US employees in the IT division were eligible for the study. We also talked with union leaders, because one small unit within the IT division was covered by a collective bargaining agreement (although the professionals and managers we have described here were not covered by the agreement or connected to the union at all). The union leaders were intrigued by STAR and the study but suggested the simplest decision was to exclude that unit, which we did, so they could continue operating under their negotiated agreement. The union leaders just asked that we confer with them if and when the program was going to be expanded beyond the initial pilot groups.

Decisions regarding who would participate in STAR were a bit different. Because the work redesign unfolds in teams or work groups, we randomized all IT work groups to either participate in STAR or continue working under the company's usual practices. All employees in work groups randomized to STAR were invited to participate in STAR trainings—although only those in the two largest metro areas would be able to do that in person rather than via web conference. For example, let's consider a work group with a manager based in one of those cities and his ten employees. The manager and the eight employees working in that city are also invited to participate in the study, but the two employees who work in a smaller location across the country are not asked to be part of the study (because we could not send field interviewers to every office). When the STAR pilot is launched, this work group is randomized to STAR and the manager and all ten employees are invited to all STAR trainings. The eight employees working in the larger sites come in to a conference room and experience the trainings in person; the two located elsewhere log in to the web conference system, hear the facilitator in real time, see the slides in real time, and can ask questions and participate both via chat and by talking. The facilitator and STAR coordinator in the room actively include the remote participants, but because we did not include them in the data collection, we cannot assess whether those who went through STAR via web conference changed as much as those who participated in person.

The most consequential exclusions were leaving out contractors who work in the United States alongside the employees and managers we studied and excluding all of the offshore staff. We recognize that we have studied the most privileged of this global workforce and not learned from the many workers who contribute to the work of the TOMO IT division without being so-called regular employees. This was a tough compromise, particularly since we came to see the global labor chain and insecurity as critical parts of the US employees' experience. We wish we could also have studied the global labor chain and insecurity from the perspective of offshore workers and contractors working in the United States.

But US employment law means firms try to keep a clear line between their employees and contractors. Officially, the company does not direct the work conditions or work environment for independent contractors. Any contractors working through a third party (like an IT consulting firm that sends IT professionals to do a specific project at TOMO) are considered employees of that organization. Government guidelines suggest that if a business controls what specific work tasks are done or directs how the work is performed, then the contractor is likely misclassified—and should be counted and taxed as an employee. It is our impression that TOMO executives believed they needed to exclude all contractors from STAR because including them would have opened questions about misclassification. If contractors participated in STAR discussions about TOMO rules and expectations and were invited to be part of team reflections and redesign efforts, that would suggest they are not actually *independent* contractors, but part of the firm. The firm might have been asked (by the IRS or others) to justify the status of those contractors. The safer course for TOMO's larger staffing strategy and financial liability was to leave contractors out of STAR, and the study evaluating it, altogether.

TOMO's offshore staff included contractors hired through Indian IT staffing agencies and some employees of a TOMO subsidiary. Excluding all offshore staff made sense, since we did not have funding to study the experiences and well-being of workers in India and elsewhere; important as those questions are, our grants had not been written to address them nor did we have the budget to do any data collection outside the United States. We accepted these exclusions (with some regrets) because the project required the close cooperation of the firm and the firm had legitimate concerns about any project that reached beyond its US employees.

Team Ethnography in a Corporate Setting

This study was an adventure in team ethnography and in combining field-work and project management. Erin and Phyllis were in TOMO often, both for short visits lasting a few days and for a few months at a time, and we were on the phone with our key contacts in human resources and the executive team much more than we had ever expected to be. But we also relied on wonderful research staff, divided into those who represented the study and those who coordinated STAR, located on-site at the largest TOMO IT office for the duration of the project. Kim Fox was the study project manager within TOMO, and her work was critical for building and maintaining relationships with a wide variety of stakeholders. She became the in-house expert on all the logistics and relationships required to get the survey data collected, introduce the study in person or by phone to teams, book the conference rooms for the field interviewers to conduct the interviews privately, plan data collection around key deadlines and deliverables that each team faced, and much more. Kim is also a gifted interviewer who conducted many of the context interviews where frontline managers and directors shared their perspective on what was going on, how they were feeling, and how the merger and documentation changes were unfolding. These interviews deliberately did not focus on STAR, but the interview respondents often discussed those changes too. We also benefited from the excellent work of Julia Miller-Cantzler and Jon Vaughn, who served as secondary site managers and conducted these interviews too.

In the STAR coordination role, we were lucky to work with Holly Whitesides and Laurie Pasricha, who brought both interpersonal savvy and strong interviewing skills to the project. STAR coordinators were the in-house face of the initiative, sending invitations to trainings to managers and employees, booking rooms and setting up the web conference system, coordinating with the CultureRx facilitators, and also addressing questions from participants. They wrote full field notes on over fifty training sessions and attended many more to make sure they went smoothly and to observe participants' responses. In addition, Holly and Laurie did one-on-one training sessions with managers to introduce STAR and then guided managers through the supportive behavior tracking exercises (where they were asked to set goals on how they would interact with their employees and then track those over the course of a week). STAR coordinators also conducted semistructured feedback interviews with employees and managers that asked more directly and in more detail about experiences with STAR. This was a complex role; we asked STAR coordinators to provide practical support to the initiative while also conveying to employees and managers that they wanted to hear whatever feedback the participants had. They said, over and over, that they wanted to hear everyone's experiences—good, bad, and mixed—and these interviews explicitly probed for problems and concerns about STAR. We had identified a smaller number of teams moving into STAR as our in-depth sites, with variation by job role and by the vice president supervising those teams. We observed all of these teams' training sessions and conducted more interviews, talking with more employees as well as with the frontline managers, and interviewing them several times as STAR unfolded. Those teams are heavily represented in the book, since we got to know them better (and Erin and Phyllis did more of these teams' interviews), and we returned to them for more of the later interviews after the official end of STAR.

We relied on University of Minnesota PhD students working as research assistants, including Kelly Chermack, Rachelle Hill, Erin

Hoekstra, Erik Kojola, Sarah Lageson, and Jack Lam, for additional interviews at TOMO and for survey administration for the final web-based survey. Our network colleagues Ellen Kossek and Leslie Hammer conducted a few interviews as well. We encouraged interviews in person (usually on-site but sometimes at a coffee shop and occasionally in an employee's home). But particularly because STAR told people they could decide when, where, and how they did their work, we did phone interviews when respondents requested that.

The distributed data collection allowed us to do many interviews (with about 400 conducted over the course of the study) and to take field notes covering many different meetings, trainings, and events as well as routine interactions and conversations in the office. This strategy required more standardization than one would see in an organizational ethnography conducted by one researcher. We developed protocols for introductions (so that the different roles were described to everyone in the same way) and discussed how we would respond to common questions like "What are you learning?" and "Will STAR survive the merger?" We used semistructured interview guides where the same questions were asked in roughly the same order, although all the interviewers were adept at probing and at following the lead of the respondent to learn more about topics of interest to them. We had routines for writing interview summaries, so that Erin and Phyllis could easily review interview highlights as they came in (and before our undergraduate RAs got busy transcribing the recorded interviews). And we had regular meetings to discuss both practical questions about the rollout of the study and STAR and what we were seeing, hearing, and wondering about these professionals' and managers' experiences. We also met regularly with the STAR coordinators and the facilitators to assess fidelity, or how closely the training sessions had stuck to the planned material, and to get their impressions about any teams or individuals who were particularly skeptical or who had raised questions that needed HR attention (like how to file vacation time in the HR system under STAR).

We spent less time observing daily work as it unfolded than we would have liked, although we began the project with a few months of formative research in one smaller work site where we could shadow IT professionals and managers and ask our most naïve questions about IT work. Observing work in situ was a challenge because so many work interactions occurred on IM (an internal chat application) or conference calls (although we did sit in on many calls and watched IMs as we sat in cubes with informants). We were also acutely aware that quiet time to do their technical tasks, often called their "real work," was precious. We felt reluctant to sit with the IT professionals to observe too often, even if we were mostly quiet. These challenges are common for researchers doing ethnographic fieldwork in white-collar, professional settings and so it is not surprising that many of our observations come from meetings, and from conversations on the way to or from meetings, lunch, or trainings.

All of our work at TOMO relied on the excellent work done in our own home office at the University of Minnesota. We worked through the entire study with an amazing project manager, Rachel Magennis. Rachel coordinated everything, from our calendars to our travel to TOMO, from budgeting to hiring and supervising undergraduate research assistants to transcribe and de-identify the qualitative data, from secure data transfers to fine-tuning codebooks so we and others could use the survey data with confidence. Rachel worked closely with the embedded research staff, with multiple people within TOMO, and with our network colleagues. She also facilitated and supported the work of our great graduate research assistants and postdocs during this period, including Wen Fan, Jacqui Frost, Katie Genadek, Kia Hiese, Erin Hoekstra, Anne Kaduk, Yagmur Karakaya, Erik Kojola, Sarah Lageson, Jack Lam, Shi-Rong Lee, Raphi Rechisky, and Madison Van Oort. We also benefited from the administrative and budgeting support of Jane Peterson, Hilda Mork, and Kris Michaelson, among others. We are indebted, in particular, to Yagmur Karakaya, who has worked with us as we moved through the analysis for this book, including coding, helping us craft arguments, and coordinating the bibliography.

In short, this type of research requires many people and many relationships that need to be tended to keep the research partnership going. Though our take on overload and its mitigation as presented here is our own, the actual research has very much been a collective endeavor. We are grateful for the many contributions and the goodwill of all of these collaborators.

Evolving Relationships

Because this study went on for about five years, and because the research site morphed into a new organization after experiencing major disruptions, it is not surprising that our relationships and perspectives changed over time. We have described our take on the HR partners and executives at the time we began working with TOMO. But with the merger, those HR partners were drawn into other important tasks like deciding who would keep their jobs, who would report to whom, and how benefits and bonuses would be restructured. For almost two years after the merger announcement, our key HR contacts worked to advocate thoughtfully for continuing the study and STAR while also doing that work. Sometimes this meant coaching us on how to prepare a crisper briefing for the executives who wanted an update. (Obviously, they did not weigh in on what findings we reported or the substance of our findings. But we learned from them how much detail a particular set of decision-makers could take in and how to craft slides that distracted executives could follow.)

These HR partners and other HR professionals within the TOMO IT division were skilled coaches. They could help an IT manager who thought of himself or herself as a technical expert but not a people person develop skills as a manager. And these HR partners had some great ideas on informal coaching for STAR, including having managers who were STAR enthusiasts tell their stories to other managers. In the end, less coaching happened than they wanted because the merger integration work was so pressing. If you do not have a clear reporting structure yet and have not given people their new job titles, you cannot devote as much attention to supporting an innovative practice like STAR. And after the most pressing merger integration work was done, our primary HR partners voluntarily left the company for better—or at least less stressful—jobs. As we discuss elsewhere, the new HR professionals who were assigned to manage STAR and help the executive team decide whether to expand, revoke, or revise it had absolutely no exposure to STAR trainings. One key contact was new to the firm, so she also had limited interactions with managers who were happily managing their teams under STAR. We met with these individuals and shared materials with them, but they were primarily oriented toward developing positive relationships with the executives they would be working with going forward and some (from ZZT, in particular) were not interested in STAR.

We knew that the legacy TOMO executives felt committed to seeing the study through. In line with our memorandum of understanding, they defined that as getting through the fourth wave of surveys and then giving us some time to prepare our analysis and share a final briefing. As we reached that point and as the executives anticipated making a decision about STAR, we began to feel most of them distance themselves from us and from the project. More meetings were held that did not include us. We had a sense of declining access to information. Ethnographers and fieldworkers are always intruders and, in organizational settings where doors can be closed and conversations taken elsewhere, we are privy only to what informants are open to sharing. However, we were fortunate to sit in on several meetings with the core executive team even at this stage and to attend the larger event where the decision to end STAR was announced to all managers. We also continued talking with some vice presidents and the new HR partners informally and in interviews, but we could feel the relationships shifting as the study neared its official end and as one of the most supportive vice presidents decided to leave the company.

These shifts make sense because we had partnered with TOMO— which no longer existed as an independent entity—to study STAR— which no longer existed as an official pilot or policy—as well as to investigate broader questions regarding the interplay of work, family, and health. Yet questions of sustainability and the possible dissemination of this approach to broader audiences led us to stay and to learn as long as we could. We even tried to help the executive team get better data to assess their concerns and make a decision about STAR by conducting a fifth survey, which was obviously of interest to us as well. By this point, we had reached the official end of the research partnership and they did not want us to do in-person surveys on-site, on company time. But we had emails (both company and personal) from employees and managers who had completed the first wave of the survey and given us permission to contact them again. We switched to a web-based survey, with the same questions as before plus a new battery of questions on collaboration, team performance, and communicating with coworkers and managers. And we heard back from roughly two-thirds of the original survey respondents (N = 698), including similar numbers of those who had been in STAR and those from the control groups. As we discuss in chapter 7, we did not uncover any specific problems in STAR teams and we heard much about its successes.

By this stage, we were happy to share information from the survey and our last batch of interviews, but executives were no longer asking for input. We shared what we could—with official decision-makers and with the IT professionals and managers who had so generously shared their perspectives with us—and we too moved on.

This project was clearly a large and ambitious study, involving a wide variety of stakeholders. But we did not feel overloaded or burned out—although sometimes we were tired and stretched—in part because appropriate resources were provided (in terms of staff budgets as well as intellectual capacities) from the NIH, NIOSH, the William T. Grant Foundation, Alfred P. Sloan Foundation, the Administration for Children and Families, and our home institutions. We enjoyed many supportive interactions with our fantastic collaborators across the Work, Family, and Health Network and specifically at the University of Minnesota and then at MIT. The years collecting data in TOMO and then analyzing and making sense of what we learned have been a time of real growth, enlivened by a sense of possibility as we considered how work could work better for those in this company and far beyond. We are also grateful to have had the opportunity to go deep inside corporate America and to connect with so many interesting and hard-working employees, managers, and HR specialists. This is not the style of social science that either of us was initially trained to do, but it has been rewarding and enlightening as well as genuinely enjoyable.

APPENDIX 3

⌘

IDEAS FOR ACTION

A core premise of this book is that overload is produced inside work organizations by specific management decisions and staffing strategies, together with new communication and information technologies, that push workers to do more and more, often with less and less. Work spirals in intensity, leading to feelings of chronic overload. We argue that this way of working is both unhealthy and unsustainable. Workplaces need to change—to be redesigned in ways that address the needs and health of employees as well as the needs and healthy performance of the firm. In this book, we evaluate an organizational change initiative, STAR, and discuss other work redesign initiatives that we believe to be promising. But we also recognize that many readers are not executives who can decide to implement a dual-agenda work redesign initiative. In the case of burgeoning overload yet limited prospects for official policy change, what, then, are possible responses?

Here we share some ideas about what frontline managers and individual employees can do to move toward new ways of working and to challenge the status quo of overload and work intensification. We think of these as "in the meantime" changes that will hopefully lay the groundwork for broader policy changes within work organizations and within society in terms of our cultural understandings of what constitutes both good work and the ideal worker. These ideas come from our study of professional and managers in one 24/7 global firm. While they are applicable to white-collar workers in a variety of industries, they may need to be adapted for other types of workforces and other industries, such as healthcare or manufacturing.

Ideas for Managers and Team Leads

Managers can create more flexible and supportive team cultures, even when formal company policies remain intransigent. Here are some ideas for managers, team leads, or supervisors who want to begin redesigning work for their team or department.

Focus less on when, where, and how work happens and more on results. This doesn't mean employees have permission to disappear, since many people need to collaborate in team projects, learn from one another, and build good relationships with coworkers and with clients. It does mean recognizing that managing is not about monitoring "butts in seats" or rewarding those who respond immediately to any email, text, or call.

Identify and reduce low-value work. In every bureaucracy, unnecessary forms and meetings crowd out time for the real work of an organization. Managers can work together with their teams and workgroups to ferret out the "every Monday" meeting with no real agenda, duplicative tasks, and unnecessary record-keeping.

Clarify what is expected for each employee, in terms of work products and other deliverables. Do this as a real planning exercise, with employee input, and not simply as a box to fill in on a formal performance review. Remind employees to question tasks and activities that are added to their to-do list or calendar if those do not seem to be important steps toward their primary goals. Ask them to alert you if they can't see how they will fit in something they have been asked to do without working long hours or weekends.

Encourage employees to share when they are feeling overloaded. You may not be able to hire additional staff or move a deadline in every case, but you can help prioritize tasks, take over some tasks, and look for others who can pitch in. At a minimum, you will have an early warning about overload and possible burnout and can work toward solutions.

Don't celebrate long hours or treat them as signs of commitment. This is common in hard-driving industries and organizational cultures, but instead have a goal of high performance with sustainable hours and announce that goal to the team.

Make it the default that employees decide when and where they work. If a particular work practice (like regularly working at home three days per week or working 7 a.m. to 3:30 p.m. most days) does not seem feasible to you, discuss that with the employee or with the team. Perhaps together you can identify how working at home can happen more smoothly, with new routines for updating each other. The goal is building a new team culture that assumes flexibility and then problem-solves to make it work for everyone.

Talk about how work is done too. Ask employees how they work when they feel most productive, energized, and focused. Encourage employees to work that way at least some of the time. Start team discussions about how you can collaborate and communicate as needed while people are working in these different ways. Ask employees to share examples of how they have changed their everyday routines in ways that work for them.

Recognize that concentrated time (often offline) is needed for getting real work done well. Constant interruptions and multitasking do not make for good knowledge work or foster creativity and innovation. Support employees who want to unplug for a few hours to work on particular tasks or for personal time. This is particularly important in companies with active Slack or IM conversations or organizations where emails fly back and forth with many people expected to weigh in. Discuss, as a team, what counts as an urgent need to interrupt that blocked time and how to reach one another in that situation.

Investigate performance problems to see what the issues really are for a particular employee, rather than assuming that flexible work patterns are the problem. For example, if an employee who works remotely or has a different schedule is not performing well, do not assume that coming back into the office full time or working standard hours is the solution. Explore what would work better for that person and the team, but don't frame flexible work as a privilege that can be revoked.

Be sure your own evaluations of who is performing well and who is a star are not really evaluations of who has always-on availability. Check that you are not rewarding employees based on long hours, instant responsiveness to emails, texts, or chat messages, or a willingness to prioritize work above all else. Do not praise people for how quickly they respond to you. There may be some times that quick responses and late nights are indeed required, but recognize it as a problem if that is the norm.

For positions that seem to require high availability and responsiveness (like client managers or technical support), consider having two or three employees assigned to maintaining one relationship or monitoring one system. The teams that were responsible for getting the IT systems back online at TOMO did well under STAR in part because they already had routines for rotating who was on call. Many people could be reached when needed, but only one person needed to be online, ready to respond in a moment. Joint relationship management happens at some law and consulting firms too. Like job-sharing where two people work part-time to cover a full-time role, this strategy requires building new routines and developing trust, but it pays off with time fully away from work.

Acknowledge and support people's lives and priorities outside of work. Ask about what is happening outside of work and encourage employees' efforts to do what matters to them. Be sure that parents and caregivers feel supported and also check that employees who do not have obvious family responsibilities (but do have friends and personal priorities) feel heard and respected too.

Change up your own work routines to fit in your personal, family, or health commitments. Do that publicly and without guilt, as a role model for working in more sustainable ways.

Many of these changes are simple and may even seem like the basics of good management. But many organizations have well-established cultures and incentives that push in a different direction—toward work intensification and getting more and more from employees and from frontline managers. In that situation, a team that begins operating in the way we have described here will create a counterculture at odds with the dominant culture.[1] Managers who pursue this path need to be prepared to explain why these changes are working well for their teams and to go to bat for employees who are criticized for acting in accord with the team's culture. It helps to have documented evidence of success in meeting deadlines and goals to reassure others who worry about these changes. (See the section called "What Actually Changes, on the Ground?" in chapter 5 for more on how frontline managers help work redesign initiatives succeed.)

Ideas for Individuals

What can an individual employee do to address overload and help create a better work environment when their employer and manager remain stuck in work-intensification mode? This is a tricky question for us because we do not believe individual behavior changes are effective on their own, or at least they are not sufficient for the institutional reforms we see as essential. There is also a real risk that employees who go against strong expectations for always-on availability, long hours, and getting it done no matter what may well be penalized by their supervisors and, at worst, targeted for termination. Standing out in a culture that accepts overload as inevitable feels like a gamble, and we can't advise on whether that gamble is a good one.

Still, we share some ideas here for small changes that may help others see the possibilities for working differently. These can be thought of as trial balloons to see whether the broader team or company culture adapts or pushes back, preparing you and others for broader and more collective changes.

> *Do not talk about long hours, working on vacation, interrupting sleep for work, and so on as a personal badge of honor.* Those (self)-congratulatory conversations reinforce an expectation that ideal workers will work intensively and ignore the costs of those practices for individuals, families, and the company.

Do not joke about work from home as time to eat bonbons, do laundry, or otherwise slack off. If others on your team are not doing their part to meet team goals, talk to them or to a supervisor rather than blaming their work practices. Many white-collar, professional, technical, and managerial workers (including us!) find that their most productive days are those quietly focused workdays at home, but there are also some work-at-home days that are quite unproductive. That variation in productivity occurs when people are working in the office too.

Do not comment on people's hours or how long it has been since you've seen them in the office. This reinforces the expectation that face time is valued and that work only counts if it happens in a certain place, as we described in chapter 4.[2]

Think about when, where, and how you are working when you feel most productive, energized, and focused. Talk with your manager or team about how you can work that way more often. Discuss how you can collaborate and communicate as needed. (See the earlier note, where managers initiate these conversations, but you can too.)

Consider blocking time offline for real work and discuss communication plans with your manager or team first. (See note to managers on this too.)

Broach the topic (cautiously) of trimming low-value work. You and your coworkers may recognize that certain tasks and meetings actually detract from getting the real work accomplished. You might want to begin by simply mentioning the lost productivity of unnecessary work or how particular activities crowd out the most important tasks.

Do not accept every meeting or call automatically. When you're asked to join a meeting, ask for clarification on the agenda, how you will contribute, or how the conversation is related to your primary goals and then decline the meeting if that is not clear. In this book we share stories of this happening often in STAR, but we recognize this response could get you in trouble in some workplaces. Discuss this strategy with your manager and explain the other work you are prioritizing (or the need to prioritize something personal).

Change up your own work routines to fit in your personal, family, or health commitments. Share that within your team, without guilt. It is especially useful for men to share that they are making adjustments at work because of their personal and family commitments. Mothers are often assumed to be taking care of family needs but may be penalized for doing so.

Support your coworkers' efforts to make their work sustainable and to meet their personal priorities. Offer to cover a meeting or to share notes from a call, for example, and convey that you see their personal lives as important, rather than a hassle. Be sure to do this for people of all ages, life stages, family types, and genders.

Share when you are feeling overloaded or when a particular task or time line is not realistic, from your perspective. This is challenging in settings where you have been expected to somehow do whatever is asked, but it is important to disrupt the assumption that work can expand and intensify without consequence. We have heard employees ask managers questions like "Which of my tasks would you like me to set aside, now that I need to focus on X?" or "We have talked about these six priorities, but I need you to tell me which one to treat as my top priority and whether anyone else can take something from this list."

If you're feeling burned out, that your health is at risk, or you are considering leaving the job because of its intensity or hours, say so and say it to multiple people. This may give you leverage to push for change. Even if changes don't happen, it sends a signal to the company that the current situation is problematic. Again this is particularly important for men, because women are often assumed to make career choices based on work–life balance while men are not.

These changes—particularly when multiple changes are pursued together and when others join in—may dislodge old expectations and prepare the way for redesigning work more fully.

NOTES

⌘

Chapter 1. Old Rules, New Realities

1. See Arne Kalleberg's (2009, 2011) description of good jobs and bad jobs and the polarization of American work. Economists often focus on wages as the primary measure of good jobs, but we adopt a broader perspective on job quality similar to Kalleberg's.

2. We build on the dual-agenda approach developed by Lotte Bailyn, Deborah Kolb, and their colleagues to pursue the dual goals of enhancing gender equity (often by addressing work–life challenges) and improving work effectiveness. See Bailyn (2006), Fletcher, Bailyn, and Blake Beard (2009), and Rapoport et al. (2001). Throughout the book, we use "dual agenda" broadly to refer to organizational changes that address both work effectiveness and workers' ability to live healthy lives and pursue their personal or family commitments.

3. The Work, Family, and Health Network was an interdisciplinary research team that was funded by a cooperative agreement through the National Institutes of Health and the Centers for Disease Control and Prevention: Eunice Kennedy Shriver National Institute of Child Health and Human Development (Grant # U01HD051217, U01HD051218, U01HD051256, U01HD051276), National Institute on Aging (Grant # U01AG027669), Office of Behavioral and Social Sciences Research, and National Institute for Occupational Safety and Health (Grant # U010H008788, U01HD059773). Grants from the William T. Grant Foundation, Alfred P. Sloan Foundation, and the Administration for Children and Families provided additional funding. The contents of this publication are solely the responsibility of the authors and do not necessarily represent the official views of these institutes and offices. You can learn more about this collaborative study in appendix 2, as well as chapters 4, 5, and 6 where we review specific findings from TOMO. The research team conducted a parallel study in thirty long-term care sites, which are commonly called nursing homes. The STAR initiative was customized for that workforce and that industry's concerns, with some positive effects. See Berkman et al. (2015), Hammer et al. (2016), Hurtado et al. (2016), Kossek et al. (2019), and Marino et al. (2016). Analysis of the nursing home study is still ongoing, and new publications will be posted at www.workfamilyhealthnetwork.org.

4. For studies of hourly service workers, see Schneider and Harknett (2019), Henly and Lambert (2014), and Newman (1999). For research on professional elites, see Blair-Loy (2003), Perlow (2012), Ho (2009), Wynn and Rao (2019), and Epstein et al. (2014). For an important comparison of workers' experiences and family life across class locations, see Cooper (2014).

5. See note 3 and appendix 2 for information on the funders. Our wonderful collaborators and their roles are also described in appendix 2.

6. This is a classic sociological question, often associated with Everett Hughes (see Strauss 1996), that is meant to direct attention to the possibility of institutional change. Historical research and cross-national studies also help people see that other social systems, institutional rules, and everyday practices are feasible. There is a reason that so many popular press articles about

parental leaves and public childcare start with Sweden or other Nordic countries; those comparisons are intended to reassure Americans that public policies might be otherwise without giving up a generally healthy economy.

7. This quote is attributed to Lewin, whose research is foundational for the field of organizational development. Lewin is also said to have said "nothing is so practical as a good theory" (see https://en.wikiquote.org/wiki/Kurt_Lewin). Phyllis regularly heard her mentor and friend Urie Bronfenbrenner, a famous developmental psychologist, claim that "nothing was more useful to further basic, theory-driven scholarship than research on a particular policy" as it was implemented.

8. Perceptions that mothers are less committed and less competent, while fathers are particularly dedicated and likely to be good workers, run deep and underlie well-known motherhood penalties in hiring (e.g., Correll et al. 2007).

9. A recent story on millennial burnout went viral; see Petersen (2019). Harris (2017) provides a more extended, sociological analysis of millennials' frantic efforts to do more in order to get by in an era of high inequality and low job security. He notes that many millennials "never learned to separate work and life enough to balance them" (p. 8), but recognizes that this is not simply a generational preference; instead, these patterns reflect intensified work, insecure jobs, and a need to hustle for additional gigs among those doing contingent and freelance work.

Chapter 2. Overload

1. A bit about our terminology for the different roles in the organizational hierarchy: we call all the workers who do not have managerial responsibilities "employees" or "professionals," but many corporations call these people "individual contributors." They are, of course, workers, and we use that term too. Like other white-collar organizations, TOMO uses the term manager to describe supervisors directly above the core workers in the organization chart. Managers have supervisory responsibility, including responsibility for performance reviews and related salary and bonus decisions, for at least one worker in TOMO but may supervise up to one hundred employees. We use the term "managers" and "frontline managers" for this group. Senior professionals called "leads" informally guide the work of less experienced IT professionals on their teams but they are not officially "people managers" (who do performance reviews), and so we call them employees as well. Directors oversee the work of several managers and the employees who report to them. Above managers and directors, the executive level includes vice presidents and a few senior vice presidents. An executive vice president heads the IT division and reports directly to the firm's CEO.

2. Jacobs and Gerson (2004) detail this bifurcation in their book called *The Time Divide*. See also Kalleberg (2011), Kuhn and Lorenzo (2008), Cha and Weeden (2014), and Mishel (2013). While Cha and Weeden (2014) report small declines in the 2000s, it may be that IT and other industries with extensive globalization and downsizing (in the US and other expensive markets) had different patterns.

3. Mishel (2013) describes how women's additional weeks per year contribute to this trend. On the trends for families, see Jacobs and Gerson (2004) and Boushey (2016).

4. See Kalleberg (2011) for the US situation through about 2006. For comparative analyses, see Gallie (2017) and Green (2006). Work intensity is believed to have increased because of the decline in trade unions and the rise in economic insecurity tied to offshoring and increases in the contingent and temporary workforce. Changes in technology that make it easier for management to cut out slack time and to monitor output and quality more easily also seems to foster greater intensity, although the trends in perceived intensity do not line up nicely with the introduction of key technologies (Gallie 2017).

5. See Pearlin (2010).

6. This survey measure of overload is one item from the psychological job demands scale, as conceptualized by Karasek (1979). The other two items in that scale are feeling that you need to work very hard and to work very fast in your job. See Kalleberg (2011) on changes in subjective intensity of work from the 1970s to the 2000s. Other scholars have described "overwork," usually understood as working 50+ hours per week (for example Cha and Weeden [2014]) and discussed "overload" as a feeling that there is too much to handle *across all one's roles* (Blair-Loy and Cech 2017). Brigid Schulte's book summarizing some of the same dilemmas we address discusses "overwhelm" as a subjective sense of too much to handle, again *looking across domains* (Schulte 2015). While we appreciate Schulte's wide-ranging book (and her discussion of our previous work redesign research), her focus is primarily on women's experiences and on work–life challenges. We want to bring the conversation back to work overload—on feeling there is too much to do and too few resources *with regard to one's job specifically*—because we see it is the situation at work, not necessarily the combination of work and family responsibilities, that is increasingly the root of the problem.

7. See the 2018 General Social Survey with 35% agreeing or strongly agreeing (variable: overwork), up from 27% in 2002 and 2006.

8. For example, Perlow (2012) and Reid (2015) describe expectations of responsiveness—day or night or weekend—to client questions and to coworker and manager queries, whether they are urgent or not, for management consultants. Mazmanian and Erickson (2014) argue that professional services firms (like law firms, management consulting firms, and accounting firms) do not only expect availability of their employees as a core part of evaluating their work and career potential, but these firms "are selling availability as an integral part of the product." This insight is related to economist Claudia Goldin's (Goldin 2014) analysis of the rewards for very long and specific work hours (which contribute to the gender wage gap). Goldin claims that firms pay more for these work practices in part because clients expect to be able to reach *a given person*. When a specific person is required to be available to tend a client relationship whenever the client has a need (or a question or a random thought to share), hours will stretch and instant responsiveness will likely be rewarded. In healthcare, availability expectations vary across occupations, as Clawson and Gerstel (2014) and Briscoe (2007) show. Those who are responsible primarily for direct care work, such as nurses, nursing assistants, and EMTs, have more set, bounded work hours but need to be reached to renegotiate schedules. Doctors, on the other hand, are more available for questions outside of their clinic hours and many MDs have sought certain types of practices because they can put a limit on how often and how much they are on call or informally available to patients.

9. Wynn (2018) identifies similar characteristics of long hours, constant availability, limited control over schedules, and face time in her study of management consultants. She uses the term "everwork" and describes this as a "supercharged evolution of the ideal worker norm." Our conceptualization of overload and intensive work was developed before we read Wynn's work and in a different industry.

10. See Kurutz (2018) for the pharmacist quote, Conlon (2016) for an example of nurses' tips for managing long hours, and Wollan (2016) on lunch breaks.

11. To adjust for other potential predictors of overload, we estimate a logit model where a variety of work and personal characteristics predict reporting overload (i.e., agreeing or strongly agreeing that there is not enough time to do their job). This model is based on 956 IT professionals and managers who completed our baseline survey. Conclusions were identical with probit and ordinary least squares models. Those who working 50+ hours are 2.48 times more likely than others to report overload. (A parallel model with a continuous measure of work hours suggests that each additional hour increases the odds of reporting overload by 13%.) Respondents who report working at least 10 hours per week in the evenings, nights, and early morning are 1.46 times more likely to report overload while those who work at least 4 weekend days per month are 1.74 times more likely to do so. This is an additive model, so employees and managers reporting long hours *and* working nights, mornings, and weekends are even more likely to feel this overload.

Even net of hours worked, managers are 1.8 times more likely than nonsupervisory employees to feel overload. Project managers (who coordinate projects across the software development functions but have no formal authority over the analysts, developers, and testers on those projects) are also 2.25 times more likely to feel overload than the reference category of software developers. Women are 1.8 times more likely to report overload than men in this IT workforce. We discuss gender differences later in this chapter.

IT professionals and managers are significantly *less likely* to feel overloaded when they report that they have more control over when and where they work (our schedule control measure) and when they feel more supported by their supervisors regarding their family and personal lives (our family-supportive supervisory behaviors measure). These aspects of the work environment are primary targets in the STAR intervention, as we explain in chapter 4.

12. Family caregiving demands do increase the odds that employees and managers feel that work conflicts or interferes with family, but they do not matter for overload. Being married or partnered (vs. single) does not predict overload either. Those who have a spouse who is not employed or working part-time are marginally less likely to feel there is not enough time to get their job done. This is intriguing because a spouse or partner at home may free people to work longer hours—since someone else can take up more of the housework or carework tasks—but here we see some evidence that there is a boost even after accounting for work hours. Perhaps those with a spouse or partner available at home are able to focus more fully on their work while working.

13. Chapter 3 discusses those expectations and the job insecurity that encourages compliance with them. Later chapters address how technologies can be used in ways that help employees tame overload—not only as a conduit of overload. See also Mazmanian, Orlikowski, and Yates (2013), who point out that professionals and managers often understand their technology use to be their choice rather than a compelled response to management pressures, and Wajcman (2015). Perlow (2012) documents how coworkers reinforce expectations of availability.

14. Clawson and Gerstel (2014) compare the schedules, disruptions, and controls of four different occupations in the healthcare sector. They note that unpredictability (including changes to schedules and unexpected overtime work, among other things) happens so often that it cannot be understood as unexpected, but the timing of those schedule issues or extra work is not known. This unpredictability is less common for nurses, who have more leverage in the labor market because it is difficult to recruit and retain these credentialed professionals, and more challenging when organizations are lean and any individual's absence throws an already tight system into chaos. As we will discuss in chapter 3, the IT professionals and managers at TOMO had little leverage to demand stability or limited hours both because the organization was already running lean after downsizing and because these workers worried about losing their jobs to contractors or offshore workers.

15. See Becker et al. (2018). Unfortunately, our surveys did not ask the TOMO professionals and managers about availability norms or pressure to be reachable at any time.

16. Our cut-offs here are at least 10 hours per week of evening or night work and at least 4 weekend days per month (or roughly half of the available weekend days). We also estimated multivariate models that include total hours, these measures of "stretched" hours, and other characteristics. In these regression models, night and morning work and weekend work are significant predictors when we include a categorical measure of work hours (50+ vs. less than 50 hours per week) but do not reach statistical significance in the model with continuous work hours. That is likely because there is a correlation between working these specific times and working more hours, overall.

17. See Hamermesh and Stancanelli (2015); this analysis is not limited to professionals and managers or to salaried white-collar workers, so it is not directly comparable to our TOMO study.

18. For the best estimates of exposure to unstable and unpredictable schedules, see Lambert et al. (2014). For research on retail workers, in particular, see Henly and Lambert (2014), Henly et al. (2006), and Schneider and Harknett (2019).

19. Stable routines are particularly important for children and adolescents, of course, and the predictability of parents' schedules and support available at work affects their experiences and their children's well-being. See, for example, Carillo et al. (2017), Johnson et al. (2012), Perry-Jenkins (2014).

20. In other white-collar workplaces, including our previous research in the headquarters of Best Buy Co., Inc., employees who are double- and triple-booked in meetings scheduled at the same time are viewed as having high status. Being double-booked is viewed, in these organizational cultures, as a sign of one's importance or value to the firm. But these people cannot actually attend all those meetings. With conference calls, some people at TOMO try to do just that.

21. On technology and work interruptions (which become the work itself), see Barley, Meyerson and Grodal (2010), Mazmanian, Orlikowski, and Yates (2013), Perlow (2012), Bird and Rieker (2008), Klotz and Rosen (2017), and Berdahl, Glick, and Alanso (2017). On the ways these technologically mediated communications remake bureaucracy, see Turco (2016).

22. In TOMO, phone calls between two people (as opposed to conference call meetings) seem to be reserved for issues that are either urgent—such as calling someone to inform them of an outage or other technical problem—or viewed as contentious or touchy. Because phone calls

can be more forthright and private, managers tend to view an escalation—which is reporting a problem to a higher-level manager—as less aggressive when it happens by phone rather than in an email that can be referred to later or forwarded to a larger audience.

23. We learned more about these work practices as we did our fieldwork in TOMO and unfortunately did not ask about multitasking or interruptions in our early surveys. See Perlow (1999) for an older example of real work getting pushed to evenings and nights because of excessive meetings; today, though, the technologies allow people to be easily reached at any and all times.

24. Employees and managers with more schedule control, i.e., more choice in when and where they work, are significantly less likely to feel overloaded; see note 8. "Virtual face time" in which the employee can work offsite but needs to be available via IM, email, or phone can also be problematic. But it seems to be less burdensome than being pressured to be on-site, in the office, for long workdays *and also* available via electronic means in the evenings, nights, mornings, and weekends.

25. These beliefs have also been articulated in Williams (2000) and Bailyn (2006). See also the literature on "flexibility stigma" (Williams, Blair-Loy, and Berdahl 2013) and on the benefits of "passing" by hiding flexible work patterns (Reid 2015).

26. See Noonan and Glass (2012), quote on page 40. See also Glass and Noonan (2016) and Blair-Loy (2009).

27. The other work exposures studied are unemployment, lack of health insurance, limited social support at work, and a sense that management decisions are not fair or just. The Goh, Pfeffer, and Zenios studies examine self-reported health, self-reported mental health, physician diagnosed health conditions (or chronic illnesses), and mortality. Many of these work conditions are as consequential or more consequential for these health outcomes as exposure to secondhand smoke. See summary in Pfeffer (2018) and details in Goh et al. (2015a, 2015b).

28. Because we began interviewing frontline managers and added employees as the STAR redesign was launched, this section of the book relies more heavily on managers' perspectives than on nonsupervisory employees' perspectives. Managers in our sample were working more intensively than employees (with longer hours on average, more overload reported) and they were dealing with health concerns themselves, perhaps because they were a few years older on average. But we also asked managers for their perspective on how work affected the employees who reported to them. Most of the quotes in this section come from interview questions asking "What do you hear, if anything, from your employees about how their jobs affect their health? Their personal life? Or what do you notice?" and "What is it like to be a manager here, in terms of your own personal life or your health?"

29. It is hard to conclusively tie any health condition or crisis to specific work conditions or work stress, of course. But Melissa's description of her diagnosis makes it clear that she was told stress contributed to her stroke. We should also note that Melissa's stroke occurred after STAR, the initiative we describe later in the book, was launched. Melissa described STAR very positively and reported that her employees were happier and healthier with these changes. But Melissa's director still expected her to be in the office at least four days a week and be available for extended hours, even after STAR. Additionally, around the time STAR rolled out to her team, Melissa's team doubled in size—because another manager was laid off—and her workload increased further.

30. Alexandra Michel's (2011) study of investment bankers delves into the ways that intensive work transforms the body. She also identifies how these younger professionals first railed against their bodies, seeing their bodies as objects to be disciplined or mastered and viewing health crises and exhaustion as challenges to push through. Over time, some of these bankers began to understand their bodies as subjects, as guides from whom they could listen and learn about when work intensity had become counterproductive. Perhaps because our TOMO IT professionals and managers were older than the young bankers, we had the sense that bodies—illnesses and limitations—were viewed sympathetically and as long-suffering companions. Some, like Sherwin, took health crises to heart and reorganized their sleep, their exercise, and their work practices to support their bodies better. As noted in chapter 1, STAR provided an opportunity and legitimation for those changes for Sherwin and other TOMO employees.

31. We use the K-6 measure of psychological distress (R. C. Kessler et al. 2003) in our surveys. These findings are from bivariate analysis of overload or hours and these well-being outcomes.

32. These findings come from an analysis with Anne Kaduk and Katie Genedek that analyzes the first employee survey at TOMO. These findings about involuntary variable schedules are net of personal characteristics, socioeconomic status, family demands, work hours, and numerous other measures of the work environment, and also account statistically for the clustering of employees in work groups. See Kaduk et al. (2019).

33. These findings are based on 618 IT employees for whom we have at least three days of valid actigraphy data; the actigraphy study did not include managers. See Olson et al. (2015).

34. In our study, sleep quality is measured here by questions asking employees to rate their sleep (reporting "bad" or "fairly bad" sleep) and asking how often you wake feeling rested ("never" or "rarely" waking rested). Unstable work schedules also predict poor sleep quality in a very different workforce, as Schneider and Harknett (2019) find in their study of retail workers.

35. For reviews of the research on work–family conflict, see Schieman et al. (2009), Michel et al. (2011), and Kelly et al. (2014).

36. See also Schieman (2013), Schieman and Glavin (2008), Chesley (2005, 2011, 2014), and Chesley and Moen (2006).

37. See Clawson and Gerstel (2014) for this term and an analysis of unpredictability in different healthcare occupations.

38. We do not have semistructured interviews with family members and that type of research would be valuable as well; couple analyses has been central to some of our earlier work (Moen 2003), and there is more to learn about current work conditions and couple dynamics. One recent study found that employees who feel their organization expects them to monitor their email after regular work hours are more anxious and that their spouses are, in turn, more anxious and less satisfied with their relationships (Becker et al. 2018).

39. See Ramarajan and Reid (2013). Padavic, Ely, and Reid (2019) argue that there is a "social defense" operating in which executives may prefer to define the problem of gender inequality as a work–family challenge. According to these authors, a work–family framing highlights women's supposed conflicts but overlooks the broad experience of overload; it also relieves management from taking other actions to address gender inequality in workplaces.

40. Classic research by Mirowsky and Ross (1998) finds that women are more expressive of emotions on surveys and also that they face more distress, even after adjusting for expressiveness. Rosenfeld and Mouzon (2013) provide a thorough review of research on gender and mental health.

41. See Cooper (2000), Williams (2010), and Berdahl et al. (2018) on work as a "masculinity contest" where men prove themselves as real men by their strength and stamina as well as toughness and competitiveness.

42. See Shows and Gerstel (2009) where they compare fathers who are doctors and fathers who are emergency medical technicians.

43. The men who did more daily care and mental labor included single fathers, men who were married to women in even higher-status professional jobs (such as attorneys or doctors), and a few men married to women whose jobs were so inflexible (such as teachers) that the men were cast in the role of the "default parent" who could be called when a child was sick or who might be able to take an hour off during the day for a school conference. Our survey sample included some professionals and managers in same-sex partnerships and marriages, but only a couple of our interview respondents were in same-sex families (and none openly identified as trans, nonbinary, or bisexual). So we are not able to investigate how LGBT employees at TOMO experience overload.

44. See Glavin et al. (2011), who find, in a large Canadian survey of employed adults, that being contacted by work when at home is more distressing to women and that is because women are more likely to feel guilty about those work interruptions. See also Nomaguchi et al. (2005) on similar levels of "time squeeze" for moms and dads, but a greater impact on moms' distress.

45. Of course, not all marriages and partnerships are heterosexual. We have about twenty survey respondents who are partnered or married and in a same-sex relationship; we did not ask about sexual orientation directly so can only report based on the gender of a spouse or partner. Other research suggests lesbian couples have a more equal division of paid and unpaid work than do other couples (Shafer et al. 2017). No one we interviewed who was in a same-sex marriage or partnership had a spouse/partner who was working less than full time. We expect that these spouses and partners would also be frustrated by long hours and interruptions—as we heard from one gay man who described his husband's annoyance with his work patterns in an interview—and that the spouse's own work commitments would affect the TOMO employee's overload in same-sex couples too.

46. These figures come from an analysis of 590 TOMO respondents in heterosexual couples that was led by sociologist Emily Shafer (2017). Women partnered to men working these long hours report greater stress and report lower relationship quality, specifically less "affectual solidarity" as measured by questions about feeling understood by, cared about by, and relaxed around one's spouse or partner. In contrast, men's stress and relationship quality is not affected by their partner's long hours, net of their own work situation. See also Becker and Moen (1999), Maume (2006), and Stone (2007).

47. See Chesley (2011) and Kramer, Kelly, and McCulloch (2015).

48. See Acker (1990), quotes from page 149.

49. These dynamics were recently summarized in a New York Times article titled "Women Did Everything Right. Then Work Got 'Greedy'" (Miller 2019). See Cha and Kim Weeden (2014) and Goldin (2014) for gender differences in work hours and how that increasingly fuels the

gender wage gap. On institutionalized expectations and "opting out," see Stone (2007) and Moen and Roehling (2005). See Cha (2010) on men's and women's job exits in response to their spouses' long hours.

50. See Albiston (2010) and research by Michel (2011) on the transformation of bodies with intensive work.

51. See Cooper (2000) and also Berdahl et al. (2018). Chang (2018) describes long hours and overload in Silicon Valley today, though she frames this as a work–family concern rather than a set of unsustainable and unwise practices that affect most employees.

Chapter 3. How We Got Here and Why It Matters

1. These were not our primary research questions when we came into TOMO, and we did not set up our interviews to ask directly about the perceived sources of overload (although we heard in detail about the experiences of overload). Instead, this is an inductive analysis—one we pieced together to make sense of that puzzle once it became clear how pervasive overload and related practices were.

2. See Boushey (2016), Perea (2011), and the National Domestic Workers Alliance (www .domesticworkers.org) on current campaigns to incorporate domestic workers, like nannies and cleaners, into US labor standards.

3. Professionals like attorneys and doctors were not usually embedded within large organizations at the time the Fair Labor Standards Act of 1938 was written; instead, they operated in their own practices and presumably set their own hours and work conditions. They were credentialed and regulated, in a sense, by their professional associations. There were also many fewer salaried knowledge workers like the IT professionals we studied, at the time these labor laws were crafted. The primary divisions in industrial workplaces were between management (who were salaried) and blue-collar workers (who were hourly workers, covered by labor laws regulating hours and the ability to unionize); see Kalleberg (2011) and Cappelli (1999). The FLSA exempt rules are based on annual earnings being paid on a salaried rather than hourly basis, and the type of work done (or "duties" test). Almost all managers who have a say in hiring, firing, or evaluation of employees are exempt. Deciding on the status of professionals may be more complicated. These workers are described as having "advanced knowledge" and doing work that "involves the exercise of discretion and judgment." The only TOMO employees in our study who might not have been exempt were the few administrative assistants and coordinators who were surveyed but not interviewed.

4. See Boushey (2016) or the National Partnership for Women and Families (www .nationalpartnership.org) on state and municipal leave and sick time laws. See Berg, Bosch, and Charest (2014) for the idea that the US has unilateral working time practices and comparisons to other countries.

5. For research on workaholism as a psychological trait or state, see Burke and Fiksenbaum (2009) and McMillan and O'Driscoll (2008).

6. See Blair-Loy (2003), Blair-Loy and Cech (2017), and Pugh (2015, p. 21). Michele Lamont's (1992, 2000) research demonstrates that both working class and professional men in the US draw

strong symbolic boundaries between those who work hard, which is evidenced in part by a willingness to take on unpleasant work and put in whatever hours are needed or requested by management, and those who do not. For arguments connecting masculinity (particularly white-collar, middle-class masculinity) to ideal worker norms and long hours, see Cooper (2000), Townsend (2002), and Williams (2000, 2010).

7. See Perlow (2012). Although the schema of work devotion is prominent in US culture and reinforced in many organizations, individuals may not necessarily embrace it. Even in Blair-Loy's (2003) original study of elite women in finance, only about half of women were fully and enthusiastically work devoted. Even when employees do not *want* to work this way and do not experience intensive work as a validation of their identity as moral workers or as professionals, they know that engaging in intensive work (and being seen to do so) is required to get ahead. For example, Ofer Shraone (2004) found that in an IT workforce with competitive performance reviews but little clarity on how performance is judged, employees set ambitious deadlines for themselves and then work very long hours to try to meet those in order to demonstrate their commitment and readiness for promotion.

8. See Hochschild (1997) and Gideon Kunda's (2009) classic ethnography of an engineering firm for more examples of how organizational cultures create "normative control" over workers. Professional identities can also be a source of normative control; for example, Blair-Loy and Cech (2017) find that women scientists who embrace work devotion feel less overloaded. Also see Gerstel and Clawson (2014) on the lure of an organizational culture that recognizes one's efforts and work identity.

9. On shareholder value as a primary focus and declines in working conditions for professionals and managers, see Fligstein and Shin (2004). Firms may also cut costs by reducing capital investments (such as new equipment or maintenance of old equipment) or by trying to skimp on research and development. "Short-termism" or a primary focus on "making the numbers" expected by financial analysts often drives management behavior. Graham, Harvey, and Rajgopal (2005) found that "managers describe a trade-off between the short-term need to 'deliver earnings' and the long-term objective of making value-maximizing investment decisions," and "a surprising 78% of the surveyed executives would give up economic value in exchange for smooth earnings." See also Rahmandad, Henderson, and Repenning (2018) and Kochan (2015).

10. We emphasize insecurity but do not use the terms "precarious work" or "precarity" because the TOMO employees and managers we are studying are still in regular jobs rather than contingent or contracted work. Furthermore, their higher salaries and better benefits mean they are not currently, i.e., while they keep these jobs, economically vulnerable. Our argument is that the background of precarious work and declining opportunities to find high-paying and stable jobs affects even these privileged professionals and managers—but we want to distinguish their current situation from workers facing dire and immediate economic challenges. See Kalleberg and Vallas (2018) for a recent discussion of varying definitions of precarious work.

11. See Kalleberg (2011, p. 154), as well as Peter Cappelli's early description of the "frightened worker model" (1999) and McGovern and colleagues' (2007) review of Marx's claims and recent evidence on market discipline prompting long work hours and intensive work practices.

12. Harris (2017, p. 70).

13. The links between rising insecurity, declining worker power, and intensified work are suggested by others as well, including Kalleberg (2011) and Burchell, Ladipo, and Wilkinson (2002). But sociological and organizational research has rarely explored these connections fully or delved into the subjective experiences and specific workplace practices that combine to create these pressures; for one exception, now almost twenty years ago, see Smith (2001). Yet even some studies that emphasize normative control have, lurking in the background, a hint that job insecurity and related management practices are drivers of the intense demands and overload. In fact, when Kunda (1992, 2006) and Hochschild (1997) revisit their firms in epilogues to their classic ethnographies, they see those strong and appealing organizational cultures being crowded out by leaner and meaner practices with increased insecurity and pressure. Two studies of IT workers also point out management pressures (Cooper 2000) and employability concerns in a reward system that "ranks and yanks" routinely (Sharone 2004). Pugh (2015, p. 23) argues that "some of this behavior is driven by fear—if you perceive you are more likely to lose your job, you may work harder to make the employer want to keep your job," but then turns back to work attachment and identities in her analysis.

14. In the US, the Fair Labor Standards Act requires wage premium for hours worked beyond 40 hours per week unless employees are exempt from the overtime rule. Salaried employees who earn more than about $47,000 per year and who do executive or professional work are exempt from the overtime pay requirements. See https://www.dol.gov/whd/overtime_pay.htm.

15. The fact that labor costs seem to go down when staff are cut or cheaper workers hired offshore leads the popular press to claim that "Wall Street Loves Layoffs" (La Monica 2013) and "Layoffs Make CEOs Look Like Heroes—That's Why Corporate America is Sick" (McGee 2014). The actual relationship between downsizing and subsequent stock market performance is more complicated, depending on the market's perceptions of whether demand is low for the firm's products, whether other firms in the industry are also cutting labor, and the size of the cuts (Brauer and Zimmerman 2017). But it is clear that downsizing and offshoring have indirect costs (in terms of lost sales, lost innovation, low morale, high workload, and exits by some of the strongest performers) that mean "many of the anticipated benefits of employment downsizing do not materialize" (Cascio 2010). See also Maertz et al. (2010).

16. "Agile" development represents a different process and philosophy that is deliberately less linear and involves more interactions between the clients or end users and the coders. See Repenning et al. (2017).

17. For example, Padavic, Ely, and Reid's (2019) study of work intensification and overload among management consultants discusses "overselling and overdelivery," in which managers offer unrealistic project scope or time lines to clients and sometimes push their subordinates to go above and beyond the stated work product to try to impress the client (or others inside the consulting firm) with the depth or sophistication of their analysis.

18. Others have recognized that those who solve problems are rewarded while those who instead work in ways that avoid problems in the first place are not. For example, see discussions of rewards for "arsonist firefighters" (Ely and Meyerson 2000a, Kelly et al. 2010, Perlow 1997). Jude also highlights the fact that the experts' or professionals' standards are more detailed and nuanced than the quick assessment made by the project manager and reported up to senior management.

19. TOMO officially discourages inaccurate hours reporting and, in fact, requires every employee and contractor to complete annual "compliance training" that stresses the need to report hours accurately. For that reason, we do not provide any more detail on the respondent's role or personal life in this quote. Hiding or "eating" hours likely occurs in other industries where projects are billed by the hour but clients are believed to be sensitive to the project cost. Salaried professionals may "eat" those hours, putting in unacknowledged overtime and undercutting future projects' budgets by creating unrealistic expectations. But independent contractors also bid low, promising a task in fewer hours than they know it will take and so effectively cutting their actual hourly pay rate, in order to get new business.

20. See Repenning and Sterman (2001, p. 75) as well as other research by these two scholars and their colleagues on the "capability trap."

21. McGovern et al. (2007, pp. 138–40) in large survey of British workforce. In that data from 2000, 27% of workers had seen workforce decrease (downsizing) in the past three years. In our data from TOMO, downsizing happened so often that everyone in our study would have reported a recent "exposure" to the stress of losing coworkers.

22. Other research finds evidence that the insecurity and uncertainty common in organizations that have downsized and shifted to more contracted or temporary workers is associated with less cooperation and less effective collaboration. See research by Crowley and Hodson (2014).

23. We find no relationship between subjective overload and organizational citizenship behaviors while longer work hours predict *more* of this pitching in (although the causal direction may be that those who assist coworkers end up working longer).

24. The debate on the extent and specific locations of substantial job loss is on-going, but see Autor et al. (2003) and Michaels et al. (2013) on the risk to lower- and moderate-skilled jobs.

25. Given the parameters of our research agreement with the firm, we calculated these estimates based on publicly available salary data for software developers and engineers in the US and India rather than data on TOMO's labor costs in the US and India. The 10–25% estimates provided here are based on a) comparing the median salary of a software developer in TOMO's headquarters city to the median salary of a software developer in the offshore city with the largest TOMO staff, using payscale.com, and b) comparing IT software engineers with ten years of experience in the US and in India, using wageindicator.org. This latter comparison likely understates the cost difference between the US and India because our respondents noted that Indian staff were often new graduates, while US employees were experienced professionals.

26. Our study is limited to employees in the US and so we cannot compare the perspective of TOMO employees in the US to those working for TOMO in other countries. More research is needed to understand the experience of IT workers in India, including investigating what frustrates these workers about coordinating with staff in the US and how stresses and satisfaction vary depending on whether one works for a multinational firm directly or a contracting firm that subcontracts to many large firms.

27. The standardization and documentation that we discussed earlier is not explicitly motivated by the global labor strategy, but those process changes may make employees' jobs even less secure. When everyone is following the same process and when each step of a given project is thoroughly documented, the expertise—both relational and technical—of a given employee is reduced. Any person can be downsized or replaced by an offshore worker

without much risk to the project. In a more craft-oriented or integrated system, a given developer might carry deep knowledge of a business client's needs in his or her head, know those people well, and also know what strategies and approaches have already been tried to solve a particular problem. Losing that person's expertise puts the project at much greater risk (of failure or late delivery) than is the case when everyone is following standardized procedures and providing very detailed documentation.

28. This manager's advice reflects messages heard in management circles and the popular press in which workers are advised to plan "boundaryless careers" where they are always preparing for their next job, rather than expecting job security or loyalty from their employers (Cappelli 1999, Osterman 1999, Pugh 2016b).

29. The "frightened worker model" that was described by Cappelli (1999) twenty years ago works better—generates more compliance with fewer negative consequences—when employees feel that their firm is just doing what others in industry (or US economy) are doing. If employees resented the repeated downsizings, they might withdraw more of their effort or sabotage projects in quiet ways. But they are less likely to do that when they feel this is business as usual. Our interviews suggest that downsizing is routine and not questioned while the particular offshoring strategy at TOMO receives slightly more critique—though not loud or vociferous criticism even in the confidential interviews—because the inefficiencies associated with hiring the cheapest, least experienced developers or testers in India are obvious to the US-based workforce. See also McGovern et al. (2007) on the routineness of these practices and Allison Pugh's (2015) interview study describing working Americans' low expectations of their employers, particularly with regard to long-term commitments and job security.

30. We see a very different process at work in this globalized IT workforce than the normative control and internalized self-discipline (tied to professional or organizational identity or to proving masculinity by being successful in one's career and as a breadwinner) that has been stressed in many recent studies of professionals and managers. Many of these studies were conducted just before globalization and automation made job insecurity so salient to professional and managerial workers. Another possibility for the contrast between our research and the studies discussed earlier is that the professionals and managers in our study are, for the most part, in a different life stage than the young strivers is other research (including Cooper [2000], Michel [2011], and Sharone [2004]). The average age in our survey sample is forty-six years for employees and a bit older for managers. These professionals and managers are eager to keep the jobs, and good benefits, they currently have and so the links between job insecurity and intensive work may be clearer in this population. On the realities of age discrimination in hiring and older workers' recognition of the risks they face after job loss, see Moen's (2016) book called *Encore Adulthood* and research by sociologists Lassus, Lopez, and Roscigno (2015) and economist David Neumark (2016). Two papers using data from the Work, Family, and Health Study examine the additional complication of the TOMO merger announced during the course of the study (which increased perceived job insecurity) and the heavier weight of that uncertainty on the well-being of boomers as compared to younger cohorts (Lam et al. 2015, 2016). We do not foreground discussion of the merger here because the dynamics of downsizing, offshoring, and related changes in work processes were at play well before the merger was announced. Additionally, although the merger announcement increased perceived job insecurity, layoffs did not increase within the IT

division in the first two years after the merger announcement. In other contexts, though, mergers may prompt downsizing and be the immediate catalyst for high demands and lean staffing that we describe here.

31. If this is the case, then avoiding the problems associated with this intensity and overload requires changing the cost structure for the firm. For example, higher corporate taxes might offset the lost productivity from health problems and early retirements and partially address the limited investments these workers can make in community life. Corporate taxes might also be increased for firms relying on offshore labor, effectively decreasing the labor cost savings of pushing work offshore (with onshore workers taking on additional coordination work). Alternatively, labor law might be revised to provide overtime pay for workers classified as professionals and managers too, in hopes of discouraging the work practices and related problems.

32. The results summarized here are from statistical models (estimated as ordinary least squares models) that adjust for a variety of personal and job characteristics. We focus on the effects of subjective overload and job insecurity, but these models also include work hours (estimated in separate models as a continuous measure and as a binary indicator of working 50+ hours), the amount of night/morning work and weekend work reported, schedule control, family-supportive supervision, job control (or decision-making autonomy), age, gender, marital status, whether the respondent has a spouse or partner available at home (as contrasted with a spouse employed full time or a single person), whether there are children under eighteen in the respondent's home, whether the respondent have caregiving responsibilities for an adult relative, whether the respondent is a manager, and a job function variable. For job satisfaction and turnover intentions, subjective overload is key; burnout is predicted by both actual hours and overload in this professional and managerial workforce.

33. See Sianoja et al. (2018). This analysis uses the daily diary substudy of TOMO IT professionals who are also parents. These employees were interviewed briefly on eight consecutive nights and reported each day on when they started and stopped each work spell, when they got in bed and went to sleep, and on questions about their work performance and specific situations at work. When IT professionals have less time off between their last spell of work one day and starting work the next day, they are more likely to forget tasks and meetings at work and have more trouble concentrating. Those findings show that limited time off between workdays matters net of total weekly work hours, sleep time, reports of stressful events at work, and time spent on childcare and housework.

34. See Rahmandad and Repenning (2016) and Repenning (2001) on firefighting (or time devoted to fixing problems after the initial development of a product or program) as a self-reinforcing process.

35. See Rahmandad and Repenning (2016) on "capability erosion dynamics." Job insecurity can also negatively affect the quality of the work and the extent of collaboration and engagement—and we have seen that TOMO has both high pressure and high insecurity. Job insecurity predicts less goodwill (as measured by agreement that managers and employees are "on the same side") and lower motivation. Downsizing seems to reduce creativity too, and those who are focused on surviving the next round of layoffs are unlikely to invest in either deepening their own skills (since the rewards are for just getting it done) or supporting their colleagues' development. See Amabile and Conti (1999), Crowley and Hodson (2014) on the effects of insecurity and downsizing.

36. See Weil (2014).

37. See Acemoglu et al. (2016), who report an 18.7% decline in US manufacturing jobs between 2000 and 2007 and then quantitatively estimate that 10% of the job decline in manufacturing can be attributed to Chinese imports directly with a larger "downstream effect."

38. See Kuruvilla and Noronha (2016) on legal offshoring, Riordan (2018) on restructuring of work processes, and Remus and Levy (2016) and Khalid (2017) on automation of legal work.

39. See Sako (2013, p. 186) and Kuruvilla and Rangathan (2008) on offshoring of various business tasks and professional work. See Blinder (2006) on which jobs and tasks are more susceptible to offshoring and Brynolfsson, Mitchell, and Rock (2018) on which jobs and tasks are more susceptible to automation.

40. On the "one-way honor system," where workers expect to give their all to their employer but do not expect job security or loyalty in return, see Allison Pugh's *The Tumbleweed Society* (2015), and Pugh (2016). On professional workers' understanding of and occasional resistance to "personal branding" as a strategy for getting and keeping work, see Vallas and Christin (2018).

41. On physician burnout, see the Agency for Healthcare Research and Quality's reports and trainings at https://www.ahrq.gov/professionals/clinicians-providers/ahrq-works/burnout /index.html. See also Gawande's (2018) aptly titled article "Why Doctors Hate Their Computers" and Babbott et al. (2014) linking technologies to physician stress. External pressures to change professional practice, combined with new technologies, have prompted healthcare organizations to give certain tasks to "semiprofessionals" (like medical assistants) who are paid much less than doctors or nurses. But it turns out to be complicated, in practice, to get the higher status professionals and the other workers to coordinate effectively, as Kellogg (2018) describes. See also Petrakaki et al. (2016).

42. This is reminiscent of Padavic et al.'s (2019) discussion of "overdelivery" in management consulting, where there is pressure to "kill the client with a 100-slide deck," even if that means excessive hours and is not of use to the client.

43. The start-up description is partially based on MBA teams Erin has advised. These student teams try to help a firm see its way through an important organizational change and those working with start-ups report story after story of confusion, exhaustion, and chaos. See also Gulati and DeSantola (2016).

44. See Cooper (2014) for a vivid description of economic anxiety and insecurity affecting upper middle class and upper class families and Lowe (2018) for a recent discussion of fear of losing this job vs. employability concerns.

Chapter 4. Dual-Agenda Work Redesign: Understanding STAR at TOMO

1. See the notes for chapter 1 as well as Bailyn (2006), which was originally published in 1993, Fletcher, Bailyn, and Blake Beard (2009) and Rapoport et al. (2001). As we discuss later on, the work redesign initiative we study does not proclaim gender equity goals explicitly (Kolb and Meyerson 1999).

2. We describe the roles of various contributors in appendix 2. See also note 3 (from chapter 1) and workfamilyhealthnetwork.org. We also relied on organizational development experts

Cali Ressler and Jody Thompson of CultureRx, the founders of ROWE. See Chapter 4, 5, appendix 2, and www.gorowe.com.

3. The next chapter describes the experimental design in more detail. See also Bray et al. (2013), Kelly et al. (2014).

4. The definition of primary prevention is elaborated in an earlier description of STAR in Kossek et al. (2014), p. 58. This approach is also described as one that targets the "organization of work."

5. See Jones, Molitor, and Reif (2018).

6. The evidence on the effects of workplace wellness programs is decidedly mixed. A review found significant and "clinically meaningful improvements in exercise frequency, smoking behavior, and weight control," and a survey of employers found most were convinced "that workplace wellness programs reduce medical cost, absenteeism, and health-related productivity losses" (Mattke et al. 2013). But few companies actually evaluate those claims carefully, and a major experimental study found no causal evidence that the wellness program affected health behaviors, self-reported health, or medical expenditures. See Jones et al. (2018).

7. See appendix 2 for more information on our collaboration with Leslie Hammer, Ellen Kossek, Kent Anger, Ryan Olson, Cali Ressler, and Jody Thompson to develop STAR by integrating workplace changes we had studied in pilot projects in a white-collar workplace and grocery stores.

8. See Karasek (1979) and Karasek and Theorell (1990) for more on the Job Demands-Control-Support model. There are many different models or theories regarding the work–health link, and many of them point to similar hypotheses. Parker, Morgeson, and Johns (2017) recently reviewed "One Hundred Years of Work Design Research" and summarize these models well. We emphasize the Job Demands-Control-Support model in our description of STAR because it is where we (Phyllis and Erin) began our thinking about schedule control when we started working together on changing workplaces and joined the Work, Family, and Health Network. This model is also appropriate for our purposes because there is a robust literature on health and well-being outcomes that explicitly investigates this model and because Karasek and Theorell (1990) consider work redesign as a strategy for improving work environments, addressing health problems, and encouraging positive well-being. The Job Demands-Resources model associated with Bakker and Demerouti (2009) also suggests that worker well-being is affected by the mix of demands and resources (including control and support, but also other work conditions).

9. Job control involves both decision authority or latitude over key decisions regarding how work is done and the sense that one's skills are utilized (Karasek and Theorell 1990). We emphasize decision authority in our discussion of job control. Schedule control is distinctive from job control, but our research shows that those who have more control over how they work (job control) also tend to have more control over when and where they work (schedule control). This is not surprising since, in many organizations, higher-status employees tend to have more autonomy and more flexibility, while those at lower ranks have less freedom to decide how they approach their tasks and are monitored more closely with regard to schedules too.

10. See Kelly et al. (2011), Moen et al. (2008), Moen, Kelly, and Hill (2011), Moen et al. (2011), Moen et al. (2013).

11. Leslie Hammer and Ellen Kossek drew on the work of Sheldon Cohen and Thomas Wills, seminal theorists of social support, to hypothesize how social support might affect positive psychological well-being and workers' performance on the job. They then identified concrete behaviors that are interpreted as indicators of managers' support for personal and family life, developed training to encourage frontline managers to enact those behaviors more consistently, and evaluated that training initiative in grocery stores as part of the network's pilot stage. Again, this form of support does not replace or fall under the older conceptualization of support from previous theory. Instead, this work emphasizes that specific forms of manager support, oriented to the employee's personal and family life, should be examined to understand job quality fully. See Hammer et al. (2009), Hammer et al. (2011), Hammer et al. (2013), Kossek et al. (2011), and Kossek et al. (2018).

12. For critiques of the "ideal worker norm," see Williams (2000), Acker (1990), Bailyn (1993/2006), and Moen and Roehling (2005). We studied ROWE as a challenge to this "gendered ideal worker norm," as described in Kelly, Moen, Chermack, and Ammons (2010).

13. Although the idea of results orientation did not arise from occupational health theories, we came to see how these messages helped people question and manage high work demands.

14. See Perlow (2012) and Turco (2016).

15. The flow of the STAR training and the detailed scripts used by facilitators can be found (and downloaded for free) at www.workfamilyhealthnetwork.org under Toolkits. Here is more information on managers' experiences, though. Managers are first oriented to the STAR initiative in a short training session with a facilitator. Employees are not present, and managers are encouraged to share any anxieties or worries about the initiative. They then complete a self-paced, computer-based training lasting about an hour. The computer-based training reviews demographic changes that mean more employees in the US also have substantial family and caregiving responsibilities, describes the impact of stress and work–family conflict on business outcomes (e.g., turnover and low employee engagement), and claims that demonstrating support for subordinates' personal and family lives can benefit both employees and the organization. In a short video, a senior TOMO executive explains his interest in STAR and urges managers to get on board. The training reviews ways managers can demonstrate "personal support" and "performance support," and asks managers to set goals for exhibiting supportive behaviors over the coming week. Managers then carry a device (an iPod Touch in our study) with an alarm reminder to log these behaviors in the installed app. A couple weeks later, each manager receives a personalized feedback chart. The feedback reminds managers of the types of supportive behaviors they concentrated on, whether they met their goals, and the mean scores for other managers in STAR. Feedback is delivered individually, and information is not shared with executives. A second self-monitoring task is completed about one month after the first. Managers also participate in a facilitated "managers only" training session toward the end of the STAR rollout where they have an opportunity to share what was working well in their teams and to ask questions of facilitators and their peers.

16. See Matos and Galinsky (2015). The National Survey of Employers study was conducted in 2014 and includes 1,051 employers with fifty or more employees. The sample includes both for-profit organizations (67%) and nonprofit organizations (33%).

17. See Kelly et al. (2010), Kelly and Moen (2007), and Kelly and Kalev (2006) for earlier discussions of the limitations of flexibility as accommodation. See also Perlow and Kelly (2014)

on contrasts between flexibility as accommodation and work redesign that attends to both workplace and personal concerns. Note that flexible hours or telecommuting is often an appropriate accommodation under the Americans with Disabilities Act, but we do not use flexibility as accommodation to refer to changes that are backed by law.

18. The same survey reveals that only 27% of organizations allow most employees to change their starting and stopping times (vs. 81%) and only 8% allow most employees to work at home occasionally (vs. 67%). See Matos and Galinsky (2015).

19. It is difficult to predict who will get flexibility even when a company has a clear policy because managers serve as gatekeepers. Sweet and colleagues (2016) examine the complicated ways that managers' characteristics and attitudes affect subordinates' flexible work practices. Leslie and colleagues (2012) find that managers' beliefs about why an employee is seeking a flexible work arrangement are critical to understanding how the work practices affect the employees' career.

20. See Golden (2001), Glauber (2011), and Swanberg et al. (2005). However, research also suggests countervailing strategies for gaining flexibility, depending on occupation. For example, Wharton, Chivers, and Blair-Loy (2008) find that hourly workers are more likely to use available flexible work policies because they are less concerned about potential negative consequences for their careers but managers are more likely to negotiate informal flexibility. Clawson and Gerstel (2014) highlight the class and gender dynamics of negotiating schedule control in different occupations.

21. There is a growing literature from lab or online experiments showing negative evaluations of workers who pursue flexible work options; see Williams et al. (2013) and Munsch (2016) for overviews. Experimental research finds strong evidence of evaluators docking the pay (and promotion likelihood) of those using flexible work arrangements, but research following workers over time is more mixed. On flex practices affecting performance ratings, see Wharton, Chivers, and Blair-Loy (2008), Leslie et al. (2012). On promotions, see Judiesh and Lyness (1999). On wages, see Glass (2004), Coltrane et al. (2013), and Goldin (2014). The research findings in this area are complex partly because it is often the high performers who win the opportunity to work in these ways—and those workers are also likely to be paid well (Kelly and Kalev 2006, Weeden 2005). Additionally, when flexible work arrangements are uncommon, those who negotiate them may put in extra effort out of gratitude that their manager or organization allowed the arrangement (Kelliher and Anderson 2010). Third, if a flexible work arrangement makes it easier for a worker to do good work (by removing strain or increasing concentration, for example) then these "happy workers" may be more productive and legitimately earn more (Konrad and Yang 2012, Weeden 2005). All of this means that there may be offsetting processes affecting the wages of people using flexible work arrangements: "flex stigma" or negative evaluations of their commitment and promise counterbalanced by financial rewards for high performance and extra effort. Men's career interruptions and part-time work is clearly penalized, though, as both lab studies by Laurie Rudman and Kris Mescher (2013) and field experiments by David Pedulla (2016) demonstrate.

22. See Reid (2015, p. 16). See also Bailyn (2006), Moen and Roehling (2005), Becker and Moen (1999).

23. See a related critique of work–family framings in Padavic, Ely, and Reid (2019).

24. There are many, many definitions of institutions in social science; we are focusing on "middle range institutions" in part because we are looking within organizations (rather than in

broader organizational fields or across the society) and because the "institutional work" literature that we draw on generally looks at this level of institutions. See Hampel, Lawrence, and Tracey (2017).

25. There are also roles that guide behavior by describing who does what and who gets to make what kinds of decisions; these roles may be codified in formal job descriptions but they are also evident in unwritten norms about what particular people can and should do. Institutions have social power. When people act in the expected ways, their actions may not even be noticed (or at least not be worthy of comment) but when people act in ways that do not align with those beliefs and common practices, they are either sanctioned or called to account by having their actions questioned.

26. Institutional work has been defined as "the practices and processes associated with actors' endeavors to build up, tear down, elaborate and contain institutions" (Hampel et al. [2017]); see also Lawrence and Suddaby (2006).

27. When STAR rolled out at TOMO, there was a partial policy change that facilitated the work redesign experience. The TOMO telecommuting policy had been that employees who wanted to regularly work from home (rather than do so on a very occasional and ad hoc basis) needed approval from their manager and the vice president above them to do that. Groups that moved into STAR were granted "blanket approval" for telecommuting with the relevant VPs signing off for all of the employees in that group, regardless of an individual person's interest or plans to work at home. This was a work-around to reassure employees they were covered under the formal policy (that required VP permission) while also conveying that STAR was changing those rules for the groups participating in the STAR pilot. A multilevel change strategy that works with top down and bottom-up changes is also advocated in recent stress intervention research tied to the occupational health literature (see Kossek et al. [2014], Semmer [2006]).

28. Again, see Bailyn (1993/2006), Rappoport et al. (2001). The focus on employees' wellbeing and particularly on their lives outside of work distinguishes a dual-agenda work redesign approach from many "job redesign" initiatives that prompt changes in employees' control over some work processes and from "lean management" initiatives that optimize efficiency or effectiveness doing work tasks, but the focus is squarely on the work domain. Employees are asked to reconsider how they get their work done, aiming to improve more productivity or quality, but there is often no attention to how work could fit better with their personal commitments (to their health, their community, their further education) or family responsibilities.

29. See Williams (2010), for example, on the ways that upper middle class masculinity assumes a work-first identity and polices men who do not perform as ideal workers. See Kelly et al. (2010) on men's interest in "working smarter" as they encountered a very similar work redesign initiative, ROWE at Best Buy Co., Inc. See also Kellogg's (2011) study of surgeons' response to a mandated decrease in work hours (to no more than 120 hours per week!). Kellogg found that those who supported the changes in work hours were more likely to be women (along with some men), while "Iron Men" who had thrived in the old system or viewed surviving long work hours as a testament to their strength and masculinity actively resisted the change. When personal and family benefits are discussed in STAR training, there is a deliberate effort to keep the discussions broad. Facilitators emphasize personal situations that are less consistently tied to women or mothers (e.g., dentist appointments, supporting an elderly parent's recovery from surgery rather than

caring for an infant) and often choose men for the few parenting-focused role-plays in the training.

30. See Lee, Mazmanian, and Perlow (2018) on the importance of creating spaces for reflection and experimentation for organizational changes that affect the social dynamics of a team. See Kellogg (2009, 2011) on "relational spaces" where advocates of institutional change can strategize together on how to promote new ways of working.

31. Both the facilitators who conduct STAR training and the TOMO insiders who pushed for STAR and guided its implementation are *institutional entrepreneurs*, "change agents" who "initiate divergent changes" (that contradict the existing institutions already operating in that setting) and "actively mobilize resources to implement change" (Battilana, Leca, and Boxenbaum 2009). This study relied on key HR managers who went well beyond a narrower understanding of HR's role as enacting compliance with employment law to imagine how work might be reorganized to address workers' needs and the firm's goals (see Dobbin 2009). These HR managers planned how to "socialize the change" with top management and how to use executives who got on board early to influence their peers. Success as an institutional entrepreneur requires excellent social skills, including empathy and deep understanding of others' interests and anxieties, and good strategy for garnering support and avoiding or defusing opposition. See Battilana et al. (2009), Fligstein (1997, 2001), and Canales (2016) on the "invisible institutional work" that is required to make the public institutional work (like STAR training sessions) succeed. Action researchers—people who work with affected groups to implement a change and study it simultaneously—need to develop some of these skills themselves and also find insider allies who can guide them through this type of project. See Hampel, Lawrence, and Tracey (2017) on "applied institutional work" conducted through participatory action research.

32. Theoretical descriptions of institutional entrepreneurship and institutional work emphasize the framing strategies (including framing the old as problematic and the new as a viable solution) and symbolic work (including drawing on larger narratives and identities that appeal to a given audience) that is required to create institutional change. Battilana et al. (2009) and Hampel et al. (2017) provide useful overviews of these literatures. See also Fletcher et al. (2009) on similar efforts to change the narrative and enable early changes ("seed carriers") in dual-agenda redesigns that draw on feminist poststructural theory.

33. These questions were asked in training sessions for all groups. We have full lists of every word shared for these ten training sessions but the types of words shared were consistent across other trainings we observed.

34. These sessions can be understood as a poststructuralist discursive intervention as well, as described in Fletcher, Bailyn, and Blake Beard (2009). From this perspective, STAR provides a discursive space in which voices that are usually silenced or marginalized are welcomed and brought into the mainstream. In this case, the marginalized voices that are given space and attention are the frontline employees and many frontline managers who recognize that current ways of working are untenable. The voices that were previously recognized as knowledgeable and legitimate are those of top management who set up the staffing plans, global labor chains, and unrealistic time lines discussed previously. See also Ewick and Silbey (1995) on "subversive stories" that challenge the taken-for-granted rules of the game.

35. Some common practices are questioned but other common practices—including the frequency of downsizing and the reliance on offshore labor—that are critical contributors to overload are not questioned explicitly in STAR. The focus is more on how the work is done (covered in chapter 2) than on the underlying business strategy and related management decisions (covered in chapter 3). This raises an important question: Do more limited changes like those put on the table with STAR help given the larger context of globalized capitalism, job insecurity, and related market pressures on firms? Our analysis finds benefits of STAR, described in later chapters, even in this context, but it is an open question how the changes we study might stack up against other changes in staffing practices or greater worker voice regarding key business decisions. This is an important area of inquiry.

36. The STAR initiative at TOMO was led by skilled and savvy outside facilitators, and we see that outsider status as useful for prompting these kinds of changes. Outsider's challenges may be heard less defensively (since the outsider isn't being disloyal by being critical) and outsiders are not working against a history of previous interactions or against the official chain of authority. They can challenge leaders in a way that insiders often can't. However, insiders who are able to get cognitive and psychological distance from the current organizational practices and norms may be able to lead these changes as well. See Debra Meyerson's work on "tempered radicals" or insiders who have firm commitments to a cause or new practices that are not currently accepted in their organization and encourage significant change through moderate, often quiet means (see Meyerson [2001a]). Perlow first developed the PTO initiative—another important work redesign—as an outside researcher, but the change efforts were led by insiders at the consulting company as the rollout expanded (Perlow 2012). We need more research comparing the success and the process of insider- and outsider-led initiatives of this type.

37. STAR sessions at TOMO were facilitated by CultureRx consultants. In this chapter, we name the two founders of CultureRx, Cali Ressler and Jody Thompson, who were intimately involved in developing STAR training but we do not name the other facilitators who delivered the training. Our observations of training sessions under multiple facilitators reassured us that TOMO teams received the same messages regardless of who led the training. The one exception was quickly dealt with; Ressler and Thompson replaced a facilitator who struggled with this audience and gave those teams additional coaching to bring them up to speed.

38. See Perlow (2012) and Kellogg (2011).

39. See chapter 3 and appendix 1 for a discussion of the intended and actual flow of the work. We now believe that STAR could have been customized better for IT by devoting more time to detailed discussions of each team's and role's actual need to respond quickly and their current routines for doing so. A standard set of questions might have helped groups recognize when they needed quick responsiveness and when those practices reflected a culture where responsiveness is rewarded and always-on availability viewed as a sign of commitment. Sharing the practices of production support teams (who had rotating pager duty and clear protocols for real emergencies) with other teams might also have led groups to see how to develop new availability expectations.

40. See Ressler and Thompson (2008).

41. Scholars have long recognized that professionals can promote institutional change (i.e., advocate for new rules of the game) by claiming that new practices will further their autonomy

as professionals. This was described in a very different case—elite French chefs' advocacy of nouvelle cuisine—by organizational scholars Rao, Monin, and Durand (2003). In our case, the discussion of professional autonomy and empowerment via STAR may also serve as a salve to counteract other recent changes that TOMO employees and managers experience as disempowering or restricting their autonomy. New models of software development can be viewed as the deskilling of technical projects that used to be guided by broadly trained and autonomous professional experts. The recent push in this firm and others has been to divide software development projects more and more narrowly, across different roles and across continents as we described in chapter 3. STAR offers employees more control over when and where the work is done *and* provides employees with a legitimate say in how some aspects of the work (like coordination via meetings) are done. Work redesign may be especially appealing for workers facing the deskilling and narrowing of their work. Top management may hope that it will offset some of the employees' frustrations with other changes in work processes. Executives at TOMO never explicitly told us that they hoped STAR and its experience of autonomy would counterbalance the perceived deskilling of professional work, but that motivation seems plausible.

42. Most of these managers rose up through the ranks of some software development role themselves, and they often had long tenure at TOMO. There is relatively little social distance (in terms of education, skills, and often common class background) between these frontline managers and the employees they supervise. Their assumption is most often that their subordinates are already capable and dedicated to meeting their work goals. In her review of another type of organizational change that also addresses the relationships of coworkers and managers, Gittell (2016, p. 10) notes that new ways of interacting "often disrupt our sense of professional identity" and "disrupt the existing, taken-for-granted, often invisible patterns of privilege and power." Because of those disruptions, these changes may be "painful . . . with many defensive reactions and false starts" (Gittell 2016, p. 10). We suggest that the pain and middle-manager resistance was minimal at TOMO because STAR was convincingly presented as consistent with the valued identities of IT professional and IT manager.

43. There were some positive effects of the customized STAR in the nursing home industry. See Hammer et al. (2016) on pitching in and safety culture, Hurtado et al. (2016) on smoking, as well as Kossek and colleagues' (2019) study that finds STAR benefited those employees who had elder care responsibilities in terms of stress and psychological distress. Okechukwu et al. (2016) also find evidence of the benefits of more family-supportive managers and cultures for the health of residents.

44. There are other real challenges with implementing a work redesign intervention like STAR in nursing homes. Each site is fairly autonomous and has its own history of change initiatives and different relationships between management and staff. Ellen Kossek and colleagues (2019) are currently analyzing how the STAR intervention unfolded across different work sites. Additionally, there are challenges that are consistent across the industry. Variable schedules and other changes in work processes are harder to implement in a tightly coordinated and regulated setting, though there are examples of successful work redesigns regarding scheduling in healthcare (Pryce, Albertsen, and Nielsen 2006) and worker input into operational decisions in many industries (see Parker et al. 2017 for a review). In long-term care, profit margins are thin and there is pressure, from headquarters, to manage labor costs very carefully—creating lean staffing

and unpredictable overtime. See Clawson and Gerstel (2014), Kossek et al. (2016). Additionally, demonstrating support for subordinates' and coworkers' personal and family lives may feel like an extra burden in an industry where emotional labor and care work demands are already very high. In short, there are many reasons that it was difficult to take STAR into nursing homes, but one of those challenges was that some frontline managers and more senior administrators did not believe their employees were actually professionals who were routinely bringing expert knowledge and their best effort to their work. Looking beyond the nursing home case, it may be more difficult to implement work redesign in unionized settings if the history of collective bargaining has reinforced an us vs. them culture. IT professionals and managers at TOMO saw their interests as aligned and there was relatively high trust in employees. While unionized workplaces vary considerably, it may be more challenging to align employees and managers' interests in shifting more *individual* control to employees when there is an established system of collective bargaining as shared management-employee control. We see unionization as a form of collective control and voice that represents an alternative—and historically important— channel for redesigning work and promoting employee health, well-being, and sustainable productivity. However, it is not a likely path in white-collar US workplaces today. We address broader changes in policy and the employment relationship further in the last chapter.

45. Sometimes the participants in a session will bring up "old-school managers," but employees and managers are generally cautious about criticizing particular people within the firm. The exception was manager-only sessions where peer managers will name a particular vice president or executive whom they view as a barrier to change. TOMO's organizational culture was not brash or highly conflictual, so managing these dynamics might be more challenging in other settings.

46. Organizational scholars Michael Lee, Melissa Mazmanian, and Leslie Perlow (2018) discuss the importance of providing "interaction scripts" that provide concrete guidance to teams trying to change how they interact. Here, teaching people to use this redirecting question ("Is there something you need?") helps lower-status employees avoid explaining themselves to a boss, which would reinstate the previous expectation that managers direct when, where, and how subordinates work. Poststructuralists also recognize that language routinely reconstitutes power and so new language is needed to shift power. See Fletcher et al. (2009) applying a feminist poststructural perspective to dual-agenda work redesign initiatives.

47. Managers' anxiety needs to be carefully managed so that these critical players feel their worries have been heard but they are also encouraged to experiment and to allow employees to begin making changes. The private space of the managers-only training sessions allows frontline managers to talk freely and strategize about how they might promote changes in the face of cautious executives above them (Kellogg 2009, 2011). The more public sessions that include both employees and managers set up the expectation that these changes will be moving forward and make it more difficult for managers to try to limit the implementation of STAR.

48. See, for example, Correll (2017), Meyerson (2001b), Weick (1984).

49. Other dual-agenda work redesign initiatives have leveraged insider support more actively than we did at TOMO. For example, when ROWE was implemented at the corporate headquarters of Best Buy Co., Inc., a speaker's panel that included a variety of managers and employees came to early training sessions to share their positive experiences with ROWE and answer

questions from those just beginning the change process. The ROWE team also prepared short video interviews with enthusiastic Best Buy employees, to show in sessions or make available for executives considering whether they wanted to bring their department into ROWE at that time. (See Ressler and Thompson [2008] for more details on ROWE at Best Buy.) When the management consulting firm BCG implemented a different work redesign initiative, called PTO, in consulting teams across the US and beyond, enthusiastic insiders were trained as facilitators who led new teams through the change process (Perlow 2012).

50. Private spaces for strategizing and mobilizing allies have long been seen as key to social change in social movement theory and have also been viewed as important for institutional change within organizations. For example, Kellogg (2009, 2011) identifies how important "relational spaces" were in her study of hospitals' implementation of a regulatory requirement to cut residents' hours. The hospitals where change advocates found and fostered relational spaces where people in a variety of roles who supported the change could affirm their ties and plan how to respond to "defenders of the status quo" saw full implementation of the hours changes, while the hospitals where these spaces were not utilized did not.

51. In retrospect, we see that the facilitators did not directly address these concerns when they were voiced, either because they did not fully understand the concerns or because they realized that the obvious fix—adjusting the workload to fit the existing staff or increasing skilled staff— was not going to be accepted by top management. To be fair, we did not fully understand these issues at the time of the STAR training sessions either. We came to see the underlying causes—how interrelated management strategies and associated job insecurity leaves these workers with little leverage to resist the ratcheting up of workload and work pace—more clearly as we were analyzing interviews and observations for this book (which was after the STAR training sessions had occurred). And these issues were only referenced in fleeting or coded ways in the STAR training. Managers asked questions like "With accountability, do you have authority?" We interpreted this question (raised by Felicia, who became a strong advocate for STAR) as follows: If she as a manager is charged with getting to a given result, does she have the authority to make the decisions that would allow her team to achieve that result? In her case managing a production support team, Felicia might be evaluated by the amount of time that the systems they support are "down" or offline. Felicia is asking whether she has the authority to hire enough staff or people with the right skills to keep the systems up and running—or not. If STAR does not address lean staffing, she seems to be asking, will it solve the root problem?

52. This analysis comes from Lam et al. (2015), where we compared the baseline survey responses of employees who completed data collection after the merger announcement with those who completed the survey before the announcement. Other key predictors of perceived job insecurity were age, race (with Hispanics and African Americans reporting higher insecurity than whites or Asians), income, education, and reported job control. We also found that employees who reported to an Asian manager reported less job insecurity in this organization and employees reported more job insecurity when the manager's own insecurity was higher.

53. See Kelly, Moen, Chermack, and Ammons (2010). In our Best Buy study, we also described different ways that men and women managers expressed concerns about the work redesign initiative. Women managers at Best Buy sometimes expressed worries that employees who were not in the office during standard hours "were dead, killed on the highway" and referenced the

"common courtesy" of letting your manager know. We called that "monitoring by mothering" and noted that men managers did not use those narratives to resist the work redesign changes. We heard some common courtesy discussions in TOMO, but those did not seem to be tied to gender. Perhaps women who have made it as IT managers rely less on interpersonal ties to their subordinates that can be cast as motherly.

Chapter 5. The Business Impacts of Work Redesign

1. See Bray et al. (2017) and Kelly et al. (2014) for more on the research design. We used a modified biased coin strategy to randomize the fifty-six work groups to the two conditions but do so in a way that ensured balance with regard to size of the work unit or department, group function (e.g., software development, project management, quality assurance), and vice president. This randomization strategy ensured that all executives had some groups randomized to STAR, after insiders advised that we not leave that to chance. Findings reported here are based on intent-to-treat analyses, which means that all those randomized to STAR are compared to all those randomized to the comparison group. Some employees and managers may not have chosen to attend any STAR training sessions nor to change their behavior in any way. The intent-to-treat analysis provides a conservative estimate of the effects of STAR, since the limited changes of those who did not get on board, so to speak, would be averaged with those who enthusiastically embraced STAR.

It is important to have a comparison or control group in this type of field experiment, rather than just compare employees before and after an organizational change. In this case, all study participants were eventually exposed to a second treatment or exogenous shock tied to the unexpected merger. A simple pre–post comparison would have left us unsure how much of the changes observed were due to STAR and how much due to the merger. With a comparison group, we can utilize a differences-in-differences logic. The changes observed for the comparison group reflect the merger and other external changes such as a shift in unemployment rates but the *additional* changes for the treatment group (the differences-in-differences) can be attributed to STAR with confidence.

2. Burnout is measured with these three questions from Maslach and Jackson's established scale of emotional exhaustion (Maslach and Jackson 1986). The second element of Maslach and Jackson's burnout scale captures depersonalization— or alienation from those who need your services. Because those questions are less relevant in this IT workforce than in the human services or healthcare settings where the scale was developed, we do not include them on the survey.

3. See Moen, Kelly, et al. (2016). Frontline managers reported higher job satisfaction at baseline and there is no gap for STAR and control group managers one year in. This is reassuring, since managers who are in STAR have had their roles and rights shift somewhat and could have become frustrated with their jobs because of that.

4. See Moen, Kelly, et al. (2016). Our previous research on ROWE, another work redesign initiative that was the precursor to STAR and developed by Cali Ressler and Jody Thompson, found similar benefits. That study was not a randomized experiment and only looked at outcomes six months after the work redesign launched. We found no direct connection between

ROWE and changes in burnout or energy for the white-collar employees in that study. But there was evidence that ROWE increased employees' control over when and where they worked and decreased work–family spillover, which had indirect benefits for burnout, energy, and other well-being measures. See Moen et al. (2011) and Ressler and Thompson (2008).

5. See Moen et al. (2017). Turnover intentions are measured by questions about whether you are "seriously considering quitting TOMO" and whether "during the next twelve months, you will probably look for a new job outside TOMO." 7.6% of the STAR employees quit in the three years of study as compared to 11.3% of the control group. The executives who invited us into TOMO also worried that the firm was seen as too "corporate," too rule-bound and traditional to appeal to younger people in tech and hoped STAR would help them hire their preferred applicants. However, because the merger brought many new employees from ZZT, there was almost no outside hiring during the study period. That means we can't evaluate whether STAR helped the organization with recruitment as well as retention. We also investigated whether there were generational differences (which are called cohort differences in social science research) in the effects of STAR, in part to investigate executives' hunch that these changes would be appealing to younger workers in particular. We found very few differences by age group.

6. See Moen, Kojola, et al. (2016).

7. This interview was conducted by Kim Fox, as were many others. The research team conducted two types of in-depth interviews, using completely different staff. This interview was a "context interview," conducted with managers in both the treatment and control condition to hear what the managers were concerned with, how the merger was unfolding, and more. STAR was not an advertised focus of these interviews, and interviewers did not bring up STAR until and unless the respondent did so. The second type of interview was conducted by separate staff (primarily Holly Whitesides and Laurie Pasricha) and was introduced as a chance to provide feedback—whether positive, negative, or neutral—about STAR. We have drawn on both context and feedback interviews throughout our analysis.

8. These figures are based on 728 employees and managers who completed Waves 1–4 of the Work, Family, and Health Network survey and answered questions about weekly hours and hours worked each week at home or another offsite location. These are bivariate analyses (t-tests of means) with significant differences in the STAR and control groups at $p < .0001$ for Waves 2, 3, and 4. Multivariate, longitudinal models that track changes in work practices over Waves 2, 3, and 4 also find significant effects for the STAR*wave covariate. See Kelly et al. (2016).

9. We are always asked about what happens for employees and managers in the control group as STAR unfolds. Our control group knows there is a pilot initiative—something called STAR—going on among their peers and they ask their coworkers and managers about it (particularly because we randomized work groups, not different work sites). In experimental terms, there is a risk of "contamination" where the treatment of new messages about flexible work practices spill over to affect the behavior of those who would ideally not be exposed to the treatment at all. Our perspective is that social changes are always going to have people talking and so we would expect that TOMO employees and frontline managers in the control group do pick up some ideas and emulate some practices they have seen in STAR teams. Indeed, remote work increases among the control group, moving from an average of 22% of the total hours worked remotely at baseline

to 30% worked remotely by Wave 4. These employees may have seen others in the STAR pilot and been influenced by them—but the difference between the STAR employees is still sizable and statistically significant.

10. See Kelly et al. (2016) for use of voluntary work at home and voluntary variable schedules by gender and parental status.

11. This study is an important comparison since so few systematic evaluations of multifaceted work redesign initiatives have been conducted. However, the Dutch study is different in at least two important ways. First, the firm's management set targets for working at home; while work at home was officially voluntary, employees were expected to work in the office two or three days per week and strongly encouraged to work at home two days per week. Second, the firm reconfigured the workspace in important ways so that employees did not have their own assigned desks or cubes and the number of workspaces was cut to fit the target level of working at home. These elements likely nudge employees to work at home but this strategy may cause new problems if employees do not feel they have control or a say in where, when, and how they do their work. In this study, there were no significant differences in the intervention and reference group (that did not move into the New Ways of Working initiative) in perceived control over work time, while our study found significant increases in schedule control for STAR employees that is likely key to other effects. See Nijp et al. (2016).

12. These calculations are derived from Table 2 in Nijp et al. (2016), where we see that those in the New Ways of Working intervention averaged about 13 hours worked at home and a mean of 36.54 hours per week, while those in the reference group averaged 6.29 hours at home and a mean of 35.54 hours per week.

13. For research describing "boundary strategies" such as high integration or high segmentation of work and personal life, see Kossek et al. (1999), Rothbard et al. (2005), and Ammons (2013).

14. These figures come from a bivariate analysis comparing variable schedules reported by STAR and control-group employees and managers (in a sample of 760 people who completed our surveys at 6 months, 12 months, and 18 months after the baseline survey). Those in STAR report significantly greater odds of saying they have a variable schedule at 6 and 12 months. When we focus specifically on voluntary variable schedules, that is, respondents who said they had a variable schedule and reported high levels of control over when they did their work, we see significant differences between STAR respondents and their peers through the whole period. See also the multivariate analysis in Kelly et al. (2016).

15. See Kelly, Moen, et al. (2014) for the full analysis of changes in schedule control at the first follow-up survey (in an analysis limited to nonsupervisory employees) and details on the schedule control measure. With a simpler, bivariate analysis, we see significant differences in schedule control through the twelve-month and eighteen-month survey in the sample of 760 employees and managers who completed the four surveys.

16. In the TOMO workforce, people generally reported being friendly with their coworkers and many teams had worked together for a long time. Discussions of personal and family life were routine—but no longer offered as reasons to explain a particular schedule or decision to work at home. In other work redesign initiatives, personal sharing may be explicitly encouraged because having outside commitments is seen as more of a threat to being "professional" and an

ideal worker. In Leslie Perlow's (2012) work redesign initiative implemented in a prestigious consulting firm, a critical change was pushing for regular discussions of personal and family life and priorities. Before that initiative, many people avoided bringing up personal and family life in project team discussions because doing so would reveal that they had other commitments that they cared about.

17. These terms (sludge and sludge justification) come from the Results Only Work Environment initiative that we adapted for STAR (Ressler and Thompson 2008; Thompson and Ressler 2013).

18. It would be worthwhile to conduct research on work redesign initiatives in other settings to see how frontline managers respond there. In TOMO, frontline managers seem to build their identities based on both their technical expertise and their formal authority. They appreciate being able to "coach" their employees, rather than be "hallway monitors" (to use language that often came up in STAR training sessions) but managers in other settings might cling more to their supervision of when, where, and how the work is done. See Chermack et al. (2015) for evidence that managers with more task-specific knowledge are more comfortable embracing this type of change. See also notes for chapter 4 on professionalism and limited status distance.

19. Goldin (2014) claims that flexibility is much harder for employees in roles that involve tending relationships. Here we see that even employees whose work involves coordination and relationship maintenance are able to take control over where and how they work. The geographic dispersion of TOMO's workforce and the technology already used to facilitate coordinating across space are also useful here.

20. See Kelly, Moen et al. (2014) for the full analysis of changes in family-supportive supervisor behaviors at the first follow-up survey (in an analysis limited to nonsupervisory employees). See Hammer (2008) on the measure. There is no decrease in STAR employees' rating of their managers over the next year, but the gap between those in STAR and the control group is not significant in later survey waves. The control group's assessment of supervisor support inches up over time, and we do not know exactly why that is. Perhaps managers in the control group are influenced by their peers in STAR, suggesting that new norms for supportive and flexible management develop across the IT division even though the policies do not officially change for the control group. Alternatively, this may be tied to the merger; employees (in both the STAR and control groups) may feel supported because their TOMO managers are proactively checking in on them during the merger period. That analysis of the later waves is based on bivariate analysis comparing STAR and control group for the sample of 760 employees and managers who completed the four surveys.

21. For example, Schulte (2014) reviews advice on getting clear on what your priorities are to avoid feeling overwhelmed and discusses the suggestion made by Tony Schwartz (who is a productivity author and leads the Energy Project) to do concentrated 90-minute sprints of work, then take a real break. We do not question the wisdom of this advice, but question whether many organizations currently allow those concentrated, uninterrupted work patterns and whether employees feel able to direct their own work time in the context of unrealistic time lines and high insecurity. Certainly, a work redesign initiative (like STAR) can foster that intentionality and smart work practices when the changes are pursued by the team and when management is on board. Otherwise, though, only some people will feel able to make these changes.

22. See Perlow (1997).

23. See Mazmanian and Erickson (2014) and Mazmanian et al. (2013).

24. We have done some preliminary analysis looking across teams in TOMO to try to understand variation in whether teams talked repeatedly and proactively about the changes they were making and developed new norms or took STAR as permission for each person to do what seemed sensible to them, without explicit coordination and reflection. Managers can and do prompt these discussions but they also occurred in teams where the manager was a STAR skeptic when employees pursued these conversations. One differentiating factor seems to be the team's flexibility before STAR was introduced. Teams where flexible schedules and remote work were common but done under the radar (so hidden from upper management) more often saw STAR as legitimating their previous practices. But these teams seemed to invest less in discussing other changes—including turning off IM—that they might make with STAR. See also Chermack et al. (2014) for a discussion of variation across teams in the implementation of ROWE at Best Buy.

25. Peggy is one of the few black women in our sample and in TOMO's IT division. While we did not focus on dynamics by race (or gender or nativity) within teams, we wondered whether Peggy's previous experiences might have been affected by being a racialized token in this setting (see, for example, Wingfield 2013). She may have had a sense of distance from her team that made her less inclined to pitch in to assist them. Perhaps she felt that her own performance was scrutinized by others, so she needed to concentrate on performing her own tasks well. With less time pressure and more team conversations about working together effectively and creating a more supportive environment, Peggy seems to feel differently after STAR.

26. See, for example, Chesley (2005) and Glavin and Schieman (2010) on technology blurring the boundaries between work and nonwork time. See Kelliher and Anderson (2010) for evidence that those who gain flexibility through individual negotiations then give more time and effort in response.

27. See Glass and Noonan (2016, p. 217) and Noonan and Glass (2012, p. 45) and Lott and Chung (2016).

28. See Kelly, Moen et al. (2014) for analysis of the first six months after STAR launched. Kelly et al. (2016) presents additional analyses through the eighteen-month survey and finds no significant effects of STAR on hours worked. At the eighteen-month survey, there is a marginally significant (p = .07) difference between the two conditions because those in the control group had decreased their work hours slightly at that point. There was no significant change over time for those in STAR.

29. See Kelly et al. (2014). We found no increases in work hours for employees who were not parents or for single employees at six months into STAR, reassuring us that the small decrease in parents' work hours did not create an additional burden for others.

30. The firm shared several years of data with us and devoted significant staff time to pursuing these questions. Unfortunately, the data were quite messy for our purposes. Our study randomized work groups to the two conditions based on who they reported to. (Because changes like this require managerial buy-in, randomizing according to the organizational chart seemed essential. If employees are going to believe that they can make these changes, their manager has to have been through the process too.) But the firm's productivity and performance data captured data on large projects—applications and programs that involved the work of many groups

and teams. These data measured things like the lines of code written as compared to the labor costs for writing that code, the error rate and outage rate for given applications, and more. With support from the firm's staff, economist Jeremy Bray, project manager Kim Fox, and others in the research team matched performance data for specific applications and programs to the share of employees doing that work who were in STAR (vs. the comparison group). This allowed us to say, for example, that a new software application was 70% completed by employees in STAR and 30% completed by employees in the control group. Most applications and programs reflected the contributions of workers in both conditions. These complications may contribute to our null findings, with no positive or negative effect of STAR on productivity and performance measures. More research is needed, ideally using a variety of hard productivity and performance measures, to fully assess the impact of work redesign initiatives in different workplace contexts.

31. See Bray et al. (2017). We use the World Health Organization Health and Work Performance Questionnaire (HPQ) that asks about hours worked in the past 7 days, expected hours per week, personal job performance on a 10-point scale, and coworker job performance. Following Kessler and colleagues' (2003) guidance, we then calculate absenteeism, presenteeism (comparing own performance to others' performance), and productivity (which is hours of work relative to expectations with a reduction for presenteeism).

32. See, for example, reviews by Kelly et al. (2008) and Allen et al. (2015).

33. See Bloom et al. (2015).

34. See Godart et al. (2017).

35. See Barbosa et al. (2015). Note that the costs used in the return on investment assumed that the firm would need to pay for all staff time customizing and delivering the training when, in this case, the research grants covered much of those costs. However, the return on investment analysis is intended to give employers who are considering this type of intervention a sense of the relative costs and benefits of doing that. In this analysis, the firm savings were tied to reduced turnover, primarily, as well as presenteeism and healthcare costs.

Chapter 6. Work Redesign Benefits for Health, Well-Being, and Personal Life

1. Large firms, like TOMO, with many employees who have relatively long tenure and are middle-aged are more likely to be attentive to healthcare costs (although TOMO's primary motivation for bringing us in was burnout and turnover concerns). Firms that rely heavily on subcontracted workers, independent contractors, or have a "churn and burn" labor strategy that accepts high turnover are probably less concerned with minimizing healthcare costs because the organization does not expect to pay for health problems that arise later in the workers' lives.

2. For summaries of this literature see Berkman et al. (2014, p. 153–81) and Pfeffer (2018). See also Chandola, Brunner, and Marmot (2006), Kivimaki et al. (2002), Stansfeld and Candy (2006).

3. On social support and health generally, see Berkman, Kawachi, and Glymour (2014). On the benefits of supervisor's support for personal and family life, see Hammer et al. (2011).

4. See Nijp et al. (2012) for a systematic review of schedule control that also notes there were very few experimental or intervention studies. The Work, Family, and Health Network studies were not published in time to be included in this review, and our joint work includes several

intervention and experimental studies on the benefits of changing schedule control and supervisor support for personal and family life (e.g., Hammer et al. [2011]; Moen et al. [2011]). Findings on the health benefits of control over *how* you do your work (called job control) specifically are stronger, as noted earlier.

5. In addition to sharing evidence from our interviews and fieldwork, this chapter summarizes many of the quantitative articles from the Work, Family, and Health Network. But more research continues to be published with TOMO data and parallel data from nursing homes. See https://workfamilyhealthnetwork.org/publications for research from 2019 and beyond, as well as more publications from the long-term care (nursing home) sample.

6. Since all our respondents were healthy enough to be working, these well-being measures are useful for capturing stress and psychological distress that is troubling but not debilitating. We use the perceived stress scale developed by Cohen and colleagues (1983) and the K-6 psychological distress scale associated with Kessler and colleagues (2003). Perceived stress items were asked of employees only, while both employees and managers were asked the psychological distress questions.

7. See Moen, Kelly, et al. (2016) for the details on the subjective well-being analysis.

8. Other research finds null effects or negative effects of workplace interventions on health and well-being when organizational restructuring or downsizing is also occurring. See Egan et al. (2007).

9. See Moen, Kelly, et al. (2016); note that the interaction effect for gender and condition is only marginally significant ($p = .06$) in the stress model. This means we are slightly less confident that STAR had different effects for men and women. See Rosenfeld and Mouzon (2013) on gender differences in reported mental health.

10. Cortisol is a hormone secreted by the adrenal glands that affect the functioning of nearly every major organ in the body. Research suggests that a flat or blunted cortisol awakening response is associated with negative health outcomes, such as cardiovascular disease, depression, and diabetes. See Almeida et al. (2018) for more information on the cortisol awakening response and its health implications as well as details on these methods and findings. Note that STAR did not change employees' cortisol patterns over the one-year follow-up period on workdays. Almeida and colleagues had hypothesized greater change in nonwork or recovery days for STAR employees.

11. See Crain et al. (2014), Lee et al. (2017), and Buxton et al. (2018). At one point in time, higher work-to-nonwork conflict predicts worse sleep quality, after adjusting for the number of children and higher job demands (which both predict worse sleep quality as well). Higher work-to-nonwork conflict is also significantly associated with shorter sleep duration and less consistent sleep patterns.

12. See Olson et al. (2015) for the shorter-term effects. STAR seems to affect sleep duration directly while sleep quality is affected through increased control over when and where work is done (reported in the last chapter) and subsequent decreases in work–nonwork conflicts (which we describe later in this chapter). See Crain et al. (2018) for the sustainability analysis across eighteen months.

13. See Buxton et al. (2018) for a review of the literature on the long-term health consequences of sleep deficiency and details on this analysis.

14. See Berkman et al. (2019) on the effects of STAR on cardiometabolic risk. Similar effects are found for the long-term care sample as well (where those at higher risk initially benefit from the work redesign initiative). For a description of the cardiometabolic risk score and its relationship to later cardiovascular events, see Marino et al. (2014).

15. See Kelly et al. (2014). We use well-established scales developed by Netemeyer and colleagues (1996). In the published article, we called these work-to-family and family-to-work conflict measures, but the question wording always mentioned both family and personal life, to be sure that those who are not married, parents, or caregivers felt these questions were relevant to them as well.

16. The significant effects for nonwork-to-work conflict might seem surprising because STAR makes changes in the work domain rather than trying to change anything at home. But, with greater control and support from colleagues and bosses, employees feel free to rearrange work tasks because of personal commitments and express less concern about getting to work "on time." Going to a personal appointment or deciding not to rush a kid off to preschool on a morning that he or she is moving slower than usual is not experienced as a nonwork-to-work conflict; it is a perfectly acceptable adjustment, often made without comment and without notifying anyone at work. A second point is that the marginally significant decreases in work-to-nonwork conflicts are found in an intent-to-treat analysis where everyone who was randomly assigned to STAR is compared to everyone assigned to the control group. When we look at those who participated in at least 75% of the STAR training (as compared to the full control group), we see larger and statistically significant declines in work-to-nonwork conflict as reported in Kelly et al. (2014). All reported effects of STAR based on the survey data are from intent-to-treat analyses, unless noted otherwise.

17. This study measured time adequacy in multiple domains (not just with family); see Moen, Kelly, and Lam (2013). Also see research on parents' time adequacy and the family time squeeze in Milkie, Nomaguchi, and Schieman (2019), Nomaguchi et al. (2005), and Schulte (2015).

18. US Secretary of Labor Tom Perez used the phrase "you shouldn't have to win the boss lottery" to get flexibility at work in speeches around 2014, and this phrase seems to have come from Neera Tanden, president of the Center for American Progress, when she described how Hillary Clinton's flexibility as a boss allowed Tanden to take on important jobs in D.C. while having young children (Stevens 2014).

19. See Kelly et al. (2014) on larger effects of STAR for those with less supportive supervisors at baseline and Almeida et al. (2015) on supervisor support reducing the impact of work–nonwork conflicts on employees' stress physiology.

20. Like most companies in the US, TOMO does not offer paid family or parental leave to fathers (at least at the time of our study), and there was no federal or state law that provided paid leave for Chuck. See Boushey (2016) and the report from PEW research (2017) on access to paid family leave in the US.

21. We recruited children ages nine to seventeen years for this part of the study. Developmental scholars note some children enter adolescence at nine or ten, and the team considered how early and middle adolescent development informs the pattern of findings. See Davis et al. (2015) for details on the analysis of parent–child time. (Kelly Chandler previously published as Kelly D. Davis.)

22. The findings for the TOMO parents are reported in Davis et al. (2015) while the broader patterns regarding mother–daughter dyads are reviewed in Lam et al. (2012). That study also emphasizes the positive effects of father–child time, but it often declines more over the teen years. In our analysis of TOMO parents, it seemed that fathers' time with children was increasing in STAR; it is possible that effects for fathers would become clearer over time, but we only asked the questions about time with children at baseline and the twelve-month survey.

23. While our qualitative data suggests STAR can bring more calm and less conflict to home life, we did not see that pattern clearly in our survey data. The daily diary survey asked about stressful interactions and conflict within families, and we did not find statistically significant differences between STAR parents and control-group parents on those measures.

24. For an overview and integration of spillover and crossover concepts, see Bakker and Demerouti (2009).

25. This analysis uses data from children aged 9–17 years who have a parent employed at TOMO. See Lawson et al. (2016) for details on this analysis of affective well-being and emotional reactivity.

26. Positive and negative affect are measured using the Positive and Negative Affect Schedule (Watson, Clark, and Tellegen 1988) asking questions like "How much of the time did you feel _____ today?" with six negative affect items (e g , sad) and five positive affect items (e.g., excited) and responses from none to all of the time. Using the Daily Inventory of Stressful Events (Almeida, Wethington, and Kessler 2002), youth were asked whether any stressful experiences happened since the previous interview. Prompts included arguments and disagreements, feeling that the parent had asked them to do to more, stressful events for family or friends that affected the youth, and anything else they found to be stressful. The analysis of emotional reactivity investigates whether positive and negative affect shift more or less in response to these daily stressors for youth with a parent in STAR vs. in the control condition.

27. See McHale et al. (2015).

28. Our daily diary survey sample is too small (with around 100 parents and children who completed both waves of data collection) for us to statistically analyze how those effects unfold with mediation models. See Lawson et al. (2016) for a review of crossover research on parents' work experience and children's well-being.

29. See Reid (2015) as well as Wynn (2018) and Williams (2010).

30. See Kelly et al. (2014).

Chapter 7. Two Steps Forward, One Step Back

1. We conducted a web survey about ten months after the official end of the STAR pilot, in the period where it was unclear what the merged company would do with regard to workplace flexibility and work redesign. As we discuss later in the chapter, we did this in part to try to investigate the executives' stated concerns about STAR, with the intention that this information might help executives decide whether and which "tweaks" or modifications to STAR would be helpful. The overall response rate for this survey was 66% and included 572 respondents who still worked at ZZT and 117 respondents who had left the firm by this time. At this point, we did not work with the firm to collect data on-site but instead conducted a web survey where we

attempted to contact every person who had completed the Wave 1 survey and so been part of the Work, Family, and Health Study at any point. Here we report on the 220 employees and sixty managers who still worked at ZZT and had been randomized to STAR. STAR was seen as "very" or "somewhat" successful for the respondent's team or work group by 96% of employees and 85% of managers. For all three questions (success regarding own experience, team, and organization), nonsupervisory employees rate STAR's success significantly higher than managers though managers are still quite positive. There are no significant differences in perceived success of STAR by gender or parental status.

2. Because there were fewer than ten TOMO vice presidents in the IT division at the time of our study, we have omitted potentially identifying information like specific role, gender, or pseudonym that suggests a particular ethnicity. With executives who were publicly skeptical of STAR, we sometimes use their pseudonyms because the perspective they shared with us was also shared publicly with their subordinates and other executives.

3. Our research team was wrapping up the study as the decisions to end the pilot were occurring. We were able to conduct informal interviews with multiple executives who had been part of TOMO (and so seen STAR up close) during this period, and we sat in on several meetings with executives and HR managers as they debated what to do next. There we noted the disjuncture between what we heard from supportive VPs in conversations and interviews and what they said in the group, particularly given the top executives' clear preference for more traditional management practices. ZZT executives were explicitly aligned with moving everyone to more traditional policies and managing in more traditional ways. We also talked informally with a few executives over the next two years, to check our emerging analysis against their perspectives. Before the official announcement of the end of STAR, we attempted to interview some legacy ZZT executives and the merged firm's CEO but we did not succeed. We did not push as hard as we might have because it seemed that the legacy TOMO executives who had let us in were worried about their jobs. We were concerned that pushing them for more access or going around them would connect them even more closely with what was becoming a disfavored initiative and so increase the risk that they would be fired or (more likely) politely shown the door. A reluctance to publicly criticize the decisions made by powerful leaders is not limited to organizations going through mergers or major organizational changes of course; see Jackall (1988) on "strategic silence."

4. We used this term partly because we did not want to call it a treatment or tie the study directly to these changes. Calling STAR a pilot seemed natural (and less likely to influence participants' responses to surveys and interviews) because the company often piloted new practices and technologies before rolling them out to an entire unit or the firm.

5. On the expectation that middle managers often resist change, see Huy (2002), Balogun (2003). On managers' resistance to changes that reduce their discretion, in particular, see Dobbin et al. (2015). For a discussion of how resistance was minimized, see chapter 4.

6. These HR professionals had been charged with supporting the executive team as they decided the future of STAR. The HR professionals who had invited us in to TOMO and helped launch STAR had left the firm by this time, so the people guiding the decision about the future of STAR were new to the initiative in one case and new to the company in another. The institutional entrepreneurs who had championed STAR were gone, and these HR professionals were

busy building their alliances with the executives, with fewer established connections to the middle managers and frontline employees who appreciated STAR.

7. These anecdotes of abuse are not full-blown stories, with rich development over time, but short and often vague references to apparently outrageous actions on the part of employees. Still, like Ewick and Silbey (2003, p. 1331), we recognize that "all stories are social events" and that bringing up these situations reveals the "social structure (e.g., role, rule, hierarchy)" implicit in these interactions. Executives and sometimes managers and IT professionals reference violations of the old and still powerful expectations that managers will direct employees' actions. Framing these occasions as evidence of "abuse" reasserts the old expectations as normative, even though the actual practices that are described are sensible and acceptable within the reworked STAR teams. It was also important that executives told these stories at a large management meeting. As Allen (2001, p. 78) notes, "storytelling contributes to social cohesion through the mutual affirmation of common problems." Here the executive invokes as "we" of reasonable managers who must deal with a "them" of unreasonable employees who push too far, gaming or abusing the system when they can.

8. Patsy goes on to say that there was unlucky timing because this incident occurred around the time that other companies were revoking their work-from-home policies. See the discussion of other companies' decisions around flexibility and the salience of the Yahoo decision in particular later in the chapter.

9. The three abuse stories we heard were about the homeschooler, missed executives' meetings, and an employee who moved a few hours away from the office without alerting his manager. We never talked with anyone who knew exactly who had moved.

10. Unfortunately for the initiative, the HR professionals who had championed and observed STAR had mostly left the merged firm by the time these stories were circulating. Those who remained were legitimately focused elsewhere, on how to reorganize the whole IT division in a sensible way so that employees and managers facing changes in their titles, bonuses, and salaries would not revolt and leave the company in large numbers.

11. This vice president points to a challenge and presents a solution that others have found in other organizations. Turco (2016, p. 77–88) investigates a tech firm's broad guidance to employees that they "use good judgment." Many employees appreciated their high levels of control over when, where, and how they worked in this firm, being "trusted" and "treated like adults," which are phrases heard often in reference to STAR. But some employees and managers were concerned about a lack of clarity in what constitutes "good judgment" and how assessment of that might that vary across managers. The firm began offering manager training and job-specific training in response. Turco (2016) frames this as the clarity challenge that a broad relational contract (with its move away from binding rules and policies) can prompt; see also Gibbons and Henderson (2012).

12. This analysis is based on our last web survey (see note 1 in this chapter) with 521 employees and managers who were still working at the firm and had completed our Wave 1 survey. For the first questions, we use the full sample and the questions about open team communication and work quality are based on the 417 nonsupervisory employees. (There are no significant differences on those questions among managers completing the survey). Note that this survey was conducted almost a year after the official end of STAR. We did not ask these questions in our

Waves 1–4 surveys but added them to evaluate the collaboration concerns that a few executives raised after the merger.

13. When we found no evidence of collaboration problems with teams that had worked in STAR (in our interviews and survey analysis), we came to see that STAR was being blamed for other company decisions and strategies. That perspective was reinforced by our interviews with an experienced developer, Ewan. Ewan called himself an "Agile enthusiast" and he had some tough questions about measuring performance and quality in STAR training session so we thought he would be a good person to probe about whether communications or coordination had suffered with STAR. Ewan laid out a vision for the ideal way of working that was somewhat similar to the VP's but then explained that TOMO had moved away from this model well before STAR.

> I think software development is most efficient when everybody's colocated and nearby and can have those water cooler conversations.

When you see coworkers casually, Ewan thinks, the "younger or less experienced" developers may ask a question that they would not ask if they needed to set up a meeting or write an email. In fact, Ewan argues that productivity problems or performance crises in IT are most likely to arise when people do not work closely together but put their "faith in writing documents." Ewan notes that with the global labor chain now operating at TOMO, they are passing documents "over lots of technical distances, logistical distances, whatever" and then it is the written documents, if anything, that are consulted by those doing the work. Additionally, the TOMO offshore unit is subcontracting to other organizations. Ewan worries that those writing the code do not have

> any concept of TOMO and what it brings to customers. Yikes. It's just scary how many [people are involved]. You know the telephone game? It's 7, 8 people, degrees of separation, between the person who originally had this idea that "Oh, we should have this feature in the software." And 9 degrees of separation later, somebody in India is coding that.

While STAR may encourage more employees to work at home, which he personally thinks is less effective than working closely together in the same office, Ewan said that "STAR is not the worst of my enemies at all."

14. Other research finds that high-status supporters of an organizational change are often concerned that their advocacy for the change may threaten their status. See Kellogg (2012), which emphasizes how the "countermoves" by defenders of the status quo can limit institutional change. In this case, high-status champions of STAR back off public support of these changes when their status within the executive team is threatened (because the ZZT executives have stronger and closer connections to the top leadership) and their power (as indicated by the size and scope of their jobs) is uncertain.

15. See the previous note about the web survey conducted after the end of STAR. Here we are reporting on IT professionals who had been recruited into our study at Wave 1 and were still working at TOMO (N = 411). We consider mean hours worked at home or elsewhere (49.6% of weekly hours for those previously in STAR vs. 34.2% for those randomized to the control group, p < .0001) and whether these employees do extensive remote work equal to at least one workday at home (73% vs. 61%, p < .01). Managers who had been part of STAR also work more at home but the contrast with the control group managers is not significant, perhaps due to a smaller sample size or perhaps because managers respond to the executives' directives more.

16. See Hallett (2010) who studied recoupling in the context of school reform.

17. Our thanks to Amy Buxbaum for collecting and summarizing approximately thirty stories in the mainstream press (e.g., CNN, Time, regional newspapers), the tech business press (e.g., Fast Company, well-known tech industry blogs), and the Harvard Business Review describing the move away from flexibility initiatives in these seven cases.

18. See Kelly et al. (2010), Kelly, Moen, and Tranby (2011), Moen et al. (2011).

19. See Kessler (2017).

20. See Bloom et al. (2018).

Chapter 8. Creating Sane and Sustainable Jobs

1. We have been deeply interested in the implications of both the old patterns and new ways of working for gender inequality. In our work, see Becker and Moen (1999), Kelly et al. (2010), and Moen and Roehling (2004). Other research that has influenced our understanding of current organizational expectations reinforcing gender inequality includes Blair-Loy (2003), Cha and Weeden (2014), Gerson (1985, 1993, 2010), Stone (2007), and Williams (2000, 2010).

2. See Harris (2017) and Petersen (2019). The TOMO IT population does not include as many younger workers (in their twenties and early thirties) as we had expected but we came to learn that many young IT workers first need to prove themselves as contractors before they can get hired as regular employees at a firm like TOMO. This too confirms how insecurity and the shifting employment relationship encourage long hours and a willingness to do "whatever it takes" to either get into or stay employed in these professional jobs.

3. On the downsides of control regarding work time and work location, see Schieman and Glavin (2017), Lott and Chung (2016), Anderson and Kelliher (2010). See also Chung and van der Horst (2018) who find that flexibility initiatives that were introduced via U.K. law and explicitly focus on work–life concerns are less likely to increase work hours than "schedule control" as part of a high-performance work system.

4. Recall from chapter 6 that STAR significantly reduced stress and psychological distress for women, with no evidence, from the survey, of significantly reduced stress and distress among men. Most STAR effects are felt broadly, but this is one important case of a gender difference in the initiative's impact. See also Moen, Kelly, et al. (2016).

5. See previous chapters for references, plus Pfeffer (2018). Large companies that self-insure and have fairly stable workforces are the most likely to be motivated by the potential reductions in healthcare costs. TOMO fits that bill. In the service sector, many retail, food, and hospitality organizations either do not offer healthcare coverage to employees or assume that high turnover means the health problems that are prompted or exacerbated by poor work conditions will not create direct costs for the company.

6. See https://workfamilyhealthnetwork.org. The materials used for STAR in TOMO are available in the Toolkits section, under Office employees.

7. See Fletcher, Bailyn, and Blake Beard (2009) for a summary of this approach. See also Rapoport et al. (2002), Meyerson and Kolb (2000), Bailyn (2011), Ely and Meyerson (2000b).

8. See Perlow (2012), Ressler and Thompson (2008, 2013), and gorowe.com. See Perlow and Kelly (2014) for an extended comparison of PTO and ROWE and description of these work redesign approaches.

9. See Blok et al. (2012) for one study of New Ways of Working that does address management's assumptions and the broader organizational culture. See also Nijp et al. (2016), who describe New Ways of Working as "a type of work organization that is characterized by temporal and spatial flexibility, often combined with extensive use of information and communication technologies (ICT) and performance-based management."

10. See http://www.wfd.com/index.html. We also interviewed Debbie Phillips, president of WFD, and Bara Litman, liaison for MIT's pilot, to learn more about WFD's Team FlexWork Process. We note that STAR may seem more onerous or intimidating than WFD's Team FlexWork Process for two reasons. First, WFD's process requires less time on the part of employees and frontline managers than STAR. Second, this approach is a bit more contained—because there is more managerial control—and so the initiative may be less intimidating to executives. Senior managers hear about the proposed principles in private where they can raise concerns or veto a particular proposed change. The risk, though, is that without a real shift in employees' ability to decide when, where, and how they work, the impact of these initiatives will be more limited than what we see with STAR. However, Erin observed one of the review sessions where new guidelines were discussed when a department within MIT implemented WFD's Team FlexWork Process and could see the value of the collective conversation about how people will work effectively and more flexibly. We have not formally studied this approach and so we can't compare its effects to the initiatives we have studied. We do note that the MIT pilots are seen as successful by insiders. Peter Hirst, the executive whose group participated in the first pilot at MIT, has touted this approach as improving "productivity, resilience, and trust." That group's guidelines clearly encouraged more work at home and customized schedules while also addressing the perceived pressure to be always available. Peter and his employees have become local champions of this team-based approach. See Hirst (2016), Plumb (2015).

11. See Connolly et al. (2017), Schulte (2017).

12. See Schulte (2014), quotes from page 125, and Sheridan (2013). Menlo Innovations' approach combines a specific software development process (Extreme Agile) with these dual-agenda work redesign goals—pointing to the possibility of doing the type of work we studied in TOMO quite differently but in a saner, more sustainable way. One major difference, of course, is that TOMO's software development process was based on a global labor chain where cheaper offshore staff was working nights and so onshore employees needed to coordinate during their "off" time with those workers.

13. See Moen (2016) for a discussion of "not-so-big jobs" and redesigning work for older workers.

14. For a discussion of part-time in professional work, see Lee et al. (2000) and for relevant laws elsewhere see Berg et al. (2014).

15. See, for example, Lambert et al. (2014; 2012), Schneider and Harknett (2019).

16. For just-in-time staffing in retail, see Henly et al. (2006), Lambert et al. (2012). For recent research on workplace monitoring via technologies, see van Oort (2018) and Mateescu and Nguyen (2019).

17. On a different staffing strategy called the "good jobs strategy," see Ton (2014). On the scheduling experiment at the GAP, see Williams, Lambert, Kesavan, et al. (2018). See Bloom et al. (2015) on the call center experiment.

18. See Meyerson (2001b, p. 46) for this quote and for the phrase about rocking the boat without falling out of it in the previous paragraph.

19. Ellen Kossek and Brenda Lautsch (2007) provide a practical guide for reflection on preferred work styles and considering what is needed to support coworkers or subordinates who prefer compartmentalizing vs. integrating work and nonwork.

20. See Boushey (2016), Moen and Roehling (2005), and Williams (2000) for a discussion of the gendered history of the old organizational practices and policies.

21. See Society for Human Resources Professionals (2018) summary of the starts and stops of the Obama administration proposed rule to increase the income threshold for salaried workers to be covered by overtime regulations and US Department of Labor (2019) for the proposed rules as of March 2019.

22. See Berg, Bosch, and Charest (2014) on the French 35-hour law. See Rubin (2017) and Wolfe (2018) on the "right to disconnect" law in France and the New York proposal, respectively.

23. Berg, Bosch, and Charest (2014) analyze three different "work-time configurations" and provide details on Sweden as their example of a negotiated system. Swedish labor law and European Union directives set minimum standards regarding hours and leaves, but over 90% of workers are covered by a collective bargaining agreement that can include scheduling rules that are mutually acceptable to management and workers.

24. See Cooper and Baird (2015).

25. See, for example, Lott and Klenner (2016).

26. 76% of private-sector workers had access to paid vacation days and paid holidays in 2017, while 93% of those in "management, business, and financial" occupations did. See US Department of Labor (2017).

27. Only 13% of private-sector workers in the US are eligible for paid family leave through their employers while 68% have at least some paid sick leave; see Department of Labor (2017). For a recent review on leaves' effects on economic outcomes and child well-being, see Rossin-Slater (2018). On the experience of workers and employers in California, see also Milkman and Appelbaum (2013).

28. Even with a leave law in place, it is difficult for many workers to access their leave rights without penalty. See Albiston and O'Connor (2016) and Albiston (2010).

29. See, for example, Silver-Greenberg and Kitroeff (2018) on pregnant warehouse workers' health concerns specifically. See also Weise (2018) on efforts to organize Amazon workers and negotiate better conditions. For pickers, in particular, collective efforts to push for better conditions are made more difficult by the growing threat that their jobs will soon be automated (and done by "robots") anyway.

30. More research is needed on whether and how limiting overtime helps warehouse workers, drivers, and the organizations employing them. The research from retail (e.g., Ton 2014) and healthcare (e.g., Kellogg 2011) suggests that it may.

31. On recent fair workweek and schedules laws in US cities and states, see Boushey (2016), Wolfe et al. (2018).

32. See Buhl (2017).

33. We draw heavily on Berg, Bosch, and Charest's (2014) discussion of unilateral, negotiated, and mandated working-time configurations here and in the next paragraphs. See also Gerstel and

Clawson (2018) for a review that stresses class differences in access to supportive, flexible schedules.

34. See Kochan et al. (2019) (Table 2). As the authors of this paper (including Erin) recognize, a survey response that one would vote for a union is not the same as actively organizing for one or supporting a union drive in the face of active management opposition. Additionally, we note that the gap between expected input and actual input is even larger for compensation, benefits, and job security than for having a say in when and how work is done. So schedule control and job control matter—but workers want a say regarding wages, benefits, and security too.

35. See Berg et al. (2014) for a discussion of works councils as well as the three broader strategies (unilateral, mandated, and negotiated) we outline here.

36. For some ideas on strengthening the safety net to reflect the realities of more job loss and insecurity, see Kalleberg (2011), Kochan (2016), Krueger (2018). One important part of updating the safety net is thoughtful enforcement of the line between contractor and employee, so that workers are not "misclassified" as independent of the firm when they should be counted as employees, with employer contributions to social security, unemployment insurance, and more. See Weil (2014) on subcontracting and misclassification.

37. In addition to Harris (2017), sociologists Kathleen Gerson (2010), David Pedulla, and Sarah Thebaud (Pedulla and Thebaud 2015, Thebaud and Pedulla 2016) have examined the preferences of young adults as well as the "institutional constraints" of limited public policies and rigid organizational expectations that push them toward less egalitarian decisions about how they manage their careers and family lives. Additionally, Barbara Risman (2018) captures the various ways that this generation "wrestles with the gender structure."

Appendix 3. Ideas for Action

1. Some of the ideas here are based on our observations of ROWE and discussions with Jody Thompson and Cali Ressler, in addition to STAR and other work redesign initiatives reviewed in chapter 8. See Thompson and Ressler (2013) for more guidance for managers.

2. Ressler and Thompson (2008) emphasize changing communications by "eliminating sludge" (such as these comments about hours, schedules, and work location) as a critical part of changing the organizational culture. See chapter 4 as well.

REFERENCES

⌘

Acemoglu, Daron, David Autor, David Dorn, Gordon H. Hanson, and Brendan Price. 2016. "Import Competition and the Great US Employment Sag of the 2000s." *Journal of Labor Economics* 34(1): S141–98.

Acker, Joan. 1990. "Hierarchies, Jobs, Bodies: A Theory of Gendered Organizations." *Gender & Society* 4(2): 139–58.

Albiston, Catherine, and Lindsey O'Connor. 2016. "Just Leave." *Harvard Women's Law Journal* (39)1: 1–65.

Albiston, Catherine Ruth. 2010. *Institutional Inequality and the Mobilization of the Family and Medical Leave Act: Rights on Leave*. New York: Cambridge University Press.

Allen, Davina. 2001. "Narrating Nursing Jurisdiction: 'Atrocity Stories' and 'Boundary-Work.'" *Symbolic Interaction* 24(1): 75–103.

Allen, Tammy D., Timothy D. Golden, and Kristen M. Shockley. 2015. "How Effective Is Telecommuting? Assessing the Status of Our Scientific Findings." *Psychological Science in the Public Interest* 16(2): 40–68.

Almeida, David M., Kelly D. Davis, Soomi Lee, Katie M. Lawson, Kimberly N. Walter, and Phyllis Moen. 2015. "Supervisor Support Buffers Daily Psychological and Physiological Reactivity to Work-to-Family Conflict." *Journal of Marriage and Family* 78(1): 165–179.

Almeida, David M., Soomi Lee, Kimberly N. Walter, Katie M. Lawson, Erin L. Kelly, and Orfeu M. Buxton. 2018. "The Effects of a Workplace Intervention on Employees' Cortisol Awakening Response." *Community, Work & Family* 21(2): 151–67.

Almeida, David M., Elaine Wethington, and Ronald C. Kessler. 2002. "The Daily Inventory of Stressful Events: An Interview-Based Approach for Measuring Daily Stressors." *Assessment* 9(1): 41–55.

Amabile, Teresa M., and Regina Conti. 1999. "Changes in the Work Environment for Creativity during Downsizing." *Academy of Management Journal* 42(6): 630–40.

Ammons, Samantha K. 2013. "Work–Family Boundary Strategies: Stability and Alignment between Preferred and Enacted Boundaries." *Journal of Vocational Behavior* 82(1): 49–58.

Autor, David H., Frank Levy, and Richard J. Murnane. 2003. "The Skill Content of Recent Technological Change: An Empirical Exploration." *Quarterly Journal of Economics* 118(4): 1279–1333.

Babbott, Stewart, Linda Baier Manwell, Roger Brown, Enid Montague, Eric Williams, Mark Schwartz, Erik Hess, and Mark Linzer. 2014. "Electronic Medical Records and Physician Stress in Primary Care: Results from the MEMO Study." *Journal of the American Medical Informatics Association: JAMIA* 21(e1): e100–106.

Bailyn, Lotte. 2006. *Breaking the Mold: Redesigning Work for Productive and Satisfying Lives*. 2nd ed. Ithaca, NY: ILR Press/Cornell University Press.

Bailyn, Lotte. 2011. "Redesigning Work for Gender Equity and Work-Personal Life Integration." *Community, Work & Family* 14(1): 97–112.

Bakker, Arnold B., and Evangelia Demerouti. 2009. "The Crossover of Work Engagement between Working Couples: A Closer Look at the Role of Empathy." *Journal of Managerial Psychology* 24(3): 220–36.

Balogun, J. 2003. "From Blaming the Middle to Harnessing Its Potential: Creating Change Intermediaries." *British Journal of Management* 14(1): 69–83.

Barbosa, Carolina, Jeremy W. Bray, William N. Dowd, Michael J. Mills, Phyllis Moen, Brad Wipfli, Ryan Olson, and Erin L. Kelly. 2015. "Return on Investment of a Work-Family Intervention: Evidence from the Work, Family, and Health Network." *Journal of Occupational and Environmental Medicine* 57(9): 943–51.

Barley, Stephen R., Debra E. Meyerson, and Stine Grodal. 2010. "E-Mail as a Source and Symbol of Stress." *Organization Science* 22(4): 887–906.

Battilana, Julie, Bernard Leca, and Eva Boxenbaum. 2009. "How Actors Change Institutions: Towards a Theory of Institutional Entrepreneurship." *Academy of Management Annals* 3(1): 65–107.

Becker, Penny Edgell, and Phyllis Moen. 1999. "Scaling Back: Dual-Earner Couples' Work-Family Strategies." *Journal of Marriage and the Family* 61(4): 995–1007.

Becker, William J., Liuba Belkin, and Sarah Tuskey. 2018. "Killing Me Softly: Electronic Communications Monitoring and Employee and Spouse Well-Being." *Academy of Management Proceedings* 2018(1): 1–6.

Berdahl, Jennifer L., Marianne Cooper, Peter Glick, Robert W. Livingston, and Joan C. Williams. 2018. "Work as a Masculinity Contest." *Journal of Social Issues* 74(3): 422–48.

Berg, Peter, Gerhard Bosch, and Jean Charest. 2014. "Working-Time Configurations: A Framework for Analyzing Diversity across Countries." *Industrial & Labor Relations Review* 67(3): 805–37.

Berkman, Lisa F., Ichirō Kawachi, and M. Maria Glymour. 2014. *Social Epidemiology.* 2nd ed. Oxford: Oxford University Press.

Berkman, Lisa F., Erin L. Kelly, Leslie B. Hammer, Frank Mierzwa, Todd Bodner, Tay MacNamara, Soomi Lee, Miguel Marino, Thomas W. McDade, Ginger Hanson, Phyllis Moen, and Orfeu M. Buxton. 2019. "Effects of a Workplace Intervention on Employee Cardiometabolic Risk: Evidence from the Work, Family, and Health Network." Harvard Center for Population and Development Studies Working Paper, Cambridge, MA.

Berkman, Lisa F., Sze Yan Liu, Leslie Hammer, Phyllis Moen, Laura Cousino Klein, Erin Kelly, Martha Fay, Kelly Davis, Mary Durham, Georgia Karuntzos, and Orfeu M. Buxton. 2015. "Work–Family Conflict, Cardiometabolic Risk, and Sleep Duration in Nursing Employees." *Journal of Occupational Health Psychology* 20(4): 420–33.

Bird, Chloe E., and Patricia P. Rieker. 2008. *Gender and Health: The Effects of Constrained Choices and Social Policies.* New York: Cambridge University Press.

Blair-Loy, Mary. 2003. *Competing Devotions: Career and Family among Women Executives.* Cambridge, MA: Harvard University Press.

Blair-Loy, Mary. 2009. "Work Without End? Scheduling Flexibility and Work-to-Family Conflict Among Stockbrokers." *Work and Occupations* 36(4): 279–317.

Blair-Loy, Mary, and Erin A. Cech. 2017. "Demands and Devotion: Cultural Meanings of Work and Overload Among Women Researchers and Professionals in Science and Technology Industries." *Sociological Forum* 32(1): 5–27.

Blinder, Alan S. 2006. "Offshoring: The Next Industrial Revolution?" *Foreign Affairs* 85(2): 113–28.

Bloom, Nicholas, James Liang, John Roberts, and Zhichun Jenny Ying. 2015. "Does Working from Home Work? Evidence from a Chinese Experiment." *Quarterly Journal of Economics* 130(1): 165–218.

Bloom, Nicholas, Aprajit Mahajan, David McKenzie, and John Roberts. 2018. "Do Management Interventions Last? Evidence from India." Working Paper 24249, National Bureau of Economic Research, Cambridge, Massachusetts.

Boushey, Heather. 2016. *Finding Time*. Cambridge, MA: Harvard University Press.

Bray, Jeremy, Erin L. Kelly, Leslie Hammer, David Almeida, James Dearing, Rosalind King, and Orfeu Buxton. 2013. *An Integrative, Multilevel, and Transdisciplinary Research Approach to Challenges of Work, Family, and Health*. MR-0024–1303. Research Triangle Park, NC: RTI Press.

Bray, Jeremy W., Jesse M. Hinde, David J. Kaiser, Michael J. Mills, Georgia T. Karuntzos, Katie R. Genadek, Erin L. Kelly, Ellen E. Kossek, and David A. Hurtado. 2017. "Effects of a Flexibility/Support Intervention on Work Performance: Evidence from the Work, Family, and Health Network." *American Journal of Health Promotion* 32(4): 963–70.

Briscoe, Forrest. 2007. "From Iron Cage to Iron Shield? How Bureaucracy Enables Temporal Flexibility for Professional Service Workers." *Organization Science* 18(2): 297–314.

Brynjolfsson, Erik, Tom Mitchell, and Daniel Rock. 2018. "What Can Machines Learn, and What Does It Mean for Occupations and the Economy?" *AEA Papers and Proceedings* 108: 43–47.

Buhl, Larry. 2017. "The Latest Fight for Employee Rights: Work Schedule Predictability." *Marketplace*. www.marketplace.org/2017/09/04/business/latest-fight-employee-rights-work-schedule-predictability.

Burchell, Brendan, David Ladipo, and Frank Wilkinson. 2002. *Job Insecurity and Work Intensification*. London: Routledge.

Burke, Ronald J., and Cary L. Cooper. 2008. *The Long Work Hours Culture: Causes, Consequences and Choices*. London: Emerald Group Publishing.

Burke, Ronald J., and Lisa Fiksenbaum. 2009. "Work Motivations, Satisfactions, and Health Among Managers: Passion Versus Addiction." *Cross-Cultural Research* 43(4): 349–65.

Buxton, Orfeu M., Soomi Lee, Miguel Marino, Chloe Beverly, David M. Almeida, and Lisa Berkman. 2018. "Sleep Health and Predicted Cardiometabolic Risk Scores in Employed Adults from Two Industries." *Journal of Clinical Sleep Medicine: JCSM: Official Publication of the American Academy of Sleep Medicine* 14(3): 371–83.

Canales, Rodrigo. 2016. "From Ideals to Institutions: Institutional Entrepreneurship and the Growth of Mexican Small Business Finance." *Organization Science* 27(6): 1548–73.

Cappelli, Peter. 1999. *The New Deal at Work: Managing the Market-Driven Workforce*. Cambridge, MA: Harvard Business School Press.

Carrillo, Dani, Kristen Harknett, Allison Logan, Sigrid Luhr, and Daniel Schneider. 2017. "Instability of Work and Care: How Work Schedules Shape Child-Care Arrangements for Parents Working in the Service Sector." *Social Service Review* 91(3): 422–55.

Cascio, Wayne F. 2010. "Employment Downsizing: Causes, Costs, and Consequences." In *More than Bricks in the Wall: Organizational Perspectives for Sustainable Success,* edited by Lea Stadtler, Achim Schmitt, Patricia Klarner, Thomas Straub, 87–96. Wiesbaden: Gabler Verlag / Springer Science & Business Media.

Cha, Youngjoo. 2010. "Reinforcing Separate Spheres: The Effect of Spousal Overwork on Men's and Women's Employment in Dual-Earner Households." *American Sociological Review* 75(2): 303–29.

Cha, Youngjoo, and Kim A. Weeden. 2014. "Overwork and the Slow Convergence in the Gender Gap in Wages." *American Sociological Review* 79(3): 457–84.

Chandola, Tarani, Eric Brunner, and Michael Marmot. 2006. "Chronic Stress at Work and the Metabolic Syndrome: Prospective Study." *British Medical Journal* 332(7540): 521–25.

Chang, Emily. 2018. *Brotopia: Breaking Up the Boys' Club of Silicon Valley.* New York: Penguin.

Chermack, Kelly, Erin L. Kelly, Phyllis Moen, and Samantha K. Ammons. 2015. "Implementing Institutional Change: Flexible Work and Team Processes in a White Collar Organization." *Research in the Sociology of Work* 26: 331–59.

Chesley, Noelle. 2005. "Blurring Boundaries? Linking Technology Use, Spillover, Individual Distress, and Family Satisfaction." *Journal of Marriage and Family* 67(5): 1237–48.

Chesley, Noelle. 2011. "Stay-at-Home Fathers and Breadwinning Mothers: Gender, Couple Dynamics, and Social Change." *Gender & Society* 25(5): 642–64.

Chesley, Noelle. 2014. "Information and Communication Technology Use, Work Intensification and Employee Strain and Distress." *Work, Employment & Society* 28(4): 589–610.

Chesley, Noelle, and Phyllis Moen. 2006. "When Workers Care: Dual-Earner Couples' Caregiving Strategies, Benefit Use, and Psychological Well-Being." *American Behavioral Scientist* 49(9): 1248–69.

Chung, Heejung, and Mariska van der Horst. 2018. "Flexible Working and Unpaid Overtime in the UK: The Role of Gender, Parental and Occupational Status." *Social Indicators Research.* https://doi.org/10.1007/s11205-018-2028-7.

Clawson, Dan, and Naomi Gerstel. 2014. *Unequal Time: Gender, Class, and Family in Employment Schedules.* New York: Russell Sage Foundation.

Cohen, Sheldon, Tom Kamarck, and Robin Mermelstein. 1983. "A Global Measure of Perceived Stress." *Journal of Health and Social Behavior* 24(4): 385–96.

Coltrane, Scott, Elizabeth C. Miller, Tracy DeHaan, and Lauren Stewart. 2013. "Fathers and the Flexibility Stigma." *Journal of Social Issues* 69(2): 279–302.

Conlan, Catherine. 2016. "Nurses, Here's How to Cope with Your Long Hours." *Monster Career Advice.* www.monster.com/career-advice/article/nurses-how-to-cope-long-hours-0716.

Connoly, Dan, Ung Uyhun, Mattew Darling, Ted Robertson, and Suman Gidwani. 2017. *Work and Life: A Behavioral Approach to Solving Work-Life Conflict (An Ideas42 Report).* www.ideas42.org/wp-content/uploads/2017/03/I42-863_RWJ_Report_DesignSolution_final.pdf.

Cooper, Marianne. 2000. "Being the 'Go-To Guy': Fatherhood, Masculinity, and the Organization of Work in Silicon Valley." *Qualitative Sociology* 23(4): 379–405.

Cooper, Marianne. 2014. *Cut Adrift: Families in Insecure Times.* Berkeley: University of California Press.

Cooper, Rae, and Marian Baird. 2015. "Bringing the 'Right to Request' Flexible Working Arrangements to Life: From Policies to Practices." *Employee Relations* 37(5): 568–81.

Correll, Shelley J. 2017. "SWS 2016 Feminist Lecture: Reducing Gender Biases in Modern Work-places: A Small Wins Approach to Organizational Change." *Gender & Society* 31(6): 725–50.

Correll, Shelley J., Stephen Benard, and In Paik. 2007. "Getting a Job: Is There a Motherhood Penalty?" *American Journal of Sociology* 11(5): 1297–1338.

Crain, Tori L., Leslie B. Hammer, Todd Bodner, Ellen Ernst Kossek, Phyllis Moen, Richard Lilienthal, and Orfeu M. Buxton. 2014. "Work–Family Conflict, Family-Supportive Supervisor Behaviors (FSSB), and Sleep Outcomes." *Journal of Occupational Health Psychology* 19(2): 155–67.

Crowley, Martha, and Randy Hodson. 2014. "Neoliberalism at Work." *Social Currents* 1(1): 91–108.

Davis, Kelly D., Katie M. Lawson, David M. Almeida, Erin L. Kelly, Rosalind B. King, Leslie Hammer, Lynne M. Casper, Cassandra A. Okechukwu, Ginger Hanson, and Susan M. McHale. 2015. "Parents' Daily Time with Their Children: A Workplace Intervention." *Pediatrics* 135(5): 875–82.

Desilver, Drew. 2017. "Access to Paid Family Leave Varies Widely in U.S." Pew Research Center. www.pewresearch.org/fact-tank/2017/03/23/access-to-paid-family-leave-varies-widely-across-employers-industries/.

Dobbin, Frank. 2009. *Inventing Equal Opportunity*. Princeton, NJ: Princeton University Press.

Dobbin, Frank, Daniel Schrage, and Alexandra Kalev. 2015. "Rage against the Iron Cage: The Varied Effects of Bureaucratic Personnel Reforms on Diversity." *American Sociological Review* 80(5): 1014–44.

Egan, Matt, Clare Bambra, Sian Thomas, Mark Petticrew, Margaret Whitehead, and Hilary Thomson. 2007. "The Psychosocial and Health Effects of Workplace Reorganisation. 1. A Systematic Review of Organisational-Level Interventions That Aim to Increase Employee Control." *Journal of Epidemiology and Community Health* 61(11): 945–54.

Ely, Robin J., and Debra E. Meyerson. 2000a. "Advancing Gender Equity in Organizations: The Challenge and Importance of Maintaining a Gender Narrative." *Organization* 7(4): 589–608.

Ely, Robin J., and Debra E. Meyerson. 2000b. "Theories of Gender in Organizations: A New Approach to Organizational Analysis and Change." *Research in Organizational Behavior* 22:103–151.

Epstein, Cynthia Fuchs, and Arne L. Kalleberg. 2004. *Fighting for Time: Shifting Boundaries of Work and Social Life*. New York: Russell Sage Foundation.

Epstein, Cynthia Fuchs, Carroll Seron, Bonnie Oglensky, and Robert Sauté. 2014. *The Part-Time Paradox: Time Norms, Professional Life, Family and Gender*. New York: Routledge.

Ewick, Patricia, and Susan S. Silbey. 1995. "Subversive Stories and Hegemonic Tales: Toward a Sociology of Narrative." *Law & Society Review* 29(2): 197–226.

Ewick, Patricia, and Susan Silbey. 2003. "Narrating Social Structure: Stories of Resistance to Legal Authority." *American Journal of Sociology* 108(6): 1328–72.

Fletcher, Joyce K., Bailyn Lotte, and Stacy Blake Beard. 2009. "Practical Pushing: Creating Discursive Space in Organizational Narratives." In *Critical Management Studies at Work: Negotiating Tensions between Theory and Practice*, edited by J. W. Cox, 82–93. Northampton, MA: Edward Elgar.

Fligstein, Neil. 1997. "Social Skill and Institutional Theory." *American Behavioral Scientist* 40(4): 397–405.

Fligstein, Neil. 2001. "Social Skill and the Theory of Fields." *Sociological Theory* 19(2): 105–25.

Fligstein, Neil, and Taek-Jin Shin. 2004. "The Shareholder Value Society: A Review of the Changes in Working Conditions and Inequality in the United States, 1976 to 2000." In *Social Inequality*, edited by K. M. Neckerman, 401–32. New York: Russell Sage Foundation.

Gallie, Duncan. 2017. "The Quality of Work in a Changing Labour Market." *Social Policy & Administration* 51(2): 226–43.

Gawande, Atul. 2018. "Why Doctors Hate Their Computers." *New Yorker*, November 5. www .newyorker.com/magazine/2018/11/12/why-doctors-hate-their-computers.

Gerson, Kathleen. 1985. *Hard Choices: How Women Decide About Work, Career and Motherhood.* Berkeley: University of California Press.

Gerson, Kathleen. 1993. *No Man's Land: Men's Changing Commitments to Family and Work.* New York: Basic Books.

Gerson, Kathleen. 2010. *The Unfinished Revolution: How a New Generation Is Reshaping Family, Work, and Gender in America.* New York: Oxford University Press.

Gerstel, Naomi, and Dan Clawson. 2014. "Class Advantage and the Gender Divide: Flexibility on the Job and at Home." *American Journal of Sociology* 120(2): 395–431.

Gerstel, Naomi, and Dan Clawson. 2018. "Control over Time: Employers, Workers, and Families Shaping Work Schedules." *Annual Review of Sociology* 44(1): 77–97.

Gibbons, Robert, and Rebecca Henderson. 2012. "Relational Contracts and Organizational Capabilities." *Organization Science* 23(5): 1350–64.

Gittell, Jody Hoffer. 2016. *Transforming Relationships for High Performance: The Power of Relational Coordination.* Palo Alto, CA: Stanford University Press.

Glass, Jennifer L. 2004. "Blessing or Curse?: Work-Family Policies and Mother's Wage Growth Over Time." *Work and Occupations* 31(3): 367–94.

Glass, Jennifer L., and Mary C. Noonan. 2016. "Telecommuting and Earnings Trajectories Among American Women and Men 1989–2008." *Social Forces* 95(1): 217–50.

Glauber, Rebecca. 2011. "Limited Access: Gender, Occupational Composition, and Flexible Work Scheduling." *Sociological Quarterly* 52(3): 472–94.

Glavin, Paul, and Scott Schieman. 2010. "Interpersonal Context at Work and the Frequency, Appraisal, and Consequences of Boundary-Spanning Demands." *Sociological Quarterly* 51(2): 205–25.

Glavin, Paul, Scott Schieman, and Sarah Reid. 2011. "Boundary-Spanning Work Demands and Their Consequences for Guilt and Psychological Distress." *Journal of Health and Social Behavior* 52(1): 43–57.

Godart, Olivier N., Holger Görg, and Aoife Hanley. 2017. "Trust-Based Work Time and Innovation: Evidence from Firm-Level Data." *ILR Review* 70(4): 894–918.

Goh, Joel, Jeffrey Pfeffer, and Stefanos Zenios. 2015a. "Exposure to Harmful Workplace Practices Could Account for Inequality in Life Spans across Different Demographic Groups." *Health Affairs (Project Hope)* 34(10): 1761–68.

Goh, Joel, Jeffrey Pfeffer, and Stefanos A. Zenios. 2015b. "The Relationship Between Workplace Stressors and Mortality and Health Costs in the United States." *Management Science* 62(2): 608–28.

Golden, Lonnie. 2001. "Flexible Work Schedules: Which Workers Get Them?" *American Behavioral Scientist* 44(7): 1157–78.

Goldin, Claudia. 2014. "A Grand Gender Convergence: Its Last Chapter." *American Economic Review* 104(4): 1091–1119.

Graham, John R., Campbell R. Harvey, and Shiva Rajgopal. 2005. "The Economic Implications of Corporate Financial Reporting." *Journal of Accounting and Economics* 40(1): 3–73.

Green, Francis. 2006. *Demanding Work: The Paradox of Job Quality in the Affluent Economy*. Princeton, NJ: Princeton University Press.

Gulati, Ranjay, and Alicia Desantola. 2016. "Start-Ups That Last: How to Scale Your Business. (Spotlight on Entrepreneurship for the Long Term)." *Harvard Business Review* 94(3): 54–61.

Hallett, Tim. 2010. "The Myth Incarnate: Recoupling Processes, Turmoil, and Inhabited Institutions in an Urban Elementary School." *American Sociological Review* 75(1): 52–74.

Hamermesh, Daniel S., and Elena Stancanelli. 2015. "Long Workweeks and Strange Hours." *ILR Review* 68(5): 1007–18.

Hammer, Leslie B., Ryan C. Johnson, Tori L. Crain, Todd Bodner, Ellen Ernst Kossek, Kelly D. Davis, Erin L. Kelly, Orfeu M. Buxton, Georgia Karuntzos, L. Casey Chosewood, and Lisa Berkman. 2016. "Intervention Effects on Safety Compliance and Citizenship Behaviors: Evidence from the Work, Family, and Health Study." *Journal of Applied Psychology* 101(2): 190–208.

Hammer, Leslie B., Ellen Ernst Kossek, W. K. Anger, T. Bodner, and K. L. Zimmerman. 2011. "Clarifying Work–Family Intervention Processes: The Roles of Work–Family Conflict and Family-Supportive Supervisor Behaviors." *Journal of Applied Psychology* 96(1): 134–150.

Hammer, Leslie B., Ellen Ernst Kossek, Todd Bodner, and Tori Crain. 2013. "Measurement Development and Validation of the Family Supportive Supervisor Behavior Short-Form (FSSB-SF)." *Journal of Occupational Health Psychology* 18(3): 285–96.

Hammer, Leslie B., Ellen Ernst Kossek, Nanette L. Yragui, Todd E. Bodner, and Ginger C. Hanson. 2009. "Development and Validation of a Multidimensional Measure of Family Supportive Supervisor Behaviors (FSSB)." *Journal of Management* 35(4): 837–56.

Harris, Malcolm. 2017. *Kids These Days*. New York: Little Brown and Company.

Hempel, Christian E., Thomas B. Lawrence, and Paul Tracey. 2017. "Institutional Work: Taking Stock and Making It Matter." In *The SAGE Handbook of Organizational Institutionalism*, edited by R. Greenwood, C. Oliver, K. Sahlin, and R. Suddaby, 558–590. London: Sage Publications.

Henly, Julia R., and Susan J. Lambert. 2014. "Unpredictable Work Timing in Retail Jobs: Implications for Employee Work-Life Conflict." *Industrial & Labor Relations Review* 67(3): 986–1016.

Henly, Julia R., H. Luke Shaefer, and Elaine Waxman. 2006. "Nonstandard Work Schedules: Employer- and Employee-Driven Flexibility in Retail Jobs." *Social Service Review* 80(4): 609–34.

Hirst, Peter. 2016. "How a Flex-Time Program at MIT Improved Productivity, Resilience, and Trust." *Harvard Business Review*. https://hbr.org/2016/06/how-a-flex-time-program-at-mit-improved-productivity-resilience-and-trust.

Ho, Karen Zouwen. 2009. *Liquidated: An Ethnography of Wall Street*. Durham, NC: Duke University Press.

Hochschild, Arlie Russell. 1997. *The Time Bind: When Work Becomes Home and Home Becomes Work*. New York: Henry Holt and Company.

Hurtado, David A., Cassandra A. Okechukwu, Orfeu M. Buxton, Leslie Hammer, Ginger C. Hanson, Phyllis Moen, Laura C. Klein, and Lisa F. Berkman. 2016. "Effects on Cigarette Consumption of a Work–Family Supportive Organisational Intervention: 6-Month Results from the Work, Family and Health Network Study." *Journal of Epidemiology and Community Health* 70(12): 1155–61.

Huy, Quy Nguyen. 2002. "Emotional Balancing of Organizational Continuity and Radical Change: The Contribution of Middle Managers." *Administrative Science Quarterly* 47(1): 31–69.

Jackall, Robert. 1988. *Moral Mazes: The World of Corporate Managers*. New York: Oxford University Press.

Jacobs, Jerry A., and Kathleen Gerson. 2004. *The Time Divide: Work, Family, and Gender Inequality*. Cambridge, MA: Harvard University Press.

Johnson, R. C., A. Kalil, and Re Dunifon. 2012. "Employment Patterns of Less-Skilled Workers: Links to Children's Behavior and Academic Progress." *Demography* 49(2): 747–72.

Jones, Damon, David Molitor, and Julian Reif. 2018. "What Do Workplace Wellness Programs Do? Evidence from the Illinois Workplace Wellness Study." Working Paper 24229. National Bureau of Economic Research, Cambridge, Massachusetts. www.nber.org/papers/w24229.

Judiesch, Michael K., and Karen S. Lyness. 1999. "Left Behind? The Impact of Leaves of Absence on Managers' Career Success." *Academy of Management Journal* 42(6): 641–51.

Kaduk, Anne, Katie Genadek, Erin L. Kelly, and Phyllis Moen. 2019 (forthcoming). "Involuntary vs. Voluntary Flexible Work: Insights for Scholars and Stakeholders." *Community, Work, and Family*.

Kalleberg, Arne L. 2009. "Precarious Work, Insecure Workers: Employment Relations in Transition." *American Sociological Review* 74(1): 1–22.

Kalleberg, Arne L. 2011. *Good Jobs, Bad Jobs: The Rise of Polarized and Precarious Employment Systems in the United States, 1970s to 2000s*. New York: Russell Sage Foundation.

Kalleberg, Arne L., and Steven P. Vallas. 2018. "Probing Precarious Work: Theory, Research, and Politics." *Research in the Sociology of Work* 31: 1–30.

Karasek, Robert A. 1979. "Job Demands, Job Decision Latitude, and Mental Strain: Implications for Job Redesign." *Administrative Science Quarterly* 24(2): 285–308.

Karasek, Robert A., and Tores Theorell. 1990. *Healthy Work: Stress Productivity and the Reconstruction of Working Life*. New York: Basic Books.

Kelliher, Clare, and Deirdre Anderson. 2010. "Doing More with Less? Flexible Working Practices and the Intensification of Work." *Human Relations* 63(1): 83–106.

Kellogg, Katherine C. 2009. "Operating Room: Relational Spaces and Microinstitutional Change in Surgery." *American Journal of Sociology* 115(3): 657–711.

Kellogg, Katherine C. 2011. *Challenging Operations: Medical Reform and Resistance in Surgery*. Chicago: University of Chicago Press.

Kellogg, Katherine C. 2012. "Making the Cut: Using Status-Based Countertactics to Block Social Movement Implementation and Microinstitutional Change in Surgery." *Organization Science* 23(6): 1546–70.

Kellogg, Katherine C. 2018. "Subordinate Activation Tactics: Semi-Professionals and Micro-Level Institutional Change in Professional Organizations." *Administrative Science Quarterly*. 59(3): 375–408.

Kelly, Erin L., Samantha K. Ammons, Kelly Chermack, and Phyllis Moen. 2010. "Gendered Challenge, Gendered Response: Confronting the Ideal Worker Norm in a White-Collar Organization." *Gender & Society* 24(3): 281–303.

Kelly, Erin L., Anne Kaduk, Katie Genadek, and Phyllis Moen. 2016. "Free to Flex? Work Practices and Career Consequences in an IT Workplace." Labor and Employment Relations Association Winter Meeting in conjunction with Allied Social Science Association conference, San Francisco, January 5, 2016.

Kelly, Erin L., and Alexandra Kalev. 2006. "Managing Flexible Work Arrangements in US Organizations: Formalized Discretion or 'A Right to Ask.'" *Socio-Economic Review* 4(3): 379–416.

Kelly, Erin L., Ellen Ernst Kossek, Leslie B. Hammer, Mary Durham, Jeremy Bray, Kelly Chermack, Lauren A. Murphy, and Dan Kaskubar. 2008. "Getting There from Here: Research on the Effects of Work–Family Initiatives on Work–Family Conflict and Business Outcomes." *Academy of Management Annals* 2(1): 305–49.

Kelly, Erin L., and Phyllis Moen. 2007. "Rethinking the ClockWork of Work: Why Schedule Control May Pay Off at Work and at Home." *Advances in Developing Human Resources* 9(4): 487–506.

Kelly, Erin L., Phyllis Moen, J. Michael Oakes, Wen Fan, Cassandra Okechukwu, Kelly D. Davis, Leslie B. Hammer, Ellen Ernst Kossek, Rosalind Berkowitz King, Ginger C. Hanson, Frank Mierzwa, and Lynne M. Casper. 2014. "Changing Work and Work-Family Conflict Evidence from the Work, Family, and Health Network." *American Sociological Review* 79(3): 485–516.

Kelly, Erin L., Phyllis Moen, and Eric Tranby. 2011. "Changing Workplaces to Reduce Work-Family Conflict." *American Sociological Review* 76(2): 265–90.

Kessler, Ronald, Catherine Barber, Arne Beck, Patricia Berglund, Paul Clearly, David McKenas, Nico Pronk, Gregory Simon, Paul Stang, T. Ustun, and Philip Wang. 2003. "The World Health Organization Health and Work Performance Questionnaire (HPQ)." *Journal of Occupational and Environmental Medicine* 45(2): 156–74.

Kessler, Ronald C., Peggy R. Barker, Lisa J. Colpe, Joan F. Epstein, Joseph C. Gfroerer, Eva Hiripi, Mary J. Howes, Sharon-Lise T. Normand, Ronald W. Manderscheid, Ellen E. Walters, and Alan M. Zaslavsky. 2003. "Screening for Serious Mental Illness in the General Population." *Archives of General Psychiatry* 60(2): 184–89.

Kessler, Sarah. 2017. "IBM, Remote Work Pioneer, Is Calling Thousands of Employees Back to the Office." *Quartz*. https://qz.com/924167/ibm-remote-work-pioneer-is-calling-thousands -of-employees-back-to-the-office/.

Khalid, Asma. 2017. "From Post-It Notes to Algorithms: How Automation Is Changing Legal Work." *NPR.Org*. www.npr.org/sections/alltechconsidered/2017/11/07/561631927/from-post -it-notes-to-algorithms-how-automation-is-changing-legal-work.

Kivimaki, Mika, Paivi Leino-Arjas, Ritva Luukkonen, Hilkka Riihimaki, Jussi Vahtera, and Juhani Kirjonen. 2002. "Work Stress and Risk of Cardiovascular Mortality: Prospective Cohort Study of Industrial Employees." *British Medical Journal* 325(7369): 857–62.

Klotz, Frieda, and Larry Rosen. 2017. "Heavy Toll of 'Always-On' Technology." *MIT Sloan Management Review*, Spring. https://sloanreview.mit.edu/article/the-heavy-toll-of-always-on-technology/.

Kochan, Thomas A. 2016. *Shaping the Future of Work: What Future Worker, Business, Government, and Education Leaders Need to Do for All to Prosper*. New York: Business Expert Press.

Kochan, Thomas A., Duanyi Yang, William T. Kimball, and Erin L. Kelly. 2019. "Worker Voice in America: Is There a Gap between What Workers Expect and What They Experience?" *ILR Review* 72(1): 3–38.

Kolb, Deborah M., and Debra E. Meyerson. 1999. "Keeping Gender in the Plot: A Case Study of the Body Shop." In *Gender at Work: Organizational Change for Equality*, edited by A. Rao, 129–54. West Hartford, CT: Kumarian Press.

Konrad, Alison M., and Yang Yang. 2012. "Is Using Work-Life Interface Benefits a Career-Limiting Move? An Examination of Women, Men, Lone Parents, and Parents with Partners." *Journal of Organizational Behavior* 33(8): 1095–119.

Kossek, Ellen Ernst, Alison E. Barber, and Deborah Winters. 1999. "Using Flexible Schedules in the Managerial World: The Power of Peers." *Human Resource Management* 38(1): 33–46.

Kossek, Ellen, Patricia Gettings, Lindsay Rosokha, and Rebecca Thompson. 2019. "Work-Life Intervention Crafting and Sustaining Implementation." Conference paper presented at Academy of Management Meetings, August 10–13, Boston.

Kossek, Ellen Ernst, Leslie B. Hammer, Erin L. Kelly, and Phyllis Moen. 2014. "Designing Organizational Work, Family & Health Change Initiatives." *Organizational Dynamics* 43(1): 53–63.

Kossek, Ellen Ernst, and Brenda A. Lautsch. 2007. *CEO of Me: Creating a Life That Works in the Flexible Job Age*. Upper Saddle River, NJ: Pearson Education.

Kossek, Ellen, Ryan Petty, Todd Bodner, Matthew Perrigino, Leslie Hammer, Nanette Yragui, and Jesse Michel. 2018. "Lasting Impression: Transformational Leadership and Family Supportive Supervision as Resources for Well-Being and Performance." *Occupational Health Science* 2(1): 1–24.

Kossek, Ellen Ernst, Shaun Pichler, Todd Bodner, and Leslie B. Hammer. 2011. "Workplace Social Support and Work–Family Conflict: A Meta-Analysis Clarifying the Influence of General and Work–Family-Specific Supervisor and Organizational Support." *Personnel Psychology* 64(2): 289–313.

Kossek, Ellen Ernst, Matthew M. Piszczek, Kristie L. McAlpine, Leslie B. Hammer, and Lisa Burke. 2016. "Filling the Holes: Work Schedulers as Job Crafters of Employment Practice in Long-Term Health Care." *ILR Review* 69(4): 961–90.

Kossek, Ellen Ernst, Rebecca J. Thompson, Katie M. Lawson, Todd Bodner, Matthew B. Perrigino, Leslie B. Hammer, Orfeu M. Buxton, David M. Almeida, Phyllis Moen, David A. Hurtado, Brad Wipfli, Lisa F. Berkman, and Jeremy W. Bray. 2019. "Caring for the Elderly at Work and Home: Can a Randomized Organizational Intervention Improve Psychological Health?" *Journal of Occupational Health Psychology* 24(1): 36–54.

Kramer, Karen Z., Erin L. Kelly, and Jan B. McCulloch. 2015. "Stay-at-Home Fathers: Definition and Characteristics Based on 34 Years of CPS Data." *Journal of Family Issues* 36(12): 1651–73.

Krueger, Alan B. 2018. "Independent Workers: What Role for Public Policy?" *ANNALS of the American Academy of Political and Social Science* 675(1): 8–25.

Kuhn, Peter, and Fernando Lozano. 2008. "The Expanding Workweek? Understanding Trends in Long Work Hours among U.S. Men, 1979–2006." *Journal of Labor Economics* 26(2): 311–43.

Kunda, Gideon. 1992. *Engineering Culture: Control and Commitment in a High-Tech Corporation.* Philadelphia: Temple University Press.

Kunda, Gideon. 2006. *Engineering Culture: Control and Commitment in a High-Tech Corporation.* Rev. ed. Philadelphia: Temple University Press.

Kurutz, Steven. 2018. "How to Retire in Your 30s with $1 Million in the Bank." *New York Times,* September 1.

Kuruvilla, Sarosh, and Ernesto Noronha. 2016. "From Pyramids to Diamonds: Legal Process Offshoring, Employment Systems, and Labor Markets for Lawyers in the United States and India." *ILR Review* 69(2): 354–77.

Kuruvilla, Sarosh, and Aruna Ranganathan. 2008. "Economic Development Strategies and Macro- and Micro-Level Human Resource Policies: The Case of India's 'Outsourcing' Industry." *Industrial & Labor Relations Review* 62(1): 39–72.

Lam, Chun Bun, Susan M. McHale, and Ann C. Crouter. 2012. "Parent-Child Shared Time from Middle Childhood to Late Adolescence: Developmental Course and Adjustment Correlates." *Child Development* 83(6): 2089–2103.

Lam, Jack, Kimberly Fox, Wen Fan, Phyllis Moen, Erin Kelly, Leslie Hammer, and Ellen Ernst Kossek. 2015. "Manager Characteristics and Employee Job Insecurity around a Merger Announcement: The Role of Status and Crossover." *Sociological Quarterly* 56(3): 558–80.

Lam, Jack, Phyllis Moen, Shi-Rong Lee, and Orfeu M. Buxton. 2016. "Boomer and Gen X Managers and Employees at Risk: Evident from the Work, Family, and Health Network Study." In *Beyond the Cubicle: Job Insecurity, Intimacy, and the Flexible Self,* edited by A. J. Pugh, 51–74. New York: Oxford University Press.

Lambert, Susan J., Peter J. Fugiel, and Julia R. Henly. 2014. *Precarious Work Schedules among Early Career Employees in the US: A National Snapshot.* https://ssa.uchicago.edu/sites/default/files/uploads/lambert.fugiel.henly_.precarious_work_schedules.august2014_0.pdf.

Lambert, Susan J., Anna Haley-Lock, and Julia R. Henly. 2012. "Schedule Flexibility in Hourly Jobs: Unanticipated Consequences and Promising Directions." *Community, Work & Family* 15(3): 293–315.

La Monica, Paul R. 2013. "You're Fired. Stock Rises. Wall Street Loves Layoffs—The Buzz—Investment and Stock Market News." *CNNMoney.* http://buzz.money.cnn.com/2013/10/01/layoffs-stocks/.

Lamont, Michèle. 1992. *Money, Morals, and Manners: The Culture of the French and American Upper-Middle Class.* Chicago: University of Chicago Press.

Lamont, Michèle. 2000. *The Dignity of Working Men: Morality and the Boundaries of Race, Class, and Immigration.* Cambridge, MA: Russell Sage Foundation and Harvard University Press.

Lassus, Lora A. Phillips, Steven Lopez, and Vincent J. Roscigno. 2015. "Aging Workers and the Experience of Job Loss." *Research in Social Stratification and Mobility* 41: 81–91.

Lawrence, Thomas B., and Roy Suddaby. 2006. "Institutions and Institutional Work." In *Handbook of Organization Studies*, edited by S. R. Clegg, C. Hardy, T. B. Lawrence, and W. R. Nord, 215–254. London: Sage Publications.

Lawson, Katie M., Kelly D. Davis, Susan M. McHale, David M. Almeida, Erin L. Kelly, and Rosalind B. King. 2016. "Effects of Workplace Intervention on Affective Well-Being in Employees' Children." *Developmental Psychology* 52(5): 772–77.

Lee, Mary Dean, Shelley MacDermid, and Michelle L. Buck. 2000. "Organizational Paradigms of Reduced-load Work: Accommodation, Elaboration, and Transformation." *Academy of Management Journal* 43(6): 1211–26.

Lee, Michael, Melissa Mazmanian, and Leslie Perlow. 2019. "Fostering Positive Relational Dynamics in Teams: The Power of Interaction Scripts as a Resource for Change." *Academy of Management Journal.* doi.org/10.5465/amj.2016.0685.

Lee, Soomi, Tori L. Crain, Susan M. McHale, David M. Almeida, and Orfeu M. Buxton. 2017. "Daily Antecedents and Consequences of Nightly Sleep." *Journal of Sleep Research* 26(4): 498–509.

Leslie, Lisa, Colleen Manchester, Tae-Youn Park, and Si Ahn Mehng. 2012. "Flexible Work Practices: A Source of Career Premiums or Penalties?" *Academy of Management Journal* 55(6): 1407–28.

Lott, Yvonne, and Heejung Chung. 2016. "Gender Discrepancies in the Outcomes of Schedule Control on Overtime Hours and Income in Germany." *European Sociological Review* 32(6): 752–65.

Lott, Yvonne, and Christina Klenner. 2016. "Ideal Workers and Ideal Parents: Working-Time Norms and the Acceptance of Part-Time and Parental Leave at the Workplace in Germany." WSI Working Papers 204, The Institute of Economic and Social Research, (WSI), Hans-Böckler-Foundation, Düsseldorf.

Lowe, Travis Scott. 2018. "Perceived Job and Labor Market Insecurity in the United States: An Assessment of Workers' Attitudes from 2002 to 2014." *Work and Occupations* 45(3): 313–45.

Maertz, Carl P., Jack W. Wiley, Cynthia Lerouge, and Michael A. Campion. 2010. "Downsizing Effects on Survivors: Layoffs, Offshoring, and Outsourcing." *Industrial Relations: A Journal of Economy and Society* 49(2): 275–85.

Marino, Miguel, Marie Killerby, Soomi Lee, Laura C. Klein, Phyllis Moen, Ryan Olson, Ellen E. Kossek, Rosalind King, Leslie Erickson, Lisa F. Berkman, and Orfeu M. Buxton. 2016. "The Effects of a Cluster Randomized Controlled Workplace Intervention on Sleep and Work-Family Conflict Outcomes in an Extended Care Setting." *Sleep Health* 2(4): 297–308.

Marino, Miguel, Yi Li, Michael J. Pencina, Ralph B. D'Agostino, Lisa F. Berkman, and Orfeu M. Buxton. 2014. "Quantifying Cardiometabolic Risk Using Modifiable Non–Self-Reported Risk Factors." *American Journal of Preventive Medicine* 47(2): 131–40.

Maslach, Christina, and Susan E. Jackson. 1986. *Maslach Burnout Inventory Manual.* 2nd ed. Palo Alto, CA: Consulting Psychologists Press.

Matos, Kenneth, and Ellen Galinsky. 2015. "Commentary on How Effective Is Telecommuting? Assessing the Status of Our Scientific Findings." *Psychological Science in the Public Interest* 16(2): 38–39.

Matteescu, Alexandra, and Aiha Nguyen. 2019. "Explainer: Workplace Monitoring & Surveillance." https://datasociety.net/output/explainer-workplace-monitoring-surveillance.

Mattke, Soeren, Harry H. Liu, John P. Caloyeras, Christina Y. Huang, Kristin R. Van Busum, Dmitry Khodyakov, and Victoria Shier. 2013. *Workplace Wellness Programs Study*. Santa Monica, CA: RAND Corporation.

Maume, David J. 2006. "Gender Differences in Restricting Work Efforts Because of Family Responsibilities." *Journal of Marriage and Family* 68(4): 859–69.

Mazmanian, Melissa, and Ingrid Erickson. 2014. "The Product of Availability: Understanding the Economic Underpinnings of Constant Connectivity." In *Proceedings of the SIGCHI Conference on Human Factors in Computing Systems, CHI '14*, 763–72. New York: Association for Computing Machinery.

Mazmanian, Melissa, Wanda J. Orlikowski, and JoAnne Yates. 2013. "The Autonomy Paradox: The Implications of Mobile Email Devices for Knowledge Professionals." *Organization Science* 24 (5) (October 2013): 1337–57.

McGee, Suzanne. 2014. "Layoffs Make CEOs Look like Heroes—That's Why Corporate America Is Sick | Money | The Guardian." *The Guardian*, July 24.

McGovern, Patrick, Stephen Hill, Colin Mills, and Michael White. 2007. *Market, Class, and Employment*. Oxford: Oxford University Press.

McHale, Susan M., Katie M. Lawson, Kelly D. Davis, Lynne Casper, Erin L. Kelly, and Orfeu Buxton. 2015. "Effects of a Workplace Intervention on Sleep in Employees' Children." *Journal of Adolescent Health* 56(6): 672–77.

Meyerson, Debra E. 2001a. *Tempered Radicals: How People Use Difference to Inspire Change at Work*. Cambridge, MA: Harvard Business School Press.

Meyerson, Debra E. 2001b. "Radical Change, the Quiet Way (Changing Corporate Culture)." *Harvard Business Review* 79(9): 92–104.

Meyerson, Debra E., and Deborah M. Kolb. 2000. "Moving out of the 'Armchair': Developing a Framework to Bridge the Gap between Feminist Theory and Practice." *Organization* 7(4): 553–71.

Michaels, Guy, Ashwini Natraj, and John Van Reenen. 2013. "Has ICT Polarized Skill Demand? Evidence from Eleven Countries over Twenty-Five Years." *Review of Economics and Statistics* 96(1): 60–77.

Michel, Jesse S., Lindsey M. Kotrba, Jacqueline K. Mitchelson, Malissa A. Clark, and Boris B. Baltes. 2011. "Antecedents of Work–Family Conflict: A Meta-Analytic Review." *Journal of Organizational Behavior* 32(5): 689–725.

Milkie, Melissa A., Kei Nomaguchi, and Scott Schieman. 2019. "Time Deficits with Children: The Link to Parents' Mental and Physical Health." *Society and Mental Health* 9(3): 277–95. doi/10.1177/2156869318767488.

Milkman, Ruth, and Eileen Appelbaum. 2013. *Unfinished Business: Paid Family Leave in California and the Future of U.S. Work-Family Policy*. Ithaca, NY: ILR Press.

Miller, Claire Cain. 2019. "Women Did Everything Right. Then Work Got 'Greedy.'" *New York Times*, April 26.

Mirowsky, John, and Catherine E. Ross. 1998. "Education, Personal Control, Lifestyle and Health: A Human Capital Hypothesis." *Research on Aging* 20(4): 415–49.

Mishel, Lawrence R. 2013. *Vast Majority of Wage Earners Are Working Harder, and for Not Much More: Trends in U.S. Work Hours and Wages over 1979–2007*. Washington, DC: Economic Policy Institute.

Moen, Phyllis. 2003. *It's About Time: Couples and Careers*. Ithaca, NY: Cornell University Press.

Moen, Phyllis. 2016. *Encore Adulthood: Boomers on the Edge of Risk, Renewal, and Purpose*. New York: Oxford University Press.

Moen, Phyllis, Wen Fan, and Erin L. Kelly. 2013. "Team-Level Flexibility, Work-Home Spillover, and Health Behavior." *Social Science & Medicine* 84 (May): 69–79.

Moen, Phyllis, Erin L. Kelly, Wen Fan, Shi-Rong Lee, David Almeida, Ellen Ernst Kossek, and Orfeu M. Buxton. 2016. "Does a Flexibility/Support Organizational Initiative Improve High-Tech Employees' Well-Being? Evidence from the Work, Family, and Health Network." *American Sociological Review* 81(1): 134–64.

Moen, Phyllis, Erin L. Kelly, and Rachelle Hill. 2011. "Does Enhancing Work-Time Control and Flexibility Reduce Turnover? A Naturally Occurring Experiment." *Social Problems* 58(1): 69–98.

Moen, Phyllis, Erin L. Kelly, and Qinlei Huang. 2008. "Work, Family and Life-Course Fit: Does Control Over Work Time Matter?" *Journal of Vocational Behavior* 73(3): 414–25.

Moen, Phyllis, Erin L. Kelly, and Jack Lam. 2013. "Healthy Work Revisited: Do Changes in Time Strain Predict Well-Being?" *Journal of Occupational Health Psychology* 18(2): 157–72.

Moen, Phyllis, Erin L. Kelly, Shi-Rong Lee, J. Michael Oakes, Wen Fan, Jeremy Bray, David Almeida, Leslie Hammer, David Hurtado, and Orfeu Buxton. 2017. "Can a Flexibility/Support Initiative Reduce Turnover Intentions and Exits? Results from the Work, Family, and Health Network." *Social Problems* 64(1): 53–85.

Moen, Phyllis, Erin L. Kelly, Eric Tranby, and Qinlei Huang. 2011. "Changing Work, Changing Health: Can Real Work-Time Flexibility Promote Health Behaviors and Well-Being?" *Journal of Health and Social Behavior* 52(4): 404–29.

Moen, Phyllis, Erik Kojola, Erin L. Kelly, and Yagmur Karakaya. 2016. "Men and Women Expecting to Work Longer: Do Changing Work Conditions Matter?" *Work, Aging and Retirement* 2(3): 321–44.

Moen, Phyllis, and Patricia Roehling. 2005. *The Career Mystique: Cracks in the American Dream*. Lanham, MD: Rowman & Littlefield.

Munsch, Christin L. 2016. "Flexible Work, Flexible Penalties: The Effect of Gender, Childcare, and Type of Request on the Flexibility Bias." *Social Forces* 94(4): 1567–91.

Netemeyer, Richard G., James S. Boles, and Robert McMurrian. 1996. "Development and Validation of Work–Family Conflict and Family–Work Conflict Scales." *Journal of Applied Psychology* 81(4): 400–10.

Neumark, David. 2016. "Policy Levers to Increase Jobs and Increase Income from Work after the Great Recession." *IZA Journal of Labor Policy* 5(1): 1–38.

Newman, Katherine S. 1999. *Falling from Grace: Downward Mobility in the Age of Affluence*. Berkeley: University of California Press.

Nijp, Hylco H., Debby G. J. Beckers, Sabine A. E. Geurts, Philip Tucker, and Michiel A. J. Kompier. 2012. "Systematic Review on the Association Between Employee Worktime Control and Work–Non-Work Balance, Health and Well-Being, and Job-Related Outcomes." *Scandinavian Journal of Work, Environment & Health* 38(4): 299–313.

Nijp, Hylco H., Debby G. J. Beckers, Karina van de Voorde, Sabine A. E. Geurts, and Michiel A. J. Kompier. 2016. "Effects of New Ways of Working on Work Hours and Work Location, Health and Job-Related Outcomes." *Chronobiology International* 33(6): 604–18.

Nomaguchi, Kei M., Melissa A. Milkie, and Suzanne M. Bianchi. 2005. "Time Strains and Psychological Well-Being Do Dual-Earner Mothers and Fathers Differ?" *Journal of Family Issues* 26(6): 756–92.

Noonan, Mary C., and Jennifer L. Glass. 2012. "The Hard Truth About Telecommuting." *Monthly Labor Review* (June): 38–45.

Norbert, K. Semmer. 2006. "Job Stress Interventions and the Organization of Work." *Scandinavian Journal of Work, Environment & Health* 32(6): 515–27.

Okechukwu, Cassandra A., Erin L. Kelly, Janine Bacic, Nicole DePasquale, David Hurtado, Ellen Kossek, and Grace Sembajwe. 2016. "Supporting Employees' Work-Family Needs Improves Health Care Quality: Longitudinal Evidence from Long-Term Care." *Social Science & Medicine* 157 (May): 111–19.

Olson, Ryan, Tori L. Crain, Todd E. Bodner, Rosalind King, Leslie B. Hammer, Laura Cousino Klein, Leslie Erickson, Phyllis Moen, Lisa F. Berkman, and Orfeu M. Buxton. 2015. "A Workplace Intervention Improves Sleep: Results from the Randomized Controlled Work, Family, and Health Study." *Sleep Health: Journal of the National Sleep Foundation* 1(1): 55–65.

Osterman, Paul. 1999. *Securing Prosperity: The American Labor Market: How It Has Changed and What to Do about It*. Princeton, NJ: Princeton University Press.

Padavic, Irene, Robin J. Ely, and Erin M. Reid. 2019. "Explaining the Persistence of Gender Inequality: The Work-Family Narrative as a Social Defense against the 24/7 Work Culture." *Administrative Science Quarterly*. https://doi.org/10.1177/0001839219832310.

Parker, Sharon K., Frederick P. Morgeson, and Gary Johns. 2017. "One Hundred Years of Work Design Research: Looking Back and Looking Forward." *Journal of Applied Psychology* 102(3): 403–20.

Pearlin, Leonard I. 2010. "The Life Course and the Stress Process: Some Conceptual Comparisons." *Journals of Gerontology Series B: Psychological Sciences and Social Sciences* 65B(2): 207–15.

Pedulla, David S. 2016. "Penalized or Protected? Gender and the Consequences of Nonstandard and Mismatched Employment Histories." *American Sociological Review* 81(2): 262–89.

Pedulla, David S., and Sarah Thebaud. 2015. "Can We Finish the Revolution? Gender, Work-Family Ideals, and Institutional Constraint." *American Sociological Review* 80(1): 116–39.

Perea, Juan F. 2011. "The Echoes of Slavery: Recognizing the Racist Origins of the Agricultural and Domestic Worker Exclusion from the National Labor Relations Act." *Ohio State Law Journal* 72(1): 95–138.

Perlow, Leslie A. 1997. *Finding Time: How Corporations, Individuals, and Families Can Benefit from New Work Practices*. Ithaca, NY: Cornell University Press.

Perlow, Leslie A. 1999. "The Time Famine: Toward a Sociology of Work Time." *Administrative Science Quarterly* 44(1): 57–81.

Perlow, Leslie A. 2012. *Sleeping with Your Smartphone: How to Break the 24/7 Habit and Change the Way You Work*. Cambridge, MA: Harvard Business Review Press.

Perlow, Leslie A., and Erin L. Kelly. 2014. "Toward a Model of Work Redesign for Better Work and Better Life." *Work and Occupations* 41(1): 111–34.

Perry-Jenkins, Maureen. 2014. "The Time and Timing of Work: Unique Challenges for Low-Income Families." In *Work-Family Challenges for Low-Income Children and their Parents*, edited by Ann C. Crouter and Alan Booth, 119–28. New York: Routledge.

Petersen, Anne Helen. 2019. "How Millennials Became the Burnout Generation." *BuzzFeed News*. www.buzzfeednews.com/article/annehelenpetersen/millennials-burnout-generation-debt -work.

Petrakaki, Dimitra, Ela Klecun, and Tony Cornford. 2016. "Changes in Healthcare Professional Work Afforded by Technology: The Introduction of a National Electronic Patient Record in an English Hospital." *Organization* 23(2): 206–26.

Pfeffer, Jeffrey. 2018. *Dying for a Paycheck: How Modern Management Harms Employee Health and Company Performance—and What We Can Do about It*. New York: HarperCollins.

Plumb, Emma. 2015. "Tips for Successful Flex from Peter Hirst, MIT Sloan—1MFWF." *1 Million for Work Flexibility*. www.workflexibility.org/tips-for-successful-flex-from-peter-hirst -executive-director-of-executive-education-mit-sloan/.

Pryce, Joanna, Karen Albertsen, and Karina Nielsen. 2006. "Evaluation of an Open-Rota System in a Danish Psychiatric Hospital: A Mechanism for Improving Job Satisfaction and Work–Life Balance." *Journal of Nursing Management* 14(4): 282–88.

Pugh, Allison J. 2015. *The Tumbleweed Society: Working and Caring in an Age of Insecurity*. New York: Oxford University Press.

Pugh, Allison J. 2016. *Beyond the Cubicle: Job Insecurity, Intimacy, and the Flexible Self*. New York: Oxford University Press.

Rahmandad, Hazhir, Rebecca Henderson, and Nelson P. Repenning. 2018. "Making the Numbers? 'Short Termism' and the Puzzle of Only Occasional Disaster." *Management Science* 64(3): 1328–47.

Rahmandad, Hazhir, and Nelson Repenning. 2016. "Capability Erosion Dynamics." *Strategic Management Journal* 37(4): 649–72.

Ramarajan, Lakshmi, and Erin Reid. 2013. "Shattering the Myth of Separate Worlds: Negotiating Nonwork Identities at Work." *Academy of Management Review* 38(4): 621–44.

Rao, Hayagreeva, Philippe Monin, and Rodolphe Durand. 2003. "Institutional Change in Toque Ville: Nouvelle Cuisine as an Identity Movement in French Gastronomy." *American Journal of Sociology* 108(4): 795–843.

Rapoport, Rhona, Lotte Bailyn, Joyce K. Fletcher, and Bettye H. Pruitt. 2001. *Beyond Work-Family Balance: Advancing Gender Equity and Workplace Performance*. San Francisco: Jossey-Bass.

Reid, Erin. 2015. "Embracing, Passing, Revealing, and the Ideal Worker Image: How People Navigate Expected and Experienced Professional Identities." *Organization Science* 26(4): 997–1017.

Remus, Dana, and Frank S. Levy. 2016. "Can Robots Be Lawyers? Computers, Lawyers, and the Practice of Law." https://papers.ssrn.com/sol3/papers.cfm?abstract_id=2701092.

Repenning, James, Donald Kieffer, and Nelson Repenning. 2017. "Agile for Everyone Else: Using Triggers and Checks to Create Agility Outside of Software Development." MIT Sloan Working Paper 5198-17, Cambridge, MA.

Repenning, Nelson P. 2001. "Understanding Fire Fighting in New Product Development." *Journal of Product Innovation Management* 18(5): 285–300.

Repenning, Nelson P., and John D. Sterman. 2001. "Nobody Ever Gets Credit for Fixing Problems That Never Happened: Creating and Sustaining Process Improvement." *California Management Review* 43(4): 64–88.

Ressler, Cali, and Jody Thompson. 2008. *Why Work Sucks and How to Fix It: No Schedules, No Meetings, No Joke . . .* New York: Portfolio.

Riordan, Christine. 2018. "Task-Based Stratification: How Technical, Social and Relational Characteristics of Tasks Drive Stratification in Corporate Law." MIT Sloan Working Paper, Cambridge, MA.

Risman, Barbara. 2018. *Where Millennials Will Take Us: A New Generation Wrestles with the Gender Structure.* New York: Oxford University Press.

Rosenfield, Sarah, and Dawne Mouzon. 2013. "Gender and Mental Health." In *Handbook of the Sociology of Mental Health, Handbooks of Sociology and Social Research,* edited by Carol S. Aneshensel, Jo C. Phelan, and Alex Bierman, 277–96. Dordrecht: Springer.

Rossin-Slater, Maya. 2018. "Maternity and Family Leave Policy." In *The Oxford Handbook of Women and the Economy,* edited by Susan L. Averett, Laura M. Argys, and Saul D. Hoffman, 323–342. New York: Oxford University Press.

Rothbard, Nancy P., Katherine W. Phillips, and Tracy L. Dumas. 2005. "Managing Multiple Roles: Work-Family Policies and Individuals' Desires for Segmentation." *Organization Science* 16(3): 243–58.

Rubin, Alissa J. 2017. "France Lets Workers Turn Off, Tune Out and Live Life." *New York Times,* December 22.

Rudman, Laurie A., and Kris Mescher. 2013. "Penalizing Men Who Request a Family Leave: Is Flexibility Stigma a Femininity Stigma?" *Journal of Social Issues* 69(2): 322–40.

Sako, Mari. 2013. "Professionals between Market and Hierarchy: A Comparative Political Economy Perspective." *Socio-Economic Review* 11(1): 185–212.

Schieman, Scott. 2013. "Job-Related Resources and the Pressures of Working Life." *Social Science Research* 42(2): 271–82.

Schieman, Scott, and Paul Glavin. 2008. "Trouble at the Border?: Gender, Flexibility at Work, and the Work-Home Interface." *Social Problems* 55(4): 590–611.

Schieman, Scott, and Paul Glavin. 2017. "Ironic Flexibility: When Normative Role Blurring Undermines the Benefits of Schedule Control." *Sociological Quarterly* 58(1): 51–71.

Schneider, Daniel, and Kristen Harknett. 2019. "Consequences of Routine Work Schedule Instability for Worker Health and Wellbeing." *American Sociological Review* 84(1): 82–114.

Schulte, Brigid. 2014. *Overwhelmed: How to Work, Love, and Play When No One Has the Time.* New York: Macmillan.

Schulte, Brigid. 2017. "Why Your Best Productivity Hacks Still Come Up Short (And What Really Needs to Change)." www.fastcompany.com/40400900/why-your-best-productivity-hacks-still-come-up-short-and-what-really-needs-to-change.

Shafer, Emily Fitzgibbons, Erin L. Kelly, Orfeu M. Buxton, and Lisa F. Berkman. 2017. "Partners' Overwork and Individuals' Wellbeing and Experienced Relationship Quality." *Community, Work & Family* 21(4): 410–28.

Sheridan, Richard. 2013. *Joy, Inc.: How We Built a Workplace People Love.* New York: Penguin.

Shows, Carla, and Naomi Gerstel. 2009. "Fathering, Class, and Gender: A Comparison of Physicians and Emergency Medical Technicians." *Gender & Society* 23(2): 161–87.

Sianoja, Marjaana, Erin L. Kelly, Lee Soomi, and David M. Almeida. 2018. "Working Around the Clock: How Uninterrupted Off-Job Time Between Workdays Relates to Energy Levels and Cognitive Functioning at Work." Working paper.

Silver-Greenberg, Jessica, and Natalie Kitroeff. 2018. "Miscarrying at Work: The Physical Toll of Pregnancy Discrimination." *New York Times,* October 21.

Smith, Vicki. 2001. *Crossing the Great Divide: Worker Risk and Opportunity in the New Economy.* Ithaca, NY: Cornell University Press.

Society for Human Resources Professionals. 2018. *FLSA Overtime Rule Resources.* www.shrm.org /resourcesandtools/legal-and-compliance/employment-law/pages/flsa-overtime-rule -resources.aspx.

Stansfeld, S., and B. Candy. 2006. "Psychosocial Work Environment and Mental Health—a Meta-Analytic Review." *Scandinavian Journal of Work Environment & Health* 32(6): 443–62.

Stevens, Allison. 2014. "Let's Take Luck Out of the 'Boss Lottery.'" *Women's ENews.* https:// womensenews.org/2014/10/lets-take-luck-out-of-the-boss-lottery/.

Stone, Pamela. 2007. *Opting Out?: Why Women Really Quit Careers and Head Home.* Berkeley: University of California Press.

Strauss, Anselm. 1996. "Everett Hughes: Sociology's Mission." *Symbolic Interaction* 19(4): 271–83.

Swanberg, Jennifer E., Marcie Pitt-Catsouphes, and Krista Drescher-Burke. 2005. "A Question of Justice: Disparities in Employees' Access to Flexible Schedule Arrangements." *Journal of Family Issues* 26(6): 866–95.

Sweet, Stephen, Marcie Pitt-Catsouphes, and Jacquelyn Boone James. 2016. "Successes in Changing Flexible Work Arrangement Use: Managers and Work-Unit Variation in a Financial Services Organization." *Work and Occupations* 43(1): 75–109.

Thébaud, Sarah, and David S. Pedulla. 2016. "Masculinity and the Stalled Revolution: How Gender Ideologies and Norms Shape Young Men's Responses to Work–Family Policies." *Gender & Society* 30(4): 590–617.

Thompson, Jody, and Cali Ressler. 2013. *Why Managing Sucks and How to Fix It: A Results-Only Guide to Taking Control of Work, Not People.* New York: Wiley.

Townsend, Nicholas W. 2002. *The Package Deal: Marriage, Work, and Fatherhood in Men's Lives.* Philadelphia: Temple University Press.

Turco, Catherine. 2016. *The Conversational Firm: Rethinking Bureaucracy in the Age of Social Media.* New York: Columbia University Press.

US Department of Labor, Bureau of Labor Statistics. 2017. "National Compensation Survey: Employee Benefits in the United States, March 2017." www.bls.gov/ncs/ebs/benefits/2017 /ownership/private/table32a.htm.

US Department of Labor, Wages and Hours Division. 2019. "Notice of Proposed Rule-Making: Overtime Exemption." www.dol.gov/whd/overtime2019/.

Vallas, Steven P., and Angèle Christin. 2018. "Work and Identity in an Era of Precarious Employment: How Workers Respond to 'Personal Branding' Discourse." *Work and Occupations* 45(1): 3–37.

Van Oort, Madison. 2018. "The Emotional Labor of Surveillance: Digital Control in Fast Fashion Retail." *Critical Sociology.* https://doi.org/10.1177/0896920518778087.

Wajcman, Judy. 2015. *Pressed for Time: The Acceleration of Life in Digital Capitalism.* Chicago: University of Chicago Press.

Watson, David, Lee Anna Clark, and Auke Tellegen. 1988. "Development and Validation of Brief Measures of Positive and Negative Affect: The PANAS Scales." *Journal of Personality and Social Psychology* 54(6): 1063–70.

Weeden, Kim A. 2005. "Is There a Flexiglass Ceiling? Flexible Work Arrangements and Wages in the United States." *Social Science Research* 34(2): 454–82.

Weick, Karl E. 1984. "Small Wins: Redefining the Scale of Social Problems." *American Psychologist* 39(1): 40–49.

Weil, David. 2014. *The Fissured Workplace: Why Work Became So Bad for so Many and What Can Be Done to Improve It.* Cambridge, MA: Harvard University Press.

Weise, Karen. 2018. "Somali Workers in Minnesota Force Amazon to Negotiate." *New York Times,* November 21.

Wharton, Amy S., Sarah Chivers, and Mary Blair-Loy. 2008. "Use of Formal and Informal Work–Family Policies on the Digital Assembly Line." *Work and Occupations* 35(3): 327–50.

Williams, Christine L. 2013. "The Glass Escalator, Revisited: Gender Inequality in Neoliberal Times." *Gender & Society* 27(5): 609–29.

Williams, Joan C. 2000. *Unbending Gender: Why Family and Work Conflict and What to Do about It.* New York: Oxford University Press.

Williams, Joan C. 2010. *Reshaping the Work-Family Debate: Why Men and Class Matter.* Cambridge, MA: Harvard University Press.

Williams, Joan C., Mary Blair-Loy, and Jennifer L. Berdahl. 2013. "Cultural Schemas, Social Class, and the Flexibility Stigma." *Journal of Social Issues* 69(2): 209–34.

Williams, Joan C., Susan Lambert, Saravanan Kesavan, Peter J. Fugiel, Lori Ann Ospina, Erin Devorah Rapoport, Meghan Jarpe, Dylan Bellisle, Pendem Pradeep, Lisa McCorkell, and Sarah Adler-Milstein. 2018. "Stable Scheduling Increases Productivity and Sales: The Stable Scheduling Study." *WorkLife Law.* https://worklifelaw.org/projects/stable-scheduling-study/report/.

Wingfield, Adia Harvey. 2013. *No More Invisible Man: Race and Gender in Men's Work.* Philadelphia, PA: Temple University Press.

Wolfe, Jonathon. 2018. "New York Today: The Right to Disconnect." *New York Times.* www.nytimes.com/2018/03/23/nyregion/new-york-today-the-right-to-disconnect.html.

Wolfe, Julia, Janelle Jones, and David Cooper. 2018. "'Fair Workweek' Laws Help More than 1.8 Million Workers: Laws Promote Workplace Flexibility and Protect against Unfair Scheduling Practices." Washington, DC: Economic Policy Institute.

Wollan, Malie. 2016. "Failure to Lunch." *New York Times,* February 25.

Wynn, Alison T. 2018. "Misery Has Company: The Shared Emotional Consequences of Everwork Among Women and Men." *Sociological Forum* 33(3): 712–34.

Wynn, Alison T., and Aliya Hamid Rao. 2019. "Failures of Flexibility: How Perceived Control Motivates the Individualization of Work–Life Conflict." *ILR Review.* https://doi.org/10.1177/0019793919848426.

INDEX

⌘

Page numbers in italics refer to illustrations.